W9-CKR-431

# VOICES OF
# THE FALL

# BAEN BOOKS by JOHN RINGO

### BLACK TIDE RISING:

*Under a Graveyard Sky* • *To Sail a Darkling Sea* • *Islands of Rage and Hope* • *Strands of Sorrow* • *The Valley of Shadows* (with Mike Massa) • *Black Tide Rising* (edited with Gary Poole) • *Voices of the Fall* (edited with Gary Poole) • *River of Night* (with Mike Massa; forthcoming)

### TROY RISING:

*Live Free or Die* • *Citadel* • *The Hot Gate*

### LEGACY OF THE ALDENATA:

*A Hymn Before Battle* • *Gust Front* • *When the Devil Dances* • *Hell's Faire* • *The Hero* (with Michael Z. Williamson) • *Cally's War* (with Julie Cochrane) • *Watch on the Rhine* (with Tom Kratman) • *Sister Time* (with Julie Cochrane) • *Yellow Eyes* (with Tom Kratman) • *Honor of the Clan* (with Julie Cochrane) • *Eye of the Storm*

### COUNCIL WARS:

*There Will Be Dragons* • *Emerald Sea* • *Against the Tide* • *East of the Sun, West of the Moon*

### INTO THE LOOKING GLASS:

*Into the Looking Glass* • *Vorpal Blade* (with Travis S. Taylor) • *Manxome Foe* (with Travis S. Taylor) • *Claws that Catch* (with Travis S. Taylor)

### EMPIRE OF MAN:

*March Upcountry* (with David Weber) • *March to the Sea* (with David Weber) • *March to the Stars* (with David Weber) • *We Few* (with David Weber)

### SPECIAL CIRCUMSTANCES:

*Princess of Wands* • *Queen of Wands*

### PALADIN OF SHADOWS:

*Ghost* • *Kildar* • *Choosers of the Slain* • *Unto the Breach* • *A Deeper Blue* • *Tiger by the Tail* (with Ryan Sear)

### STANDALONE TITLES:

*The Last Centurion*

*Citizens* (ed. with Brian M. Thomsen)

To purchase these and all Baen Book titles in e-book format, please go to www.baen.com.

# VOICES OF THE FALL

## EDITED BY
## JOHN RINGO
## & GARY POOLE

This is a work of fiction. All the characters and events portrayed in this book are fictional, and any resemblance to real people or incidents is purely coincidental.

Copyright © 2019 by John Ringo & Gary Poole

Additional copyright acknowledgments: Foreword © 2019 by Gary Poole; "Starry, Starry Night" © 2019 by John Ringo; "Spectrum" © 2019 by Mike Massa; "Storming the Tower of Babel" © 2019 by Sarah A. Hoyt; "Return to Mayberry" © 2019 by Rob Hampson; "It Just Might Matter in the End" © 2019 by Travis S. Taylor; "Inhale to the King, Baby!" © 2019 by Michael Z. Williamson; "Ham Sandwich" © 2019 by Jody Lynn Nye; "The Downeasters" © 2019 by Brendan DuBois; "The Species as Big as the Ritz" © 2019 by Robert Buettner; "The Cat Hunters" © 2019 by Dave Freer; "Alpha Gamers" © 2019 by Griffin Barber; "True Faith and Allegiance" © 2019 by Michael Gants; "The Killer Awoke" © 2019 by John Birmingham.

All rights reserved, including the right to reproduce this book or portions thereof in any form.

A Baen Books Original

Baen Publishing Enterprises
P.O. Box 1403
Riverdale, NY 10471
www.baen.com

ISBN: 978-1-4814-8382-7

Cover art by Kurt Miller

First printing, March 2019

Distributed by Simon & Schuster
1230 Avenue of the Americas
New York, NY 10020

Library of Congress Cataloging-in-Publication Data

Names: Ringo, John, 1963– editor, writer of afterword. | Poole, Gary, writer of foreword.
Title: Voices of the fall / edited by John Ringo & Gary Poole.
Description: Riverdale, NY : Baen, 2019. | Series: Black tide rising ; 7 | "A Baen Books Original"—Title page verso.
Identifiers: LCCN 2018055725 | ISBN 9781481483827 (hardback)
Subjects: | BISAC: FICTION / Science Fiction / Short Stories. | FICTION / Science Fiction / Military. | GSAFD: Science fiction. | War stories.
Classification: LCC PS3568.I577 V65 2019 | DDC 813/.54—dc23 LC record available at https://lccn.loc.gov/2018055725

10  9  8  7  6  5  4  3  2  1

Pages by Joy Freeman (www.pagesbyjoy.com)
Printed in the United States of America

As always

For Captain Tamara Long, USAF

Born: May 12, 1979

Died: March 23, 2003, Afghanistan

You fly with the angels now.

For Airman First Class William Lockhart, USAF

Born: October 14, 1937

Died: July 19, 2017

Always in my heart and my soul.

# CONTENTS

# Foreword

## GARY POOLE

One of the common refrains I hear from people when talking about postapocalyptic fiction in general—and the Black Tide books in particular—is a general level of disbelief that people would actually band together for a common cause and work together (or mostly together) to overcome what often appears to be insurmountable odds.

Which always confuses me, as the evidence that such happens is all around us.

No, I'm not saying we are actually living through a [insert type of apocalypse] event as you read this—or, at least I sincerely hope nothing has happened since this book was sent off to the printer—what I am saying is that there is plenty of evidence that people do indeed band together for a common cause when faced with disaster, especially large-scale disasters.

Don't believe me? The next time a disaster, large or small, happens, look for neighbors helping neighbors as well as strangers helping strangers. We've seen it firsthand in Texas and Florida and New Jersey and Louisiana and many other parts of the country where major storms wreaked havoc on our communities. Where governments failed, either through a lack of planning or resources, individual people stood up when it was needed and pitched in to help. Because that's what people do.

I personally experienced a hurricane when I lived in Florida in the '80s. As soon as it was safe to go outside, I saw literally hundreds of people, "regular folks" like you and me, coming outside along with me to see what needed to be done. I saw it again, firsthand, nearly three decades later during a day of horrific tornadoes that ravaged Southern Tennessee and North Georgia.

Whether it was sharing water or food, maybe a blanket or a tarp, or picking up a shovel or a chainsaw, people did what they could with what they had. To help. Not for profit, not for fame, and not because some "higher up" told them to. They did it because that is what people do.

Yet it has become fashionable in certain circles to decry the selfishness and narcissism of the "modern world." And while there are many who do, indeed, fall into that category, the vast majority of people set aside their differences and lend a hand when it's needed.

The reason I bring this up is that this mindset, the resiliency of people, is one of the major underlying themes of the Black Tide universe, and what in many ways sets it apart from other postapocalyptic fiction.

Resiliency.

That's the key word.

And it's a word that comes to mind a lot when diving into the world that John has created. Most advanced nations can absorb the impact of major storms, earthquakes, tsunamis, and other natural disasters, and with a few minor blips here and there, keep moving forward.

But what if the world of Black Tide came to be real? A biological plague would make a Category 5 hurricane or a magnitude 8 earthquake look like a toddler kicking over a sandcastle at the beach. Multiply the devastation of any of the natural disasters of the past several years a thousandfold (at least) and you might start to grasp the calamity such a plague would wreak on the world.

But while even as the most advanced nations in the world would fall to such an apocalyptic catastrophe, there would still be resilience. Not from the fallen nations, obviously, but from people.

For amidst all the incredible loss of life, through the ravages of a plague that turns people into something akin to our small-brained human forebears of tens of thousands of years ago, the *Homo habilis* and *Homo erectus* whose skeletal remains live on in our natural history museums, I firmly believe those that did survive would not give up. Even when the odds against them are overwhelming and couldn't be beat. They simply would not give in to the darkness and go gently into the good night.

Now certainly people can become very predatory. We've seen that happen many, many times throughout history. And when the choice is feeding your children or letting the "other" live, well...we've seen what happens to those "others." I am not an ivory tower type who believes in the innate goodness of all mankind and envisions a day when we will all sit around singing "Kumbaya" in perfect peace and harmony. I am fully aware that people can be vicious, predatory, and all too shortsighted in trying to meet their basic needs.

But we are resilient in dealing with those people as well. Which we've also seen time and time again throughout history. I most certainly would never want to see something akin to Black Tide come to happen in the real world. And as much as I believe that I would be able to survive it, at least for a while, I am all too aware that the odds are not in my favor. Or yours.

But I do know, not believe, but *know*, that the human race itself would survive. And maybe even, when all is said and done, thrive.

Because we are resilient.

# Starry, Starry Night

## JOHN RINGO

"Granma?" Sarah said, running into the cluttered living room. "Ronnie says Old Man Klunder isn't real! Tell him he's real! Tell him, Gran!"

Virginia Hanning removed her glasses and set down her sewing as the children charged into the room.

"Is not!" one of the boys shouted. "Old Man Klunder's a made-up story! My big brother says so!"

"Inside voice, young man!" Virginia snapped. "So, your brother says Old Man Klunder isn't real, does he? Did he live through the Fall, young man?"

"No, ma'am," Ronnie said.

Given that Ronnie was about the age she had been that terrible year and Old Man Klunder had been . . . well, amazingly, not that much older than she was now, there was no way his brother lived through the Fall. So few were left who had. All the giants—the Wolves, the Reavers, the Irregulars—gone like the snows of a Minnesota winter.

How the years and memories passed.

"Did he live through that terrible fall and winter when the world was covered in the zombies?" Virginia asked. She didn't recognize him. He must be new to Sewanee. So many new faces,

1

*it was hard to keep up. "Did he watch Old Man Klunder ride out into the night? Did he help him with the radio? Is he one of the Voices of the Fall? I think not."*

*"Tell him, Granma!" Sarah said. "Tell him the story!"*

*"Please tell it!" the children begged.*

*"Very well," Virginia said. "If you insist. It was long ago and far away, when the world was covered in the monster when Old Man Klunder saved us all. His true name was Bjorn Klunder and Bjorn Klunder was a giant of a man, with shoulders wide as two axe handles..."*

Bjorn Klorno Klunder, five feet five inches tall and down to one hundred and twenty pounds with shoulders that had never, on his best day, been even one axe handle wide, took a measured bite of beans then followed it with a measured bite of hominy. He considered, as he often had since the lights went out, that it was good he'd learned hunger when he was a younger man.

One half can of beans and one half can of hominy had been his daily ration since the infected nearly caught him on the last trip to the Meijers. That was until his stash was a quarter gone. Then it was one quarter can of beans and one quarter can of hominy. The only reason he had any stash at all was from some friends who still worked at the Green Giant plant and Lars at the Walmart being a soft touch when he had to lay him off. He'd filled his tub with water before the lights and water went out. And he'd drunk of it slow, one meager cup a day. Waste went out the window, no flushing for him.

It had been two months, he'd marked off each day on the Red Dragon Chinese Restaurant calendar, since the lights went out and despite it getting colder the infected were still roaming outside. He'd see some from the window of his one-room apartment whenever he checked. It was the second-floor apartment that had saved him when others had fallen. With only the one window, facing the rear and too high for the zombies to climb... he'd stayed quiet and they'd never even rattled the doorknob. All he had to do was stay alive 'til the snows. He could go look for food and water when the snow fell....

The blizzard was thick and fast, a mass of orange white in the reflected candle light. It was very nearly his last candle as well but he cherished the view. The howl of the wind was an old and comforting friend to Bjorn and the cold that filled the apartment was nothing he had not faced many a winter before. He huddled back under the covers of aluminum foil, gathering as much of the meager candle heat as he could. As soon as the storm cleared, he would start...

*"He came in the night, after the first of the storms..."*

The storm had blown a pile of snow against the wall of the ground floor apartment. Bjorn ignored the frozen bodies on the floor as he emptied out the cupboard. He'd eaten his fill in the first apartment he'd scavenged. After so many months of starvation he'd nearly puked he'd eaten so fast. Even half frozen the can of black beans and rice had tasted too good to stop.

There was plenty of food in the apartment. The family had stocked up.

Whether it was one of them had turned or the broken windows and door told the story didn't matter. They weren't alive to eat it.

As he walked out the smashed sliding-glass door he looked back at the nearest frozen corpse.

"Thank you," he muttered, heading out into the night. "An you go home to God, now."

A Coleman heater, a bigger apartment, a thick sleeping bag that was a now-unneeded luxury. Coleman stove, piles of food, booze and jewelry. He'd even gotten a generator tinkered to life but the roar of it had caused him to shut it down almost immediately. Too likely to draw the zombies, don'cha know.

If it had only been before the Plague, he'd think he'd died and gone to heaven. This was better than he'd lived most all his life.

The howl of the storm outside, not a single speaking person to be found and the continued lack of electricity told him it was anything but.

"Mutter always told me I'd go to hell," Bjorn said. "Guess she was right, right?"

Bjorn rattled the handle of the door but it wouldn't budge. Most of the apartments and homes had been broken into by the infected. He didn't generally bother if an apartment was too hard to get into. Plenty more to scavenge.

The stores were pointless. He'd checked most of the convenience stores in the area and they had all been pillaged before the snows from the looks of it. He hadn't even seen evidence of other people. At least thinking people. There were tracks of zombies, though. Fortunately, they only seemed to come out in the daytime. Too cold at night.

He started away then stopped at a tapping sound. He always kept an eye an ear out for the zombies. They went somewhere in the darkness and it wouldn't do, not'all, to run into some. He'd picked up a revolver gun in case but it wasn't much if there was zombies. And he'd never shot it, nor any, gun in years.

He looked about then back to the apartment. There was a white face at the window in the moonlight. It just looked at him, not even moving. He wasn't sure if it was a ghost or a person.

Then a hand raised, again, and tap-tap-tapped on the window.

Bjorn walked slowly to the window. He'd been sure he was the last man left in the whole world. Now there was a human face looking at him and tapping of a window.

Would the zombies do that?

"Are you real, lady?" he asked the face in the window. "Or am I dreamin'?"

"Are you?" the woman replied.

"Yes," Bjorn caroled, trying not to cry. "I'm real. I'm real. You're real, by golly! And *I'm* real! YOU'RE REAL!"

"Do you have any food?" the girl asked.

"Do I ever, ma'am," Bjorn said.

*"A giant man, made of courage and wisdom..."*

"I wish we had a flush toilet," Charles said, grumpily.

"An you be makin' one and we'll have it," Bjorn said, stirring the soup. "If wishes were horses, beggars would ride."

Bjorn wasn't sure he liked it more nor less with company. Slowly he'd found survivors since the first lady, Victoria. But they were all city folk, scared of the night and the stars and especially the zombies. He was still the only one that went out of a night.

It wasn't zombies that were his main concern these days but the dogs who were reverted to mostly wolf. He'd had to fire some shots the night before last when a pack had come around when he was scavenging. They'd started on eating the frozen corpses and they had the taste of man in their mouths, now.

"I'm not sure that water is safe," Charles opined.

"We're boiling it," Victoria pointed out.

"Even then!" Charles said. "Nuclear power plants have probably melted down! The radiation would get into *everything*. Look at all the people who died from Chernobyl! And that was just one nuke! There are hundreds in the United States alone! And you can't smell or taste radiation! We don't have any way to *know*!"

"An you be finding a better water than melted snow we'll all be obliged," Bjorn said, trying to control his temper. Temper never did a man good. "I'll be obliged if I don't have to find the fuel to melt it an all."

"I'd like to hear if there are others," little Virginia said. He'd found the girl in a house with her parents dead and . . . not quite right at first. Having to sit vigil on your dead parents and try to figure out how to survive for months on your own could make one not quite right. But she seemed to be doing better as long as no one got so much as a sniffle. "If there's anyone else who survived."

"I'm sure there are plenty," Victoria replied, smiling. "The government is working on this right now, I'm sure of it."

"We need a radio," Charles said. "Bjorn, pick up a radio tonight. You'll need to find one of those hand-crank ones."

"Oh, I'll be doin' that, you betcha," Bjorn said, calmly. "You bet I'll get right on that."

"Charles, quit telling Bjorn what to do," Victoria snapped. "It's not as if you're helping!"

"I'm not . . . good at finding my way around in the dark," Charles muttered.

"Do we have to fight?" Virginia said, curling into a ball.

"I'll be finding one if I can," Bjorn said, smiling at the girl. "For Virginia. Don't know where they'd be one short of the Mall or the Walmart. But I'll get one, you bet."

*"He would go out into the worst of the blizzards to rescue the helpless and bring us succor . . ."*

"Gotcha by gum," Bjorn muttered, reading the sign above the emergency radios by squinting in the dim light. Batteries ran out fast in the cold and too much light drew the dogs or the zombies so he was using a meager LED penlight. But he'd found Virginia's radio.

Most of the place was stripped of emergency gear and food. Plenty of everything totally useless in a disaster, just not much of use in one. But there were a few of the radios left. He wandered through the aisles, kicking the debris on Lars' floor wondering what else he should take back. It couldn't be much with him carrying it on his old back.

He'd walked most of the night, pushing through the snows, to get to the Walmart by the Mall of America and he'd seen not a soul on the entire long trek. He was that worn out as well. It would have been quite a walk with the ways plowed. With snow piled up on 35 and 494 it had been a fair walk. He'd say it was good for the heart but he'd had to stop from time to time for that reason if none other.

He found a big pack in Sporting Goods then stopped in thought. They always stocked early for winter in Minnesota and, amazingly, they'd put up the Christmas decorations before everything came apart. He wondered if it had been Peggy who'd worked on them but Peggy was probably a goner so did it matter?

But they'd started to put out winter gear as well. Including cross-country skis.

He hadn't used skis since . . . he remembered goin' with a girl when he'd been in school. The girl, what was her name? had skied. She'd wanted to go and he'd spent most of time falling flat on his bum. What was her name? So long ago . . .

*"Night after starry night he went out into the cold and snow . . ."*

Bjorn puttered up Morgan Avenue on the Ski-Doo towards what everyone called "New House." There were too many, now, to fit in the apartment. After some considerable debate they'd moved to a solid house that had been evacuated before everything came apart, what people on the radio were calling "The Fall." Didn't make much sense of a name to Bjorn. Fall happened every year. Needed a bigger name in his opinion.

The house had a good solid basement, though, and after making sure it was sound-proof enough he'd pulled in a big generator on the sled. So, they had lights again, night and day. It also had a ham radio no one knew how to run with a big tower in the back. For some reason everyone expected him to figure it all out. When he had the time from also being the only one who'd so much as leave the confines of the house. The "big debate" had mostly been over going two blocks, could you believe it, to a better home.

He was a bit angry, though, to see someone hadn't covered all the windows. If you showed light, even in the cold and night, you could still get zomb—

*"He once battled fifty zombies in the street, battled them all night until the dawn 'til he was knee-deep in the monsters and none of them could so much as touch him for all his bravery..."*

The emaciated infected stumbled through the knee-deep snow towards the unlit snowmobile, drawn by the sound. Sound meant people and people meant food. That was about as far as zombie logic ran.

It was the first zombie Bjorn had faced down but he'd considered, often, what to do. Much noise meant more zombies. He might even be attracting them with using the Ski-Doo and all but he was getting a bit old to keep trudging or skiing out every night to feed the Colony.

Keeping his right hand on the throttle he picked up the Mackintosh axe in his left and swung as he passed the stumbling infected.

It hadn't been but a kid, maybe a teenager, and that covered in frostbite. Barely a finger and no toes, it was putting the thing down an mercy as much as anything.

Bjorn puked into the snow, then continued up to the house. He'd have to have The Talk again about showing light...

"Hullo?" Bjorn said into the microphone. "You fellas still here? You hearin' us?"

"Hey, who's this, over?" the voice on the radio replied.

Bjorn had finally figured out he had the power supply hooked up wrong from the generator.

"Bjorn Klunder I am," Bjorn replied. "An some others..."

"...got into Powderhorn on my sled and picked up some supplies from the Meijers yesterday. Any closer to downtown and the zombies are still crawlin'. Lots of them, by golly. How in tarnation are they survivin'? It's been a little cold, don'cha know..."

*"Until one night..."*

It was nearly spring but one of those late winter nights when the cold was so hard the trees cracked.

Bjorn was taking a shortcut across Grass Lake when it hit. Most people "know" that heart attacks are painful. Most myocardial infarctions are. In that case the heart strains, like any muscle, and they are intensely painful. However, in the case of congestive heart failure, the heart simply...stops. The person with that heart never even realizes they've just died.

The Ski-Doo slid to a halt in the middle of the shallow lake and continued to idle as Bjorn slumped forward.

His arms slid into the forward foot rests and against the hot engine. Even in the intense cold his polyester jacket started to smolder and melt. The heat from the engine slowly burned through the polyester down to his flesh and bones and his forearms essentially melted into the engine.

The engine continued to idle for nearly a day until a combination of poor quality siphoned gas and low fuel pressure caused it to die with a splutter.

In the middle of the lake, far from other sources of protein, the dogs never found him.

Nor did the Colony.

*"When we were ready to stand on our own two feet, when we were ready to take up the burden, he disappeared into the starry starry night...."*

The spring was slow to come in Minnesota that year but come it did as always. The ice of the lake slowly melted and well before most of it broke up the weight of the Ski-Doo caused a crack to form, then a break, and the snowmobile slid into the depths.

Glued to his trusty steed, Bjorn Klorno Klunder sank with it until it settled into the muck on the bottom....

∽ ⊖ ⌀

"When the blizzard blasts the walls of your home and you hear the sound of a Ski-Doo in the distance, always know that Old Man Klunder watches over us still . . . And that's the end of it. So, yes, Ronnie, Old Man Klunder is real."

"So he's really real?" Ronnie said, wonderingly.

"And he still watches over us all," Virginia said, definitely. "Just as Shewolf and Seawolf and General Walker protect us, still. They'll never leave our side as long as we remember them in our hearts."

# Spectrum

## MIKE MASSA

The muted whirring of the carefully padded bells from the wind-up alarm clock was enough to wake Enoch. Though he came awake slowly, he was immediately and acutely aware of the loose sheets that lay about him. Rather than rewrap the sheets snugly he forced himself upright, blinking.

*The Count is fifty-four,* was his first thought. *Time to get ready for opening.*

He swung into a comfortable routine.

First he dipped his hands into the fired clay bowl to splash yesterday's water on his face and smooth down his hair. Flossing and brushing were automatic.

Although he conceded authenticity in order to enjoy the nice minty feeling that his third to last tube of toothpaste gave him, the clothes that he donned approximated the period of the reenactment. Relaxed leather leggings went over his Hanes underwear, which in turn were concealed by brown clout, inexpertly colored with walnut dye. Hokey beaded moccasins and a vest made from cured doeskin were brightened by a red calico bandanna that restrained his wiry, shiny black hair, keeping the strands from irritating his face.

He carefully pinned the last item, a rectangle of plastic engraved with the legend "Enoch Mist Over Water" and below that "Living History Docent," on his beaded vest.

Although he had long since memorized the instructions that Mr. Listang had provided for him, step one after getting up and before eating was to always check the List.

*"I'm not saying that you are slow or nothing, Ennie,"* his boss had declaimed. *"But you gotta be on time and do the job, rain or shine, customers or no customers, see? We get paid by the good state of Colorado just the same, so long as we keep the exhibit open. You wanna live here, fine. Keeps the college kids from pulling pranks or drinking in the exhibits. Every day, I unlock the outside and you unlock the inside once you are all dressed in costume. That way, no Sunday school go-to-meeting missus is gonna get offended ifn she sees you in your Altogether, y'see? That would be not cool!"*

Enoch hadn't seen, not really. The reservation hadn't sent kids to Sunday school in town since before he was born. And the idea of being anything but dressed in public where everyone could see was mortifying. Not since he was a very young boy had Enoch ever risked such a thing.

Regardless, the List of park rules was clear.

Item One: Unlock The Inner Turnstiles.

Enoch walked over to the gate, which was wide enough to pass customers two abreast through the frontier style fence made of vertically set wooden poles. The park had paid extra to the installer to leave the rough bark on the trunks as well as to mill points onto the top of each upright. He opened the padlock and unchained the adult gate, which had remained closed for precisely fifty-four days.

At least, he thought it had been that many days. He might have lost a few at the start when he couldn't eat or drink anything. But was definitely fifty-four days since he had woken clearheaded but thirsty and started the Count.

He was sure about that.

He squinted past the locked outer gate at the waiting area for his exhibit.

Empty, same as the day before.

He sighed happily. No people meant no problems. No strutting high school senior trying to impress his girlfriend by correcting Enoch. No irritating little kids crawling in and out of the museum's children's entrance, hiding from teachers, parents and Enoch himself.

Just above head height, a bright red and white checked banner that read "Y'ALL COME BACK FOR OUR FALL HOEDOWN!" hung stretched across the exhibit atrium. It flapped intermittently, driven by the same fitful plains breeze that blew scraps of cloth and paper past the door.

In the early days of the Count, he had heard fighting and screaming beyond the ten foot walls of the stockade that housed his exhibit. Enoch supposed that park security had eventually taken care of the daytime drunks who usually created the disturbances at the park. It had been exactly thirty-three days since he heard anything at all. He had yet to actually see even a single person.

Enoch glanced outside a second time as he snapped the padlock back onto the turnstile's hasp, ensuring that no one would help themselves to a "souvenir."

That seemed unlikely.

Mr. Listang never reappeared and the outer entrance had remained empty and locked day after day.

The rest of the Genuine Year Round State Fair, Family Park and Museum was empty too. Enoch didn't particularly care about that. Not his problem.

His problem was the List.

*"Boy, Ima make it reeyul simple! I give you the List to do every day, and you just follow it. Black and white, no guessing needed. Just read the damned list. That's number one!"*

Item Two: Perform Crop Irrigation.

At the planting area he looked longingly at the hose reel. However, the rules were clear. Regardless of the presence of visitors or not, the exhibit docent was to "play along." Guiltily, he glanced up.

The cameras that had allowed park security to catch fence jumpers no longer gleamed with a little red light.

But you never knew.

Enoch plodded over to the hand pump and began filling the brown painted hardware megastore buckets that he had left there the previous day. Two buckets of water at a time, he carefully filled the dirt troughs around clusters of mounded plants.

The insects began to buzz in an agreeably soft tone.

Thirty minutes of careful work later, he had delivered one bucket each to a third of the mounds. Before the Count, he usually had help but he could only cover so much alone.

The Schedule was black and white.

Just like the rules.

Item Three: Deliver the Crop Lecture and Demonstrate the Procedure.

He carefully stepped over to the smooth patch of dirt that was surrounded by a circle of short, fat logs that were set firmly into the ground as stools. In bad times, this was when the first harassment would start, as the park customers would lounge on their stumps and question him irritatingly.

Happily, now he could demonstrate how to hoe the Three Sisters in peace. He tried to rotate among the mounds, but weeds had been getting ahead of him. The heavy clay soil shrugged off the blunt edge of the roughly forged digging adze and weeding spike unless Enoch really put his back into the chore.

He relaxed while explaining in rote form that each mound contained three mutually supporting crop plants. Golden maize to provide the uprights, pinto beans to climb the cornstalks and shade the squash, whose spiky bristles and fibers deterred crawling insects from damaging the first two.

He didn't have to endure the know-it-alls who would point out that this form of farming didn't match his tribe, or the area, or even the other technology in the exhibit.

Pretty Sue had explained that it wasn't his problem.

*"Ennie, they don't pay us to be exact, see? We just put on an educational show. Mr. Listang, he shuffles some of the profits to the elders, you get a place to stay somewhere out of their hair, the park gets the tax break and everyone is happy. Cool?"*

It all boiled down to keeping the museum open and the exhibits running.

Enoch had agreed with Sue enthusiastically.

Living at the museum was so much better than his old life. Despite the fact that he didn't understand most of the jokes made at his expense while he worked at the park, they were only jokes. Usually, words meant one thing. Sometimes the same words could mean something else.

Pretty Sue said it was called sarcasm.

Still, mean-spirited humor from strangers was better than the weekly beating he endured from the other kids on the res.

After thirty minutes of "authentically" demonstrating hoeing, pruning, weeding and reshaping the earthen mounds to precisely no audience, he returned the buckets to the pump and slipped into his longhouse for a snack. As a side effect of running the living history museum, the exhibit staff had accumulated a *lot* of dried squash, beans and corn. Enoch drew on that store as needed, but he really preferred his dwindling stash of Mountainside brand energy bars.

In between measured bites of his treat he filled the pot with exactly two cups of water and then exactly one cup of mixed dried beans, leaving them so soak as he walked back outside.

Item Four: Deliver the Hide Scraping, Tanning and Sewing Demonstration.

In front of every re-created longhouse inside the large fenced compound the park had established an "authentic North American Indian Craft activity" station. Of all the activities, Enoch preferred the leather station. Usually, Pretty Sue would be in charge there and Enoch's responsibility was limited to fetching her a scratchy deer hide from the enormous stack of exactly thirty-two hides inside the corresponding hut. Sometimes he was allowed to assist customers if they got stuck on their moccasins or vests.

Since Sue, along with everyone else, had stopped showing up to work Enoch elected to rotate through the stations, per the List.

Some, like the cowboy forge, he was explicitly forbidden to operate alone. However, he had accumulated experience as a helper on nearly every other station.

As he strolled lightly along the worn path, he caught a flicker of motion out of the corner of his eye. He stopped to look but whatever it was had been obscured by the thick plantings that were his primary responsibility.

At the leather station, he withdrew the large scraping rack and tools. He then spent thirty minutes happily droning about animal conservation, skinning, curing and tanning while simultaneously demonstrating basic leather-working skills.

As he put the exhibit items away he again glimpsed motion. It was definitely a person with long hair and a white shirt but all he got was a momentary look.

"Hello?" Enoch paused. "I said *hello*?"

No one replied.

Enoch sighed. The idyll was over. Once again he would have to deal with park guests.

Not cool.

His second heartfelt sigh was even deeper.

He knew the rule about guests. No matter how obnoxious they got, Mr. Listang insisted that he "behave." The assistant park manager hadn't been shy about reinforcing his message.

*"Boy, never you forget! The park guests are our number one responsibility! You behave. No staring, no yelling, no nothing. You stick to the list, and if you have a problem you run get me or another docent. Otherwise, you get me in trouble. And I will make you sorry you was ever born. You hear me?"*

Enoch definitely heard him. Everything Listang said was loud. Even when he wasn't talking to Enoch, he was audible from anywhere in the exhibit area. Enoch appreciated that Pretty Sue usually talked softly.

But.

Now he had a guest, again.

This time he trudged back to "his" longhouse. Rather than stare, he just tracked the flickers of motion in his peripheral vision as the park guest trailed behind.

Once back at the front of the compound, Enoch stopped short.

The outer turnstiles were still locked.

Huh.

He turned quickly and this time saw the person in the open, not even thirty feet away.

It was a girl.

Not any girl.

A mostly naked girl.

There was a *lot* of her Altogether showing.

Enoch tried not to panic. He knew from many lectures, often reinforced with Listang's patented head chop, that he was never ever never to bother girls, most especially townie customers who weren't from the reservation.

*"Don't forget this one, boy. You wanna risk a look at the girls from your res, cool. That's between you and them. You get uppity with regular guest, a white girl ... well, ifn her daddy don't set you straight, I promise that I will!"*

Listang had punctuated that lecture most firmly. He wasn't alone.

Even Pretty Sue, who was almost always nice to him, said he was to always leave all the lady guests alone and never stare at them.

*"Ennie, you be nice to everyone. The manager is a real ba— Well, he isn't always nice. So you be nice always, especially to ladies!"*

Enoch was pretty sure that staring at almost naked lady guests was the Worst Thing Ever. Before he reflexively dropped his eyes, Enoch saw that she was wearing a really stained white tank top that fell to just below her hips. Her red hair was long and in a tangled mess. When she detected his notice, she dashed back behind the plantings.

"Um, sorry." Enoch mumbled. He faltered for a moment, keeping his eyes mostly down, but checked every few moments to see if she came back into view. He did not want to deal with any complaints that could cost him this job.

Living in the park meant escaping from his earliest tormentors. It meant freedom from the elders on the reservation who would prefer that he stay hidden so that they wouldn't be embarrassed. He did not even want to think about having to move out of the Park.

The List. Gotta follow the List.

Item Five: Deliver the Mat and Rope Weaving Demonstration.

Enoch slumped over to the appropriate exhibit. However, the routine of the lecture gradually buoyed his spirits. He smoothly demonstrated how to use pliable vines, bark, cornstalks and other materials to make rope and weave a small section of fibrous matting. During the thirty minute show he darted his eyes about, but the lone park visitor didn't make an appearance and Enoch relaxed further.

Without distractions, he worked his way through the List.

There was Clay Pot Forming and Firing. Also Basic and Intermediate Shelter Construction. Before lunch he was finishing up Shucking, Cornmeal Grinding, Tortilla Making and Baking. He was putting away the grinding board, stones, baskets and unused ears of corn for reuse when he saw the flash of white again.

He determinedly ignored the movement.

Don't bother the visitors. If she wasn't going to ask him questions, so much the better. Enoch could put up with that.

He ate lunch inside the privacy of his personal longhouse and returned to the List, repeating the morning's activity.

The sun was high in the blue sky, warming his wiry hair. The Park temperatures had moderated as the fierce summer gave way to early fall. It was still hot enough to make him thirsty, and midway through his next lecture he dipped some water from the plastic bucket at his feet. He splashed a little on the ground and heard a short grunt.

Looking to his side he spotted the redhead crouching, not even ten feet away. Her wide eyes were fixed on the bucket.

"Um, hi?" Enoch offered.

She started, but didn't retreat, alternating looks from his reddening face to the bucket.

"Would you like, uh, wo-would you like some water?" Enoch proffered the dipper. When she didn't take it, he filled it with water and held it out.

She scooted forward and grabbed the ladle by the bowl portion and slurped noisily. Most of the water spilled, including some which fell on her white shirt.

"Um." Enoch dropped his eyes again. "More water?"

"Wauugh?" the girl repeated. "Waugggh?"

"Um, sure." Enoch reached for the ladle but had to tug it from her hands. Before he could finish refilling it she had scooted right up next to him and plunged her hand directly into the bucket and began messily drinking from her hand.

"Or you can have the bucket, whatever." Enoch stepped back and surreptitiously watched her for a moment. She was dirty. Really dirty.

He wrinkled his nose. She smelled, well, bad.

Enoch wanted to tell her, but remembered the rules.

*"Son, rule number one, right after being on time and leaving the customers alone is to follow all the rules! Don't be making stuff up!"*

Enoch thought that there were an awful lot of rules numbered one. Math didn't work that way for him.

"Um, I have to finish the lecture." Enoch apologized and resumed talking about the mutually beneficial relationship of the three different crop types. While he talked, he illustrated the chores of weeding, plucking any visible insects from the plants and harvesting the late season beans. The adze was too clumsy to use right next to the corn, so he switched to the sharp, narrow blade on the end of the weed pole.

Enoch tried to get back in his zone, but the new customer's scrutiny made him feel uncomfortable. She had retreated a short distance with the mostly empty bucket, sucking water from her hand and watching him warily. He tried again to find his groove, but the bucket handle periodically clattered, distracting him.

When he moved to put away all the buckets, she scrambled nearly out of sight, dragging "her" bucket with her.

Well, he had extras. He fetched a spare from the supply longhouse and lined it up by the water pump, next to the three originals.

Still, Enoch shook his head.

Customers.

When he resumed his routine at the leather crafting lodge his new customer crept closer and listened.

Throughout the afternoon she shadowed his progress. The highlight of the day was the distribution of free samples of baked corn tortillas. She ate every single one that Enoch made. After that, she stayed closer to him.

Enoch returned to his lodge. His wind-up clock read 5:30 p.m.

The List offered: Item Seventeen—Final Cleanup and Exhibit Closure.

Usually, one of the senior docents would be gathering up the remaining park guests and politely shooing them away while Enoch tidied up.

When he walked back out into the glooming dusk, his visitor was missing. He sighed in relief and began his final walk around. As usual, the absence of visitors meant that there was no trash to pick up and no little kids hiding in the empty stable.

Visitors or no visitors, he had to check. Sue reinforced the importance of routine.

*"Ennie, if Mr. Listang is late, I'll still come by to lock up after you are all done. You lock the inner gate on time, either way. If I can, I'll bring you something nice. Pizza?"*

It felt like forever since he had eaten pizza.

The last item on the List was Lock Inner Turnstile.

He twisted the bronze colored combination lock back into place and spun the knob left twice and then right once just like Mr. Listang had shown him on his first day.

With his workday done, Enoch returned to his lodge for dinner. The soaked beans were ready to drain and cook. While they heated, he went back outside to look for the girl.

"Hello?" He cast about near the entrance. "The park is closed?"

He had to be satisfied with calling into the night. She had vanished.

His dinner of stewed bean medley and tortillas wasn't his

favorite, but he no longer had Sue to bring him anything different. Besides, while his pizza count was exactly zero, his count of supplies included four heavy sisal bags of dried beans and thirty more of dried corn, still on the cob.

The alarm clock woke Enoch.

*The Count is fifty-five,* was his first thought. *Time to get ready for opening.*

Enoch began to work his way through the first part of the List, but upon turning around from his initial turnstile chore he saw the same guest again.

She stood uncertainly near the empty buckets and the pump.

She hadn't gotten any more dressed since her visit the day before.

"Um." Enoch looked down at the ground and then back up. "Good morning, miss."

Wide-eyed, she stood mute, but seemed poised to bolt. Whenever he met her gaze, she immediately looked down, much like Enoch did.

"Um, I have to begin my List." When she didn't reply he stammered, "I-I have to irrigate the Three Sisters." They alternated looking at each other, and then at the ground in turn.

He pointed to the planting area and then glanced back at her.

She flinched when he raised his arm but stayed in place.

"Um, I have to come over there to do it." Enoch offered.

Nothing.

He was in a quandary. If he was going to continue the List and keep the Schedule, he had to start right away, which meant getting a *lot* closer to the mostly naked girl. Enoch felt his bubble of apprehension begin to expand into the start of a panic attack.

His counselor had talked to him about how to head off those feelings, which had left Enoch mostly helpless in the past. He couldn't go hide now—he had, he just had to get going on the List.

Nerving himself, he strode uncertainly to the wash pump and unhooked the bail over the handle and began to fill the first bucket. He carefully didn't look at the newcomer.

As the water began to flow the girl reached her hands into the stream.

"Waugh!" she cried. "Waugh, waugh!"

She withdrew her hands and sucked her fingers.

"No, you can't do it that way." In a flash, his incipient panic subsided, to be replaced by irritation at the break in routine.

If she was going to show up at opening, then the least she could do was drink properly and let him get on with the List!

"Here, take the dipper and put it in the bucket." Even though he was annoyed, he used his polite voice and extended the empty dipper towards her.

That met first with a blank look and then frightened shyness.

"Waugh?" she asked, still looking down at the puddle on the ground.

"You put the dipper into the bucket and dip the water out." Enoch was beginning to think that this park guest needed a lot more help than usual. "Here. Like this."

He dipped the ladle and mimed sipping. She grabbed at the ladle and he backed up a step, then repeated the gesture before handing her the empty ladle. She looked at it blankly. He took it back and repeated the action with a full bucket.

"See? You have to fill it with water first."

On her next try she dunked the ladle into the water but only managed to retain a swallow, spilling the rest.

"Better." Enoch smiled encouragingly. He remembered what it was like to be taught by someone else.

He demonstrated yet again, moving very slowly and letting her see that he was taking his time. He treated this as the same sort of problem that he had when he tried to teach visiting little kids how to perform any of the exhibit's crafts.

Finally she managed to get a full ladle to her mouth and gulped down the fresh water. Though she spilled a lot, the improvement was enough encouragement to lead her to repeat the action on her own.

Enoch grinned, happy to have helped out. Three ladles later, she smiled back, briefly revealing a bright white smile.

"Okay. Now I have to water the plants." He gently tugged the empty bucket away. At the pump he noisily filled both and began the laborious irrigation process. Unseen, she had crept up behind him, watching avidly.

"Excuse me, miss." Enoch had almost stumbled over his shadow as he continued the List. "Here, if you want to help, pump the handle."

He showed her several times how to operate the handle. In the course of things, her white tank top became soaked. Enoch labored to not notice but instead focused on completing this task as fast as he could, trying to make up time on the schedule.

Mustn't stare.

Staring is rude. Doesn't matter about the "Altogether."

On the upside, the dowsing served as an impromptu wash up, knocking back some of her eye searing body odor. Enoch was rapidly coming to hate it.

Throughout the day, Enoch and the sole park guest worked their way through the List.

Once again the highlight was tortilla making. A few bad moments were the result of his guest trying to eat a tortilla while it was still much too hot. She ran around in a tight circle, trying to escape the burning sensation until Enoch got another ladle of water to her. Her relief was palpable and Enoch felt pretty good about it.

*"Whenever one of our guests wants something, you help them. If you don't understand, then come and get me, or Joey or Mr. Listang—but always try to help. Someone gets hurt, you run to get me, okay Enoch?"*

Pretty Sue had made sure that Enoch knew that helping out was on the List, sort of, even if it wasn't written down.

Helping the park guests to enjoy themselves was definitely good. Maybe that made up for some of his inadvertent staring.

At lunch time Enoch retired into his lodge and his guest immodestly squatted outside in a shady spot. He was pretty sure that no one had told her about the "Altogether" rule.

After his snack, it was back to List. During his efforts to learn her name, Enoch inadvertently taught her his name, which she reproduced as "Eena." Despite patiently asking exactly forty-two times, he wasn't able to get her to tell him hers.

It occurred to him that his new friend might be like him.

Just a little slow.

Even guests who were a little slow were still park guests, so he had to help. Her surprising white smile reminded him of Pretty Sue. Calling her "hey you" was rude, so until she decided to tell him her own name, he decided to use a name inspired by her surprisingly bright grin.

Missy White didn't object to her new name.

Enoch completed the second half of the List during the afternoon, just as he had done for fifty-five days, with one added change. Missy followed him to every station, patiently serving as an attentive audience of one.

During the tortilla-making demonstration, Enoch illustrated how to blow on the food to cool it. She beamed when her first bite didn't burn her mouth.

At day's end he watched her creeping into the Mat and Rope Weaving longhouse. Guests weren't supposed to hide inside, but there wasn't anyone to report to.

Enoch ate his dinner without any enjoyment. He was deeply worried.

Mr. Listang had been very clear that Enoch wasn't ever to confront a guest. At the same time, park guests weren't allowed inside the exhibit overnight—it was practically half the reason that Enoch was there in the first place!

He was supposed to call Listang himself or Park Security. But the phone didn't work and there was not one person to tell.

And Enoch was pretty sure that maybe Missy wasn't going to leave.

As usual, the alarm clock woke Enoch.

*The Count is fifty-six,* was his first thought. *I better see if Missy White is still here,* was his next.

As he completed his morning ritual, he heard the pump working. Outside, he found Missy dipping the ladle into a full bucket and happily, if sloppily, slaking her morning thirst.

"Waugh!" she said happily.

"Yeah, water." Enoch was glad and everything, but there was an odor of fresh poop nearby.

Little kids occasionally made messes in the exhibit, and Listang had given Enoch cleanup materials, but Enoch really, really hated that part of his job.

Though he left cleanup for later, he started his daily job somewhat aggravated with his visitor.

As he addressed each item on the List, Missy followed closely. She lugged buckets of water next to him during when he irrigated. She happily tangled dozens of hide straps during the leather crafting. If her clay pot was a highly authentic clay lump rather than a "handmade bowl" which could be sold at the park shop she didn't seem to mind. Enoch had to carefully flatten out her lumps of corn meal during tortilla making, but they tasted okay.

During lunch he thoughtfully added another cup of dried beans to the soaking pot but otherwise kept his routine.

The second half of the day was more of the same. He showed her how to look for and crush any insects in the planting beds. He guided her hands when it was time to rebuild and shape the earth troughs that captured the water for each planting mound. She was becoming more relaxed around him, even allowing him to gently place items into her hands.

That evening after they retired to their respective shelters he thought through the situation. He wasn't sure what to do about having a guest who was disobeying the rules. No park guests were supposed to stay inside the stockade after closing.

But what if she continued to come back every day? Maybe he could persuade her to help more, even be a volunteer! He could get more of the cultivated area watered. He would have someone to work the bellows on the cowboy forge, if he dared to try it.

A park volunteer was a different matter. Then Enoch wouldn't get in trouble for letting her stay inside. It wouldn't be breaking the rules!

Or at least, not as much.

First though, he would have to try getting her into some sort of uniform, because let's face it, every time she bent over in her sole garment, she was clearly dangerously close to being in her Altogether. As a bonus, once Mr. Listang returned, she would be dressed and no one would guess that Enoch had occasionally snuck a peek.

He might even have a reason to make a change to the List if he had a volunteer.

He decided to try the next day.

That night he left a bowl of beans by the door of "her" longhouse.

*Today I get to recruit a volunteer!* was his first thought. Then he added, *Also, the Count is fifty-seven.*

Missy was waiting for him by the water pump, just as she had the previous days.

The smell of poop was back, even though he had cleaned up the mess from the previous day.

Clearly, step one was going to have to be showing her the bathroom place.

Normally guests and employees used the permanent bathrooms in the park. Since the turnstiles had stayed locked and Enoch needed somewhere to do his business, he had resorted to digging a skinny, rectangular hole behind his longhouse. Every week he had to make a new one.

Today he was going to excavate the ninth trench, so the timing was right.

He led Missy around and showed her how he used a pick and a hoe to make the narrow hole.

Then he stopped short.

How was he going to show her where to go?

He just *knew* that going to the bathroom in front of a guest was *way* worse than seeing one in her almost Altogether.

"Umm, the hole is for going to the bathroom." He sputtered, pointing at the hole.

She just looked at him and the hole on the ground.

"That is where you, you know, pee," he tried.

Nothing.

"Oh man." Enoch could not believe that he was going to do this. But if she was going to stay at the park and if he wanted to not be picking up poop, then she was going to have to know where to go.

And actually "go" there.

He turned his back to her and urinated in the hole.

She scampered to one side, watching him curiously. Red faced, he finished and self-consciously rearranged his clothes.

"Okay." Enoch could feel the embarrassment burning on his face. He really didn't want to dwell on this. "That is where we pee. Okay? In the hole."

He pointed.

She didn't seem particularly interested.

"Then you take some dirt and toss it in."

Suiting action to word he used a gardening trowel to add some dirt to the slit trench and looked up at his guest.

Missy was watching a cloud scudding across the sky.

Enoch looked back at the latrine in defeat.

"We need to get going on the List." Enoch figured that he was going to have to show her how to do it again tomorrow.

Not cool.

Back by the wash pump, he showed her how he rinsed his

hands in the bucket. This was a familiar task and was a chance to play with water, which she seemed to love.

Next to the pump was a table with his spare leather vest and a woven corn husk skirt that he had watched Pretty Sue make.

"Missy, if you want to stay, you have to be a volunteer, all right?"

"Waugh?" She looked at him and then the bucket and pump.

"No, we aren't doing water yet." Enoch realized that he was going to have to show her this too. "If you are going to volunteer, you need to have a uniform, like me."

He tapped his vest.

"Eena!" Missy answered.

Enoch took a deep breath and picked up the skirt.

He mimed putting it around his waist and tied the strings while she watched, then he held it out too her.

She looked at it blankly.

"Oh man, oh man, oh man!" Enoch said, mostly to himself.

He really, really knew that *touching* an almost naked park guest was even worse that the "Altogether" business or going to the bathroom where someone could see. He also knew that volunteers *had* to have uniforms. After all, Listang had let him work that way at first.

*"Well boy, your elders say that maybe you're smart enough to work here. You are different, that's for sure, but a couple of your reservation friends say that you listen good, so maybe we give it a shot. First week, you get to volunteer and train. You volunteer, you have to have a uniform and a name tag. No uniform, no job."*

Right.

Volunteer equaled uniform equaled showing her how it went on.

Enoch took a deep breath, screwed up his courage and stepped forward.

At lunch time, he invited his new volunteer into his longhouse.

"Since you are almost an employee now, you can come inside." Enoch explained as he led her inside.

Missy's eyes were wide. She stood timidly in the middle of the room.

Her arms were folded across her chest, creasing the oversize docent vest. Getting the white shirt off her had been easy. Getting the vest on had required gentle persistence.

Enoch had taken advantage of the procedure to dump a couple buckets of water over her, greatly improving the hygiene issue.

"Lunch is a treat." Enoch almost hesitated, but handed her a precious Mountain bar. "We don't have too many left, but I'll share since this is your first official day!"

The packaging rustled as she held the object.

"You open the package and eat it," he explained to no avail.

He took it back and extracted the bar, showing her that it was food by taking a bite.

That did the trick.

She snatched the remainder from his hand and took half of it down in a huge bite. While she chewed the sticky mouthful, Enoch looked at her more closely. Her voracious appetite was explained by her very skinny arms and legs. When Missy finally forced her first bite down, he clearly saw her ribs move.

Enoch offered her a plastic glass of full of water to wash it down. She managed while making only a minor spill that didn't damage her new vest at all. Enoch smiled at her.

This was progress!

As it had for a few days, the sound of Missy White operating the water pump woke Enoch before his alarm whirred to life.

*The Count is seventy-six,* he thought. Then, *I wish she would let me sleep. Showing her how to fill the buckets on her own might have been a mistake.*

Then he heard her scream. "Eeeena!" Then there was even more screaming.

Scrambling outside, he saw another person. This time it was a skinny, naked older man. His left arm was crooked and covered in a large swollen scab. He was cringing away from Missy, who was screaming unintelligibly at him and waving her clenched fists.

A new guest?

"Missy!" Enoch yelled for the first time that he could remember. "That is not how we greet guests!"

Both his volunteer and the Park guest shrank from his yell.

"Missy, come here!" Enoch pointed to his side and she scuttled over, looking at his face fearfully.

"Excuse me, sir." He addressed the man who seemed terrified, but who was staying close to the spilled water buckets. "Sir, are you okay?"

Enoch examined the man from a few feet away. He wasn't bleeding, and he seemed to be as fearful as Missy on her first day. Enoch walked over slowly, and when he had almost reached touching distance, the man scooted backwards several feet, still looking down at the ground.

The official park docent of the Native American Living History Exhibit at the Genuine Year Round State Fair, Family Park and Museum pumped some water into a bucket. At the sound of splashing, the man looked up eagerly.

"Would you like some water, sir?" Enoch held the dipper out, just as he had for Missy on her first day.

Predictably, the man remained wary, even after drinking. He followed the two docents at a distance all day. For her part, Missy stayed very close to Enoch, rarely straying more than an arm's distance. She occasionally yelled inarticulately at the new person, but was shushed by Enoch each time.

At tortilla time, Enoch had to leave the food on a seat and back away before the man would take it. Enoch could see that his arm was really messed up. When Enoch tried to slowly walk after him, the man retreated all the way to the stockade wall, near the main atrium.

There he ducked into a small hole in the barrier.

"The children's entrance!" Enoch could make out the man on all fours inside the short tunnel to the outer turnstiles.

Some Puebloan adobe forts included holes in their outer walls. People entering the compound had to crawl inside on their hands and knees. Hostile intruders attempting to enter were left vulnerable, emerging head first to be greeted by angry, upright defenders. The fair had elected to include that feature, targeting the interested and more agile schoolkids who were the bread and butter of the weekday tours of the exhibit.

"Is that how you got in, Missy?" He turned as his volunteer tugged on his arm, hooting quietly, but clearly still upset with the visitor.

"He is a park guest, just like you were," Enoch replied, crouching a little to smile at the man. "We take care of the park guests, that's our job. See?"

Missy White didn't seem to care about Mr. Listang's rules. Enoch let the visitor be, and shadowed closely by Missy, he returned to the List.

∽⊝∾

*I hate that water pump.* Enoch woke to the now familiar sound of Missy's morning water pump action right outside his lodge. *Also, the Count is ninety.*

A moment later the alarm clock whirred, futilely.

He rose and nudged Blackie with his foot. The new man's crooked left arm was still scabbed and red, but less swollen. Persuading Blackie to hold still while Enoch washed it had been... interesting. The man's cries had upset Missy, who had cried in sympathy. Enoch had finished off the open tube of antibiotic ointment from the first aid kit before Blackie's wound was covered.

However, the newest volunteer did like his sleep. He stood up slowly, ducking his partially bald head and grinning apologetically at Enoch. His matted beard failed to conceal that one of his front teeth was dark gray, almost black. If Enoch thought that Missy had bad breath, Blackie had set a new standard.

"Time to dress, then we gotta get on with it." Every morning now, Enoch had to demonstrate washing his face before he tied his hair back with the bandanna. He would slip on his leather vest and then hold up another vest, woven of seventy-four corn husks and eleven feet of fine leather line.

The improvement in his wound allowed Blackie to slide both arms in without difficulty. He didn't wear underwear and Enoch wasn't going to share his, so Blackie had to make do with a skirt much like the existing senior volunteer.

Speaking of which.

She was outside, impatiently waiting to start the day. Missy had adapted to Blackie's presence, but she wasn't particularly happy about it. Even though she was a head shorter, she seemed to be the brighter of the two and definitely played a dominant role.

She would take his food if Enoch wasn't supervising closely, or knock over his bucket during watering chores when she felt like it. If scolded by Enoch, she immediately crouched, ducking her head and hooting softly.

In order to reduce and eventually stop the random peeing and pooping that was stinking up his exhibit, Enoch had recruited the new man. It was no more than self-defense, in Enoch's opinion. Once Blackie was an official volunteer, Enoch began to give him direction, train him and generally take advantage of having an extra pair of hands.

As a result, Enoch had added a new item to the List.

Item Two was now the morning pee.

Enoch led both volunteers over to the twelfth slit latrine trench and went first. Neither volunteer was bashful, but while Missy quickly did her business and moved on, Blackie seemed to take enjoyment in playfully waggling his Altogether around and spraying everywhere.

Not cool.

Still, it kept the mess in one place.

More or less.

Okay, it was only an improvement, but one that Enoch would take. He would work on ideas to improve the whole "aim" thing.

Item Three: Unlock Inner Turnstile.

Item Four: Demonstrate the Shower Procedure.

Even though they had just dressed, Enoch had decided that dumping a bucket over first himself and then his "staff" would be the most effective way of coping with their body odor. At each of the twice-a-day bucketings, he mimed rubbing under his arms and between his legs.

His volunteers faithfully imitated him.

Despite the lack of soap, this had yielded good results. To Enoch's sensitive nose, the odor level had gone from almost unbearable to merely unpleasant.

With the extra help, Enoch could now irrigate the entire planted area, getting water to each mound of the Three Sisters daily. He knew from last year that in another two months the frost would begin to be an issue, but for now everything was still set.

Thus, he led the volunteer docents as they began the newly numbered Item Five: Perform Crop Irrigation followed by Item Six: Deliver the Crop Lecture and Demonstrate the Procedure.

Missy had become surprisingly precise when she watered, even though she could only comfortably carry buckets that were half full. Blackie was almost as strong as Enoch, and he easily managed two full buckets. His water pouring wasn't much more accurate than his morning pee, so Enoch used him mostly to carry full buckets to the planting area. His strength was also useful for weeding, particularly in the area that Enoch had neglected while he was alone. It had taken a while to teach Blackie which plants were "bad," but he eventually caught on.

There had been a few tense moments during Blackie's first few days. He had knocked down a few cornstalks, evoking squawks of indignation from Missy White. She had pursued him with an adze cultivator. Fortunately, her first swing missed. Enoch intervened before she could catch Blackie, who fortunately had demonstrated a surprising turn of speed.

Enoch made other changes too. He moved harvesting activities to after mealtime. Since he could spare one docent to be a human scarecrow, he could dry more of the harvest's beans, corn and squash at the same time.

Best of all, apart from his volunteers, they still didn't have any customers.

Bliss.

*Squeak, squeak, squeak.*

*The Count is one hundred and eleven.* Enoch woke groggily. He looked at the wind-up clock. It was fully an hour before the regular time. He looked at the longhouse window, and gray morning light was bleeding through the curtains.

"I never, ever should have shown her how to get her own water," he groused. Missy had been rising ever earlier and her first stop was always the squeaky water pump.

He stirred, intending to go outside and ask her to stop when he heard the first scream.

"Eeeena!"

Enoch lurched upright before he was fully awake. His first step tumbled him across the prone figure of Blackie, who was just muzzily stirring. As he regained his feet and opened the door he heard Missy still screaming, but he also heard a new sound.

A gargling roar was accompanied by the sound of clanging metal.

The run towards the commotion was short; he skidded to a halt in the museum entrance. Missy White had vanished, but her screams were clearly audible, echoing off the stockade walls. They were only slightly muffled by the hiding place in "her" longhouse. The source of her upset was clear.

Mr. Listang had returned and he was mad.

*Really* mad!

Listang gripped the uprights of the outer turnstiles, and shook them so hard that the harsh metallic clanging actually hurt Enoch's ears. As scared as Enoch was that his boss was so angry with him, he still noted that apparently the rule about being in one's Altogether was no longer in force.

Listang was stark naked.

And very dirty all over.

He had a *lot* of all over.

Despite his fear, Enoch understood that they had to unlock the gate, *right now*! It wasn't opening time yet, but Mr. Listang definitely wanted in. Up close, the body odor from the yelling and screaming figure of his boss easily bridged the gap between the outer and inner gates. As soon as he unhooked the combination lock, Enoch hastened backwards, gagging on the reek.

His backwards motion further inflamed Listang, whose shrieks seemed to reach a new, higher pitch. Enoch suspected that Listang had forgotten the combination, because he made no effort to unlock the outer gate.

"Auuugh!" A new source of shrieking opened up about an inch from Enoch's sensitive right ear. Blackie had finally caught up with his leader, but as soon as he saw Listang, he panicked and began screaming.

Enoch just *knew* that introducing Mr. Listang to the fresh volunteers while they were all in what passed for their pajamas—which in Blackie's case was also his complete Altogether—was not going to calm Listang down, no matter what the big boss was wearing at the moment.

Enoch turned to try to settle down Blackie.

The junior volunteer docent rewarded Enoch's calming efforts by screaming in Enoch's left ear, which immediately began to ring. The blast of sound was enough to make Enoch clutch at his head. Between his wrists, he saw Blackie diving for the "safe space" that he relied on when he was scared.

The good news was that this would get him out of Mr. Listang's sight.

The bad news was that Blackie's shelter was the still-dark Children's Tunnel.

The worse news was that Blackie continued to moan loudly from inside his "safe space."

Mr. Listang stopped growling for a moment. Fresh white spittle frosted his matted beard. With a glare at Enoch, he shuffled rapidly towards the exterior atrium. Moments later Blackie's screams renewed and his hairy backside scuttled backwards towards Enoch.

Reaching the interior, Blackie made towards Enoch and safety.

Still stunned by the incredible volume of all the screaming and growling, Enoch watched as Mr. Listang crawled right through the children's tunnel and got to his feet.

The park manager screamed a challenge. His bloodshot eyes held no intelligence, only rage.

And hunger.

Enoch backpedaled as his former boss sprinted directly towards a fresh target. The senior docent nearly stumbled on the wooden pallet that held the stacked brown buckets. Stepping backwards around the water pump, he tried to apologize.

"Mr. Listang, I'm really sorry about the uniforms." He pleaded. "It isn't opening time yet, and I have been all alone for a hundre—"

Enoch didn't reach the end of his first excuse as Listang, his gaze fixed upon his target, closed the distance to his intended meal. He tripped on the buckets and his grasp only reached as far as Enoch's knees. Black nails raked Enoch's shins, drawing blood and a surprised yell.

"Sir, what the hell?" he protested.

Enoch's instincts were better than his retort and he belatedly followed Blackie, whose panicked flight led them both into the heart of the planting area. Listang followed closely, and his hoarse yells spurred both of his prey to greater speeds. On the second circuit, Enoch stumbled as he passed the leather-crafting station.

Listang again dove for his prey, biting at Enoch's chest and tearing away a mouthful of skin.

Enoch screamed in real terror as he realized his boss, for some inexplicable reason, was actually trying to *eat* him. The horror lent him greater strength and he kicked his boss off, breaking two of his own toes in the process.

His screams roused Missy, and as he scrambled to his feet and began to run again, he saw her shocked face peeking out from the longhouse door she had cracked open.

"Eeenaaa!" she yelled uselessly.

"Missy, help me!" Enoch cried as he pounded past, heading back towards his own room. Listang followed closely. Enoch could see that his hunter's face was freshly painted with Enoch's own blood.

Enoch fled as fast his injured foot allowed, but a terrified glance over his shoulder showed his tormentor narrowing the gap. His fear prevented him from realizing that his path had trapped him in the entrance hall of the museum, and he fetched up against the inner turnstiles.

This wasn't fair! He had done not just the best that he could but he had helped customers. He had followed the List faithfully. Instead of appreciating that or even listening to Enoch's explanation, Mr. Listang was attacking him for no reason!

Blended with his bone-deep fear and feeling that he was going to lose no matter what, Enoch felt it.

Anger.

His schedule was ruined. His crops damaged. His work unappreciated.

Listang had never really liked him.

Had bullied him.

Even if he ended up dead, Enoch was going to fight.

He pushed off the inner gate and punched Listang in mid lunge.

Enoch's fist pounded the much larger man right in his gaping mouth.

And Enoch immediately regretted it.

Listang recoiled, screaming, but now Enoch's own hand was cut and bleeding, and his thumb stuck out at a funny angle.

Hunger overcame pain, and Listang attacked again. This time the maddened, stronger man dropped them both to the ground and the one-time park manager ducked his head down, biting at Enoch's chest.

Despite the excruciating pain, Enoch fought. Blinded by his attacker's mop of stinking hair, he clubbed ineffectually with his hands. Listang's hands tore at his face, splitting Enoch's lips and gouging his cheeks.

It was about to be over, but Enoch didn't stop fighting.

And then Listang reared up, screaming, not in hunger, but in pain. The cannibal turned just in time to catch Missy White's second earnest jab in his short ribs. The puncture from the sharp spike of the weed pole was shallow but painful. Listang instantly focused on the small naked woman, who stumbled back involuntarily, her fear written across her face.

Enoch kicked reflexively, and tangled Listang's feet. The furious man tumbled to all fours on the packed dirt, facing away from his previous target. His head snapped up, and bloodshot eyes glared at Missy.

A snarl rumbled from Listang's chest. His powerful arms and legs tensed as he stood, preparing to rush and overwhelm his next meal.

Just as Blackie ran up, nearly stumbled, and with a wild but powerful blow, swung his cultivating adze.

And buried the pick in Listang's skull.

For a moment, the tableau was frozen.

Enoch waited to see what would happen. Although it probably didn't matter, considering how much blood was splattered about, he couldn't help realizing one fact, despite his fear and pain.

There was a *lot* of Altogether in view.

Pretty much every everywhere.

Listang dropped his arms to his sides, and swayed as Missy charged forward several steps, screeching incoherently. Using both hands, she raised her weed pole overhead and with all the leverage of the long handle, swung downwards at their suddenly quiet attacker.

The pole snagged the red and white welcome banner and rapped Listang smartly on the shoulder.

The blow was heartfelt but the wooden pole rebounded harmlessly upwards.

Listang dropped limply anyway, the adze still buried in his head. One end of the torn banner still hung from the alcove ceiling while a segment emblazoned "HOEDOWN!" was draped diagonally across the fresh body before tailing off onto the ground.

Enoch's ears were still ringing from all the screaming and he had no idea what do next.

So he just lay back for a moment, his chest, hand and foot throbbing.

*I guess I better check the List.*


That morning the count was one hundred and thirty.

Enoch leaned on his weeding pole and smiled with pride as Missy dropped her empty bowl off with Blackie, who was rinsing all spoons and bowls in one of the wash buckets. Behind him, the Three Sisters were thinning out. The last of the crop was about in and first frost wasn't too far off.

With lunch over, it was about time for the afternoon List to start. As he had healed, Enoch had made a few changes to the List, adjusting to the new reality of his small world.

The new staff had been invaluable. For all that they were a bit slow, they had saved his life, literally.

Blackie suddenly growled.

Enoch followed the junior docent's gaze and saw a small naked figure emerge from the children's tunnel entrance. Blinking, the young boy looked around and, spying the scene inside, ducked back into the shadow.

Enoch smiled again.

The newest volunteer had arrived.

Cool.

# Storming the Tower of Babel

## SARAH A. HOYT

*She thought she was alone in a dead world…*

When Claire first saw the man, he looked like a zombie. In fact, the only thing that stopped her trigger finger twitching was realizing that he was in fact still dressed. The rags attached to him weren't just dirt, or an accretion of leaves, but clothes. Squinting, from her hideout, as he approached, she saw that he had, probably, once been wearing jeans and a jacket of some sort. They were now ragged and dirty, a dun color, but still clothes. On his back was one of those huge backpacks that people used to carry all their needs for a month in. And on the front… he was carrying something.

Just because he wasn't a zombie, it didn't mean he was safe, of course. He probably wasn't safe. Certainly in the old world, in the world that would never again come back, he would have been someone to stay away from. His straggly brown hair looked sun-bleached. His beard had that look like homeless men used to get, not only overgrown, but tangled and matted. And he looked straight ahead, as if he never expected to stop walking, and also as if he'd forgotten why he was walking.

When men lose their minds, Claire knew, what remained was not some great, archetypal noble savage. She'd seen that often enough while working in a hospital, in the inner city of Chicago. When men lost their minds, what remained behind was brutish and nasty whether it was short or not.

She'd taken refuge in the second floor of a bell tower in a village on the outskirts of Porto. Once she'd secured enough weapons and bullets—mostly from an abandoned police station— this refuge had proven perfect. It had one door on the bottom floor, and then no windows at all until the top floor, which was at the level of a normal third floor. Access to it was managed by a series of ladders, which could be pulled up, one after another, to leave the person at the top perfectly isolated. So far, at least, while zombies had smashed the door and made a mess of the bottommost floor, they hadn't been able to organize for an assault on the next level. And from the top of her tower, she'd shot most of the ones who approached. Unless it was darkest night, or deepest gloom, she shot them. If she could see them, she could kill them. And killing them not only kept her safe, but kept the virus away from her. She'd seen her friends succumb, and her idea had always been if she caught the flu, if formication set in, she'd eat a bullet.

When she left here—rare enough—to go find food or other necessities, she wore disposable outfits she'd found at the local medical center, mask, and coveralls, goggles and shoe coverings which she hoped minimized her chance of getting the virus.

But sometimes, after months of not hearing a human voice, nothing but the crazed keening of zombies, she wondered if it would have been better if she'd caught it and died before the world went crazy.

Only survival had become a habit. She kept her finger on the rifle trigger, lay down on the dusty, uneven boards on the floor of the bell tower, and looked as the man came closer. A few—she didn't even know how many—months ago, she would have been thrilled at this tower, with its worn floors, its stone walls, its marks of medieval workmanship. Now, as probably to the people who built it, it was a place to weather out a siege. But would the siege ever be over?

As the ragged man with the unkempt long hair drew near, she realized what he carried in his arms was a baby. At first, she thought the baby was dead, then saw it draw breath.

Her first impulse was to push the ladders down, to go welcome him in. but she stopped herself. For all she knew the baby was either a snack, or something the madman had picked up possibly after killing her parents.

He approached the tower and turned with his foot the pile of her discarded surgical coverings then looked up at the tower, his gray eyes focusing. He seemed to be making an effort of some sort, his lips working. For a moment she thought that the sound to come out of his lips would be the zombie keening.

Instead, what came out was both surprising and human, *"S'il vous plaît? J'ai besoin de lait pour ma petit fille."*

It took Claire a second to realize that what she'd heard wasn't Portuguese, one more second to realize her long-lost high school French didn't quite fit. Something about a little girl. She leaned over, just enough that he could see her, but ready to duck away should he take a potshot. There was no reason he should take a potshot, but hell, she felt like she'd gone a little crazy and she was sure he had too.

Instead, she allowed just her profile to show, and shouted, "Do you speak English?"

There was a hesitation, a clearing of throat, and then "Please, help. I need milk for my daughter."

Claire could have answered she didn't have milk—true—or that she had no idea what to do with a baby—also true—or even that she was afraid to let an unknown man into her sanctuary—still true—or even pleaded a fear of contagion. But she looked at the man, with the immobile baby in his arms. She looked dead. Was the baby dead? Or just dying, and could be killed by an unkind woman who sent them on?

So, instead of sending him on, she said, "A moment." Before lowering the stairs, and climbing down, she put one of the police handguns in her pocket. If worst came to worst, she could shoot him, or eat a bullet herself.

But when she opened the door, looking out at the man, she felt guilty for her thoughts. He didn't look dangerous. He looked dead. Physically alive, but dragging that live body through the world, long after his soul had fled.

He pushed the baby at her, on extended hands, "Please, look after her. I don't need to come in. I understand if you don't trust me."

He hadn't heard a human voice in months…

Jean Tierri had thought the worst day in his life was when he had to strangle his wife because she'd turned into a zombie. That was because he lacked an understanding of the full panoply of horror that could unfold before a single father, protecting his months-old daughter through a zombie apocalypse.

There had been the difficulty of securing milk and diapers, the problem with carrying them, and then the problem of defending himself, physically. And then there had been the problem of silence, the sense of being alone in a world where everyone else had become something less than human. His daughter Madeleine couldn't talk to him, and he'd found himself not talking to her, because his voice might attract zombies to them. The silence had settled over him, so total, so absolute, that at times he thought he was the one who'd died, and this desolate and strange place in which he walked, wholly devoid of human contact save for attackers, was his punishment, a vast, immense Tartarus in which he would wander forever.

If it were not for his daughter, for the almost atavistic need—he had no feeling left—to keep her alive, he'd have eaten a bullet, or dashed himself down some precipice, or even let one of the damned zombies eat him.

And then he'd found his first real human, and the first words he heard out of her mouth were a death sentence for his daughter.

He'd seen this tower from a distance, down the flat, straight village street, and seen the woman go into it. Normally he'd have given her a wide berth. Sure, she wasn't a zombie. She wore clothes. But she might be crazy. Or someone who wished to do him harm.

But he'd run out of milk yesterday, and Madeleine had cried out her hunger until she couldn't cry anymore. He'd stopped at every house on the way, looking for cans of formula, and found none. He only had this one hope, this one, last attempt at saving his daughter.

"I don't have any milk," the woman said. She was young, and he suspected she'd been pretty. She spoke English with an American accent, and she was clean and wearing new clothes. She smelled clean, with a touch of deodorant, which awakened in him an almost unbearable longing for a world in which young women were clean and smelled good, and didn't keen and try to tear off chunks of your flesh to eat.

She must have read his despair in his eyes, as she took Madeleine from his arms. If he'd been more aware, he'd not have let her take the baby, but all the woman did was feel over Madeleine's chest, look at Madeleine's eyes, as they tracked her, and the baby made a weak attempt to cry. "That's all right, sweetie," she said, then looked at the man. "Do you have bottles? Have you given her water?"

"Some," he said. "I have disposable bottles, but the water is not enough. I don't know what to do. There is no formula in any of the houses I looked in. The mini-mart was destroyed. Everything thrown out. I don't know what to do."

She looked him over coolly. "My name is Claire," she said. "I'm from Kansas."

"Jean Tierri," he said. "From France. I was on vacation."

"Yeah," she said. "Me too. I was in Porto for Sao Joao when the lights went out."

She must have read incomprehension in his face and said, "Never mind. I think I know where there might be some formula. Come on."

She was full of certainties, of plans, this woman. She had cars nearby—broken and dented by zombies, but still operating—and she explained, "Not many zombies here in the village. And there's a good distance before the next village. I've shot all the local ones, I think, or at least most of them. Sometimes I ring the bell to attract them, just so I can shoot them. Lately not many come."

He said, "I heard your bell. That's why I followed it. I was running out of formula. I hoped there would be someone here. I hoped—"

"A good thing, then," she said, nodding. And hesitated a moment. "We don't have a car seat. We'll try to find one. Can you hold her and shoot? We're going to the outskirts of the village and there might be zombies."

"I've had to hold her while I shoot."

"Of course."

He'd ridden shotgun while she drove madly over the bumpy Portuguese roads. Around a blind turn, a child zombie came running at them, keening, and Claire gunned the car, letting the zombie bounce over the hood, then accelerated to catch the next zombie, an adult male, before accelerating yet more, turning sharply right on the next road, to make the zombies fall off and drive over them.

He thought she was mad when she pulled right up to the store, and told him to go inside, while she held the fort.

The store looked like the little grocery stores around every corner in Portugal, except there was a heavy corrugated shutter all over the presumably glass front. It had no windows.

But Claire pushed a key at him. "I shuttered it. Open it. It's zombie free inside. I got to it before them. Smells like hell, from all the perishables going bad. But it has a lot of things I use. Grab whatever you need, besides formula. I'll hold the door."

He ended up grabbing all the formula they had on the shelves, milk, soy, rice-based, it didn't matter. It seemed impossible to him now that once, in a long-lost world, he'd thought it normal to have all sorts of baby formula, for every possible taste. He'd thought it only right. Now he wanted to cry for that lost world and his last innocence.

He grabbed all the disposable bottles, too—little sacks of plastic that took a nipple at the end—because most of the time it was impossible to sterilize the used bottles, and he took all the diapers, in all sizes, because they could be adjusted, or cut if needed and secured with tape, and he took soap and water, as Claire had suggested.

For the first time he thought of his clothes. He'd never been a good Christian. One wasn't, of course, not in modern France. One was too modern, too smart for any of that. Instead of Christianity, even through his bout in the army, in Afghanistan, he'd clung to the idea of civilization; the idea that he was living at a pinnacle of civilization, and that he must preserve it.

But now, looking at the little area with clothes the store carried, he realized the pitiful state of his own clothes and thought to himself "And Adam saw that he was naked." It hadn't mattered that he was filthy and that his clothes were tatters when there had been no one to see or notice. At any rate, he thought, he hadn't been able to take time to bathe or groom himself, because he'd have to leave Madeleine unprotected for the while. And that was unthinkable.

He was looking over the T-shirts and jeans when he heard Claire fire twice, but she didn't call him, so he thought it must be all right. In the old world, shots would be a reason to check, but this was a new world. "What a brave new world..." he murmured to himself, shocked at his own gravely, unused voice.

When he dumped things in the back of the car Claire didn't even look, up. She continued scanning the streets, watching.

He'd water, razor, soap, a lot of baby wipes—which he hadn't got before because they added to the weight he was carrying, but he hoped Claire would let him stay. He'd seen the arrangement she had in the tower, over her shoulder, while they talked, and he wanted it. The permanence and certainty of a place. Somewhere to stay. Safety for Madeleine.

He couldn't imagine hurting her to take it. It seemed a sin to destroy one of the few real humans left. And he thought that it was a real sin to return her help with fighting. Besides, he thought to himself, looking at her capable hands holding the gun, there was no guarantee he'd win.

But he hoped she'd let him stay. It would mean luxuries like wipes and maybe baths from bottled water. He'd also got a radio and batteries. He knew it would be as silent as his cell phone had gone, a useless object, no more capable of functioning than a rock. But he could hope.

He got back on the passenger seat, with a bottle of water, a disposable bottle, a can of formula. He brought out his can opener. Claire glanced over and didn't scold him, or tell him he needed his hands free to ride shotgun. Instead, she said, "Tell me when you're done." And continued scanning the street. She shot twice. He didn't know if she'd shot at zombies or if she'd hit. He didn't ask.

After Madeleine had eaten, greedily, they closed the store and drove back to the tower, which she'd also left locked. But more than that, she'd used something that looked like a shepherd's crook, to push the ladder up. When they entered, she retrieved the implement from atop the rafter where she'd hid it, and pulled the ladders down. "It's a risk, of course. And I run it, every time I go out. I don't like it, but when I need supplies, I can't stay here, holed up till I die of starvation."

She led him up the steps, to the second floor, which was full of neatly packed supplies, and the third, where she had a sleeping bag, a gas camping stove, bottled water, and a mismatched set of pans.

"However so humble it is," she said.

"I forgot to get a sleeping bag," he said.

"Next time," she said, as she showed him up the final flight of steps, that one secured, which was the bell tower proper, the bells and ropes hanging down. He tugged experimentally on one, producing a frantic ringing.

Claire reached for one of the rifles leaning against the parapet and waited, but no zombie charged.

Later, after they'd gone down the stairs, and Jean had washed as well as it was possible with a sponge and a couple gallons of water, after she'd opened and heated a couple of cans of soup and fried a few frankfurters over the gas fire of the camping stove, after Madeleine had been fed again and changed and fallen asleep on a nest of T-shirts, while wearing yet another T-shirt, Claire told him about Sao Joao, the celebration of the solstice in downtown Porto.

"I came over with my two best friends," she said. "College graduation. Pre-med. We'd heard rumors of the virus, sure, but no one was sure what it was, and we thought it was that bath salts thing again. There was this celebration in downtown Porto. June 23. We'd seen the videos on YouTube. Dancing and singing on the streets, fireworks and partying all night. Seemed just what the doctor ordered. Jill and Tammy had been sick-ish over finals, with flu, but they were better now. And then..." She shook her head. "Jill was dragged somewhere, as the lights went out and zombies charged the streets. Tammy...Tammy changed. She tore off all her clothes and started chomping."

"How did you get out of there? A major city?" He was impressed. There must have been zombies everywhere.

"I don't know. I know I hit Tammy on the head with an iron pipe, something that was just lying there, from a construction site, in downtown Porto. And then I took the pipe..." She shrugged. "I was all splattered in blood and brains by the time I made it to the beach, in the morning. There were no zombies on the beach. They must have gone towards the center, because when the lights went out, the fireworks still went up. I...I walked. I don't know how far or how fast. I walked away from people. I remember taking this track, deeper inland, not sure why, just wanting to get away. Then I found this tower. I've been here for the last few months. I thought I was the only person alive in the whole world."

"I thought it was just me and Madeleine," he said. "I thought—" and then he told her the story, the whole story. In another world, in another time, he'd not have thought to do that. Admitting to killing his wife—admitting...

"Beatrice and I saved for years," he said. "We were living together, but we thought when we married, we'd go on vacation to Portugal. Beatrice liked history, you see, and we knew there were many museums and castles and..." He shrugged. "*Enfin*, we thought it would be fun. Only when we got married, she was pregnant, and then Madeleine was born, and we waited till summer to come. Madeleine was three months old, then, and we thought it would be easier.

"Like you, I'd seen the videos of zombies, and listened to the stories of people turning in the U.S. My neighbors didn't pay much attention. After all, it was one of those things those crazy Americans were doing. Who could trust them?" He paused, his self-protection instinct telling him he was revealing too much. But once you got to the end of the world, and past it, what could threaten you? "But I'd served in Afghanistan, you see. I knew real Americans, not just what the media told us Americans were. I knew tough, competent men. I had their e-mails. From the beginning I'd asked, from the beginning I'd got back the same answer: this is a biological terrorist attack, a virus that ejects another virus, the later one of which kills all higher brain function. You can't recover from it. This is for all intents and purposes the zombie apocalypse.

"I tried to tell Beatrice. I warned her. But it's not like it would have been any easier to weather the apocalypse in Paris, would it? Still too many people, too many sources of contagion. Besides, she was so tired, so depressed. After Madeleine was born, she was so sad. They say it's normal. Postpartum depression. I thought the trip would cheer her up." He dared look up. Claire was looking at him, pityingly, the sort of look a mother gives a baby suffering from an incurable disease. "We were visiting the carriage museum, in Lisbon, where they have all the carriages of the great kings and nobles of the last five hundred years in Portugal. And right there, she started pulling at her clothes and saying something was crawling all over her. I caught Madeleine before she fell, set her on the floor and I was ready. I strangled Beatrice when she charged me, trying to bite me, and I was out of the museum before anyone discovered her. I spent all our savings in the store next door, buying the biggest backpack I could find, and formula and diapers to fill it with. I remembered disposable bottles. I took a taxi to the national preserve on the outskirts of town, and I started walking. I don't even know where I am. For weeks I waited for Madeleine to show signs of zombieing, but she behaved like any other baby. At six months, she can roll over and smile, though she doesn't smile much, perhaps because she's not seen me do it. Where did we end up?"

"North of Porto. I'm also not sure where we are. I saw a sign at the entrance to the village, but I've not been thinking about that, but more how to survive." She looked very sad. "I've come to accept I'll never return home, and I will never know if my parents survived this."

They never knew how it happened, though later they were to find it was not unusual for those in the same situation. When you find yourself at the end of the world, any human comfort is good, necessary. It reestablished their humanity. It helped them feel like not all was hopeless.

### She considered asking him to leave…

Claire didn't know how to take their relationship at first, or even she wasn't sure they had a relationship. They were chance met strangers, who could watch each other's back, which allowed them to forage faster, longer, to more distant places.

But a week later, when they went foraging, Jean acquired a lot of plastic barrels and carried them all the way up the tower, affixing them with a sort of wire frame to the pillars that supported the windows. "We'll collect the water when it rains," he said. His eyes looked distant and dreamy. "And someday we'll have a big bathtub, though I have no idea how we'll get it up here or drain it, but we'll have a big bathtub, and be able to take baths like civilized people. Possibly before Madeleine goes to colle— would have gone to college."

She spoke quickly in a rush. "Just having more water to wash in would be a great thing," she said. "I guess if we had more people we could do more, you know, but I don't even know if anyone else survived."

"Wait," he said, and brought out his transistor radio with

great ceremony. But all they heard was different types of static and sometimes, distantly, a sound like almost-voices, but not really voices. By the time the cold weather set in, they were used to living together. Perhaps they were still strangers, and yet she'd found that she couldn't imagine losing him. Madeleine was starting to sit up, and smiled a lot. They'd got more soup, more sausage and a lot of baby cereal and a propane heater that made the tower bearable when the rain-laden north wind blew.

Through those lengthening winter evenings, they listened to the radio, the differences in static, speculated about whether there were still people out there, about whether some of them were transmitting.

Then one night—they thought it was Christmas night—their scanning of AM stations brought a strange burst of language over the radio. But the language was Portuguese.

*"Castelo do Corvo, distrito de Vila Real, provincia alto Tras os Montes, Há aqui cem pessoas com provisos para passar o Inverno, e zombies sob control. Sobreviveu mais alguem em Portugal? Há alguem por aí fora ou estamos nos sós no mundo?"*

Neither of them spoke Portuguese. They listened in rapt attention as the message repeated and repeated. In a corner, in a liberated playpen Madeleine stopped playing and seemed to listen too. It was the first time the three of them had heard a stranger, since tragedy had engulfed the world.

They discussed the words they couldn't understand. It seemed to them there was the name of a city, the location, and something about a hundred people surviving—this from a resemblance to French—and a hundred people seemed like an immense number to them.

That night they opened a bottle of wine to celebrate that there were so many other people in the world, so many people it seemed to them, when they thought this had been the end of humanity.

"You know," Claire said, "they say, from our DNA that we've gone through bottlenecks like this, where there were only a few hundred people left alive in the whole world."

They waited to see if the message was repeated in other languages, but it never was. Sometimes the station wasn't even audible. Sometimes all they got was static on that dial, then it would return as though people had remembered to float the message again.

"There is no reason for them to repeat the message in English or French or any other language," Jean said, after a few hours of listening to the same message. "No reason for them to report in English or French, either," he said, since reporting of an incomprehensible nature—except they thought the number of people had increased, maybe—"even if they speak those languages, they don't think anyone in their range speaks it. They probably only transmit within a couple hundred kilometers. Maybe less."

And they'd nodded and gone to sleep, content in the knowledge that the world had people, that it wasn't just the two of them and the zombies forever.

A reason to hope...

By the end of January, or at least by about thirty days after they'd first heard the transmissions, Claire asked Jean if he thought there was any chance they could find that village. He squinted at her. "I don't know where any of those places are," he said. "And even if we found a map, and had enough gas... it will be very dangerous. And they might not accept us. We're so comfortable here, and it's safe. There aren't even that many zombies that come when we ring the bells."

She nodded, "Yes, but you see, we're going to need a doctor."

He looked alarmed. "You're ill? Madeleine is ill?" In her corner Madeleine gurgled with laughter—a new accomplishment—and returned to repeating endless strings of meaningless syllables, another new accomplishment, before rediscovering her fingers and playing with them.

"Not... ill precisely," Claire said, and seeing him look genuinely confused, she added, "You know, we've not had any kind of contraceptives..."

His eyes widened and he went red, then pale, then said, "I'm sorry. *Je suis desole.*"

"Don't be," she said. "I'm not. Someone needs to replace the hordes that died. But I... well, I studied everything about human birth. Human biology is my undergrad degree. But I don't think I can, you know, look down there, while I'm up here and pushing."

He chewed into his lip. "This village, it might have some midwife, someone?"

She nodded.

He chewed his lip. "But they might not. And we're strangers, you know? We will arrive from nowhere. We'll be lucky if someone doesn't get trigger-happy. And I'm afraid, you know, of taking you on that trip." His eyes misted. "I don't know if I could, my dear, be single father of two children. Nor having to strangle...another mother of my children."

She sighed. But the worry continued. "I'm due I think in July judging from where I stopped my cycle." She paused. "Supposing it is January now?"

"We have six months?" Jean said. "We'll think of something."

That night he tossed and turned in their nest of sleeping bags. It seemed to her that they must find a solution, but she didn't know what. She didn't want to take the long journey while pregnant, even if she thought that she must, eventually, go there, so there would be people for the children to grow up around. But while pregnant, on uncertain roads, not quite sure of their reception...she didn't want to go. She'd grown used to their tower, to the comfort and safety. Other than the Sunday bell ringing and zombie shooting, they didn't even see many zombies. If they had other people then they could rebuild the old medieval wall around the tower and the center of town, and...do something. Start a village. Other people. It seemed like a dream.

"I should have studied engineering," she said.

He half laughed. "Why?"

"Because then we could rig a transmitter, talk to that village, know if they know of anyone else, know if anyone knows of a midwife or an obstetrician."

He was silent a long time after that, then he said, "You know, there must have been a radio station around here somewhere, one with transmitters. Or someone with a shortwave radio. Or something."

She thought furiously. "I don't even know how to look for transmission equipment, and if we found it, I wouldn't know what to do to make it work, but I was thinking..."

"Yes?"

"I went through the police station in another village, to look for guns, and I saw they had a transmitter. In fact, all the police radios are transmitters and receivers, aren't they? There must be a police station around here. Perhaps we can find a phone book. They used to have maps too."

Assembling pieces...

Jean tried not to worry about Claire. If he'd thought about it, he'd not have sired a child into this world, but her idea that it was important to replace all who had died was not without merit. If humanity was to survive, there would have to be more children. He'd thought he'd have more children with Beatrice, when they could afford it, when he had found a real job, rather than the clerk job that he could find after the army. When the balance of jobs and tax burden was right, they'd have another child or two.

That was all as meaningless now as the horoscopes older civilizations used to cast to find if the gods would smile on some endeavor. Now... They'd have as many children as could survive. Unlike Beatrice, Claire either didn't have the upset stomachs, the little problems of pregnancy or she refused to give in to them. Or perhaps she wasn't familiar enough with him to let him see them. But no. That didn't make any sense. Living as they did, they had to be aware of each other, of everything the other did and felt.

But still he worried. During Beatrice's pregnancy he'd read everything about birth and giving birth, and he knew everything that could be wrong, for the baby and for the mother, particularly in a birth unattended by medical professionals. Everything could kill the mother, from an infection due to too long a birth, to a too-big baby. And even trivial things could kill the baby like a cord wrapped around the neck.

It seemed criminally neglectful, now, that he hadn't brought those pregnancy and birth books with him. Sure, there probably were some around here, somewhere, but they'd be in Portuguese, and even if he could almost guess at the meaning, he couldn't learn from them, not really. He'd miss some crucial thing.

They went out, in widening circles, finding more zombies every time they ventured farther. They found a phone book in an abandoned row house. It was curled, and had got wet in rain, when it had come through the broken windows. But it was readable, and it did have a map in the beginning.

The bad news was that the police station was...

"In zombie town," Claire said.

They called it zombie town because it was the farther end of the village on the way from the next big town, and zombies got there first. They usually got killed afterwards, when they came to the sound of the ringing bell at their next zombie-killing Sunday morning. By common consent, Jean and Claire never went there, because there was more of a chance of a random zombie showing up. Also, it was the creepy end of the village, where three or four apartment houses stood completely burned out. It was too easy to imagine the virus catching throughout all those floors, and, as the elevators stopped working, the zombies trapped in the building accidentally setting fire to it. And zombies and remaining humans burning together.

"What if we hold three days of zombie shooting parties?" Jean asked.

"Doesn't mean one won't show up the day we go into town to look for the police station," Claire said.

"No, it doesn't, but... it reduces the chances. Hey, look," he pointed across the street at a sign that said "FOGUETEIROS" with a drawing of fireworks. "Perhaps we can set off some fireworks in the night, and hold more of a zombie-shooting party."

She looked at him confused, and he realized she hadn't known him very long. It seemed so strange. He and Beatrice had dated for years, and lived together for years before they even considered having a child together.

"I was an explosives specialist in Afghanistan," he said. "I can set off the fireworks. I should also be able to make bombs to kill them, if they show up in batch lots."

There was a silence, then she nodded. She drove their car to block the door of the warehouse, as had become their custom. He didn't want her to risk herself in there, but he was holding Madeleine strapped around his middle, so neither of them really should be in there. It was just that there were only two of them. And Madeleine, who couldn't help yet.

He was incredibly relieved when the warehouse turned out to be zombie free. They had broken in, at some time, and knocked about, but since there apparently hadn't been any other humans in there, nothing held their attention. And luckily, other than throwing some things around, they hadn't caused any real damage. And fortunately the fire hadn't reached there.

Jean realized he was making sounds of excitement as he opened boxes when he heard Claire say, "Kid in a candy store?"

He laughed. "There's so many varieties here, so much fun. Okay, let me collect what I think I can to make a night-long display. We'll attract them to the tower, then shoot them, then in the morning we drive off to the police station, and we'll see what we can do. Then I'll clean the area around the tower, so that you're not exposed to any of the virus."

"I don't want you exposed to the virus, either!" she protested.

"No, of course not," he said. "But listen, there's a hierarchy, I will wear masks and protective gear, but if I catch it and zomb out, we lose me. If you catch it, we lose you and the baby."

"You'd better not catch it," she said. "I don't want to be single mother of two babies any more than you want to be single father of two babies."

"I'll take every possible precaution," he said, while piling fireworks in the trunk of the car, then throwing in some others to cannibalize for powder, in case they got a lot of zombies, now or later.

"You know," she said. "When my friend was pregnant her husband cleaned the cat box. Now you want to clean zombies."

"All the same thing," he said, and looked very serious. "Seriously, Claire, we do all this, and work this hard, and endure everything for the future, for the children. If we work really hard, and kill a lot of zombies, and create a safe environment, maybe our great-grandchildren will have civilization again, instead of living like rats in the ruins of their ancestors' achievements. Humans have always worked for their children, for the future. I think Europe lost sight of this for a while. But now? Now it's all we have. All the things that seemed important, everything that mattered? I'd have died if I didn't have Madeleine to look after. We need something to work towards."

They worked. For the next week, they held a zombie shooting party every day. Hopefully the police station also held more ammunition, because they were going to need it.

And then on the night before their proposed expedition, they set off fireworks. Claire was leaning out the tower, looking for movement in the night.

She almost shot them. They were just two figures, in the night, in the dark. But as she was about to pull the trigger, something about the figures stopped her. They were holding hands. She'd never seen zombies holding hands. She shouted into the dark, "Hello?"

"*Olá!*" came back.

"Do you speak English?"

"Yes, I do," came back in a strong accent.

They were brother and sister...

Jean was the one who let them in, leaving Claire and Madeleine upstairs, looking down. Like when they first met, while they knew these two weren't a danger because they weren't zombies, there was always the chance they were hostile anyway, or that one of them had got infected recently and would go into zombie mode any minute. Which is why he'd worn one of the disposable protective suits, and a mask and gloves.

The newcomers were young and dark in a Mediterranean sort of way. The young man had a beard, the girl had long hair. They might not have started that way, but they were better dressed or at least more composed than Jean had been. "We were in Porto, for the end-of-year celebrations for university," the boy, Pedro, said. "And then the lights went out."

"We're not exactly sure how we escaped," the girl, Laura, said. "Except for grabbing hold of what we could and killing zombies and moving, just keeping moving. By the time we got to the outskirts of town, most of the city was burning, because of the Sao Joao bonfires, and zombies, and I guess things going everywhere."

"Sometimes I worry there is something wrong with us that we could just kill people... well, used to be people. But I'd been following the outbreak on YouTube, from all over the world, and I knew that the mind was gone."

"Well, you can stay in the floor below," Jean said. "And we'll pull the ladder up. No offense, but I don't—"

"Know if one of us is infected," Pedro said. "I get that. Which is why you're wearing the medical getup."

"Right." He didn't explain to them he was afraid of other things, either. There was no point. Not that he knew if bad people had survived, but certainly if survival depended on ability to kill to survive, it was possible a great number of bad people had survived. Which is why they needed communications. They needed the ability to get a feeling for what was out there.

He hoped Pedro and Laura would be okay. They spoke Portuguese. They should be able to communicate with the faraway village. They would perhaps be able to communicate with other people.

"Change of plans," he said. "If they're a problem we should find out in two or three days. Then we'll go to the police station to find a radio."

"I figured you were trying to find a way to cut me out of all the fun," Claire said.

He tried to explain, "I'm trying to protect you because—"

Her hand grabbed his shoulder, gently. "It's all right, Jean. I get it. I was joking."

He managed a smile before they kissed.

They could fling their words into the void…

That's what it all amounted to.

Claire liked Pedro and Laura when she met them. They were what in the past, in that other, lost world, they'd have called "a nice couple of kids." They weren't infected with zombie virus, and they didn't seem interested in slitting Jean's and Claire's throat and taking the tower for themselves. Jean wasn't about to leave them alone with Madeleine, for sure, until he knew them much better, but he was willing to go with them on a raiding expedition of the police station. Willing, too, to let them clean the area around the tower of zombie bodies. They'd opened one of the marble tombs in the cemetery next door, thrown the zombies in, then slid the marble slab atop it again, all the while wearing protective clothing. Then they'd washed with antibacterial soap, and held a quarantine before returning to Claire with the scavenged police radio, which they'd attached to the car battery beneath the tower with what Jean called "the longest set of radio cables."

After that it was a matter of transmitting. Pedro, who had been studying engineering—unfortunately Laura had studied languages, not nursing or obstetrics—had done something to the radio that he thought increased its range, turning it in fact into a mini radio station. "With the antennas," he said, referring to about three car antennas bootstrapped together, "we should be able to get some distance. It's not a radio station, but Portugal is not a very big country. We should be able to transmit and receive over a lot of the North, and if we can get anyone to listen to us, and they're listening to other people … we can pass a message a long way." He'd also taken parts of the main police transmitter and done things to the little car radio. "Not too much," he said. "Too much and the car battery won't support it. But perhaps enough. I hope enough." He'd looked very sad. "They never taught us to build pirate radio stations, you know? It used to be forbidden."

On this rigged device, they caught other stations, including what seemed to be garbled Spanish stations. "There're probably others," Claire said. "In shortwave radios and other...other ways."

"I should have learned other languages," Jean said, with a slight moan. "Besides English."

"What, all of them?" Claire asked. She seemed to find the idea hilarious, but she too wished for those days of getting information painlessly, of communicating without effort across the world.

There were other stations too. For a brief moment, they caught something that sounded like German, but Laura, looking solemn, shook her head and said, "Swedish. There are other people in the world. There really are."

There was also a brief, very brief burst of English with a definite British accent, but nothing they could pinpoint.

And then they found the old station again, only different:

*"Castelo do Corvo, distrito de Vila Real, provincia alto Tras os Montes, Há aqui cento e quarenta pessoas com provisos. Estamos a reconstruir a parede da vila. Os zombies estao sob control. Sobreviveu mais alguem em Portugal? Há alguem por aí fora ou estamos nos sós no mundo? Estamos dispostos a acolher refugiados. Venham juntar-nos."*

Pedro translated, "They say, *Castelo do Corvo, Distrito de Vila Real, Provincia dos altos Tras of Montes.* We have a hundred and forty people and provisions. We're rebuilding the town wall. Zombies are under control. Did anyone else survive in Portugal? Is there anyone out there or are we alone in the world? We are willing to accept refugees. Come and join us."

When Jean and Claire repeated the other message, the one they'd memorized, it was obvious that the situation had changed for the better. This place was growing, getting established.

"I probably could find it," Pedro said.

"You're welcome to," Jean said. "But I don't want to risk Claire. Not while she's pregnant. Afterwards...and anyway, I want to get a feel for these people, to talk to them. For all we know, it's just a recorded message, even if it changed. Or just one person..."

Claire put her hand on his shoulder, "You know that's not likely. Yes, paranoia kept us alive, but at some point we'll have to trust to reach civilization ... or people, at any rate." She realized suddenly she'd come to love him. She didn't resent his protective instinct so much as found it endearing. He was trying to keep his woman and children safe. But they would have to risk something to get something, in this case the security of other humans, and a hope at a future.

"For that matter," she said, "when we communicate and give our location, it is entirely possible that people will come here, determined to fight us. Unlikely, but possible. We too have provisions, but we're only four people. But we have to risk it. I don't know how to play midwife to myself, and even if Pedro and Laura could translate books—if we can find them—for us, it could be really difficult. Or very simple, of course. Cave women gave birth. The thing is, Jean, do you want our children to grow up like this, with just the four of us, and never be able to learn anything we don't know, never be able to find someone their age to marry or fall in love or—"

He'd looked at her, suddenly, passionately, and she realized that he too had come to love her. They'd fallen together, if truth be told, out of desperation and boredom and the all-too-human need for consolation. But now there was more to it. There was a wild protectiveness. She hadn't even seen Jean give any interested looks to Laura, who was young and pretty. She guessed that Jean was a one-woman man, one of those men who are born to be married, and though they legally weren't, they really were.

"I know," he said. "I hate to risk what we have, but I know we need to risk some to get somewhere. It's just for so long my whole focus was on having Madeleine survive. When I first met you, I almost handed her to you and walked off to throw myself off the nearest tall building, because it didn't matter if I lived or died. I just wanted Madeleine to survive.

"But then there was you, and there's a baby on the way, and I realized I enjoy my life, as different as it is from everything I could have hoped for. I want to stay alive. And I want you to stay alive. We've all lost much too much. Everyone in the world has lost too much. I don't want to lose anything else, and I don't want to lose this wild, unexpected happiness I've found. I know I have to risk it. But I don't want to lose it."

She slid her hand into his. "You won't."

All the while, Pedro was waiting, holding the transmitter. "Just say when," he said. "I won't do anything you guys don't want to. You gave us shelter while we were out there. We will stay and help with Claire's baby, if no one else shows up, and if you want to brave joining Castelo de Corvo, we'll go together. I just want you to know that up front. But do you want me to talk? Reveal our position? Put ourselves out there and all? Or not?"

Jean looked at Claire and read the answer in her eyes even before she nodded.

He'd almost surely have convinced her to risk it, if she opposed it...

They needed someone to help with the birth. But, beyond all that, he realized, they needed...to be human again, to be part of a community again, to have rules and order and people they could trust again. Even if those people would end up being, of necessity, Portuguese, foreigner, strangers.

And communicating from their little holdout was the only way to get that.

He nodded.

Pedro cleared his throat and spoke, first in Portuguese, then translated in English.

"This is the Luso-Franco-American alliance," he gave a small smile towards Jean and Claire, as though afraid they'd chide him. Jean shook his head but smiled. They'd not found any other name to use, and that was as good as any, if strange for a group of only four people. "We are living in a secure building in the village of Terrafim, in the Alto Douro, Portugal. We have a pregnant woman unable to travel and due in July. We are looking for someone willing to help with the birth, and having the knowledge to do so."

He repeated the language again, in Portuguese, in English, and with Laura's help, in Swedish, German, Spanish and Dutch.

For a long time there were no answers. None at all. And they thought they were flinging their words into the void.

Claire busied herself opening cans of soup, serving a meal of sorts. Night had fallen, and the dark spread over the land.

Looking at Claire and at the world out there, Jean thought they were lost here and would always be, here, at the end of the world, and there would never be a future for Madeleine or any other children he might have. Even if people existed out there, how could they get to them?

Then the receiver crackled and there was an answer, in Spanish, in hesitant tones. "They say," Laura said, "they don't have a medical professional, and they're a hundred kilometers or so away, but they're willing to help, if they can."

Then there was another voice, in Swedish, and Laura translated, "They have a medical professional, but she's only a nurse, and they don't know how to get to you. But they'll try to figure out a way."

And then, in slow and accented English came the voice they'd first heard over the radio, "This is Castelo de Corvo. We're maybe fifty kilometers from you. We have a nurse midwife."

Jean grabbed the transmitter from Pedro's hands. "I'm afraid of having my—" He looked at Claire and smiled, and she smiled back. He guessed they'd have to start learning to do things informally. "My wife travel that far, with zombies and the possibility of blocked roads and running out of fuel."

"As you should be," the voice said, still slow, but as though it were getting its English-language feet back. "But that's all right. We have a helicopter from what used to be medical rescue. And we have fuel. We can come get you, or send a midwife to you."

Jean turned toward Claire and found her in his arms, a wild, warm, sobbing woman. He hugged her awkwardly. He'd thought all his tenderness was gone, but it was not so. Suddenly he felt himself young and foolish, capable of loving and of being hurt.

In a way he too had become a zombie when civilization died. But it was the sort of zombie who could come back to life.

"It's all right," he told her. "It's all right. We're not alone. They're willing to help us. All sorts of people are willing to help us. Humanity is going to survive. There's no reason to cry."

"I know," she said. "That's why I'm crying."

Suddenly he understood. They hadn't cried for the lost, or at least he hadn't. When Beatrice was dead, he had to leave the place fast, to rush out, to save Madeleine, to do whatever he had to do so she would survive.

He suspected Claire too hadn't cried. Or Pedro and Laura for that matter.

They'd all of them been too busy, too tired, and too broken to cry.

Crying is a human thing. You don't cry if there's no hope of consolation ever.

He petted Claire's hair, and kissed her head, as he felt tears roll down his own face. "I know," he said.

He looked out of the lonely tower at the empty countryside, but he knew that out there in the world there were other humans, there was life, there was love, and hope for the future.

The loneliness of the Fall was gone. Humans would come back.

There would be horror and blood and loss on the way there. There had been for most of human history. But Jean felt that sometime in the future civilization would live again.

And his children would be there. He hugged Claire tight. "It will be all right," he said.

# Return to Mayberry

## ROB HAMPSON

*"These are the end times! It is God's judgment! The wrath of God upon the world for its sins! Those who have been taken are the sinners of the world and the righteous have been spared..."*

"Good heavens, Munro, can't you find something else? I can't see how you can tolerate that crap. 'Brother Leonard,' indeed." Nathaniel "Nate" Kelvin made a snort of disgust and turned to stare at the older man sitting at the old chrome dinette table tuning the multiband radio. "He's insane and will give us all a bad name. Everyone probably thinks this region is full of 'religious nuts' just like him."

"Way'll...which'd be worse to a stranger, religious nuts in Lowgap or them cannibals over the ridge? Mebbe folks'd better jus' leave us all alone." The seventy-something man was the very definition of "Good Ol' Boy." Nate had been introduced to him several times over the years as a "cousin," but he'd never gotten a straight answer whether that meant first cousin, or some more distant relationship. It didn't matter, they were family, and that relationship had gained additional importance in the wake of the H7D3 epidemic.

Nate had already started hearing the rumors of attacks in the streets, stores, and offices when he'd gotten that text from his father:

61

*Pick up your sister's family and get to Munro's farm. He's expecting you.* The news had been full of official press conferences and doctors raising alarms about a new strain of influenza, but this sounded more like Pops was afraid of global thermonuclear war than just the flu. The text had been accompanied by map coordinates; it wasn't all that far away from Charlotte, just back in the hills past Elkin.

He hadn't taken the direct route to the farm. First, it was necessary for Nate to go to his sister's house in High Point. The neighborhood was quiet, but screams could be heard in the distance. Thankfully Interstate 85 had been clear, but he'd had to stop just a few blocks away to get around a naked man *biting* another in the middle of the street.

The front door was locked; despite having a key, he was unable to open it. Something was blocking it from inside. He knocked, pounded, and called his sister's name, but received no response. He went around to the back, broke a window, and climbed in over the kitchen sink. He was immediately hit by the smell, even before he saw the blood spatters. It reminded him of the time his father's game freezer had failed and the results of the previous day's hunting trip had gone rancid before they'd even had a chance to completely butcher it.

Sure enough, there was a body on the floor. Ian; probably dead. Nate might not care for his sister's "Significant Other," but he cringed at seeing him in that condition—throat torn out and mauled as if by a wild animal—or an infected. The surrounding cabinets and counters were sprayed with the bright red sprays of arterial blood and there was a spreading pool of darker blood. Again, Nate was reminded of hunting trips with his father, as well as his brief stint in the Middle East with the Corps of Engineers.

There was another smell mixed in, too. Crap. Literally—crap— the all-too-familiar smell of a person killed by an act of violence. He pulled his carry pistol out of his pocket, not that he thought a little .380 ACP would do much good short of a head-shot. He'd heard . . . stories. Pops had always ribbed him about carrying a "mouse gun" instead of a "real gun," but he figured that having something easily accessible in his pocket gave him time to get to bigger firearms in the SUV.

He cautiously and quietly moved through the house looking for his sister Sarah, or niece Anna. There was a trail of blood leading from the kitchen. He bent to touch it—not with his hands, but with a pencil he'd picked up off of the kitchen counter. Still sticky, just like the puddle in the kitchen . . . and was that a footprint? Yes, it was. He could see an outline consisting of heel, arch, and toes. Since it was a bare foot, it reinforced his suspicion that one of the infected was in the house. He tried not to think about the fact that the locked and barricaded doors meant that the infected could be one of his own family.

He heard noises from upstairs. They were moving noises, quiet and unhurried, not sounds of a struggle. Gun held shakily in front, he rounded the corner to the front stairs. There was something jammed in the front door—not a barricade at all, something like a huge wedge. There was a long-handled sledgehammer on the floor that looked like it had been used to jam the wedge in the door frame. He paused a moment and considered the caliber of his gun in light of what he'd seen in the kitchen and on the streets. He shifted the gun to his left hand and picked up the sledgehammer in his right. He'd practiced shooting one-handed and was pretty accurate. This way he had just that much more protection.

Sarah's body was at the top of the stairs, naked and bloody. The question of the infected's identity was at least partially solved. Her mouth was bloody, but then again, she was cut and bleeding from many locations. There were multiple cut and stab wounds across her neck and body, and a large kitchen knife sticking out of her chest. The blood wasn't moving—not pumping, just oozing—so she was probably dead, just like Ian.

He could hear water running and other sounds from the small bathroom at the end of the hall. Ian and Sarah had their own bathroom attached to their bedroom, so this was Anna's, and that might mean she was still alive. On the other hand, if she'd done . . . *that* . . . to her own mother, he'd best not surprise her.

"Anna?" he called. "Anna, it's Uncle Nate." He moved closer to the bathroom door, but stood to the side and raised the hammer, keeping the gun at low-ready, just in case. "Anna. It's okay. I'm here to take you to safety." The door wasn't completely closed. He could just barely see the mirror over the sink, but it was fogged with condensation. He reached out with his right hand and pushed the door with the head of the hammer.

Anna was at the sink scrubbing at her hands and arms. The water was running in the sink as well as the shower, and she was completely wet, long blonde hair hanging in strings, her clothes soaked and sticking to her body from having gotten into the shower fully clothed.

"Anna, honey. You need to stop. It's okay. It's safe. You're safe with me." He tentatively touched her on the shoulder and she turned, eyes full of tears.

"I can't get it off! It won't come off! They say the infection is in the blood and I can't get the blood off!" She started to cry.

Nate took her in his arms and held her. She sobbed for what seemed a long time, but Nate's watch said was only a few minutes before she looked up at him. "Is it really safe, Uncle Nate? Mom told me she had a message from GrandPops to leave Ian if we had to and go find *you*." She reached out and groped for a towel, then started to wipe at her face and hair.

"GrandPops was right. We need get out of here; head up north. There's someplace we're supposed to go."

She looked up at him. Her eyes were clear, her face calm. Her mouth quirked in a half smile. "I think maybe I'd better get some dry clothes on, first."

"Yeah, you dry off, while I go take care of something." He stepped out of the bathroom and closed the door. Stripping a blanket off of the bed in the master bathroom, he covered Sarah's body.

"All clear."

Anna stepped out of the bathroom, wrapped in one large towel, with another wrapped around her hair. She paused a moment and stared at the blanket-covered shape on the floor. Her mouth worked for a moment, then she continued on to her bedroom.

"I'll only be a few minutes. I was already packing. Mom said we were going up to Elkin or some place near there. Ian argued; he didn't want to go. Said something about GrandPops and his cousins being 'rednecks and myrmidons,' I think." She faltered. "Then Mom and Ian started arguing and she . . ." The sound of drawers opening and closing came from the room. She was slamming them with all her might. A muffled thump signaled something soft but heavy hitting the floor. "I will *not* cry! Mom wouldn't like it!"

Anna came out of the room. There were tears in her eyes but a determined look on her face. She was wearing a backpack and pulling on an old green duffel bag that looked just like one he had out in his SUV. Pops' Vietnam-era surplus for certain. The teenager had stuffed it full—not all of it clothes. "I need one more thing.

Are you carrying? Oh. Yeah." She nodded in his direction and Nate looked down at the gun in his left hand. "Well, mine's in a safe under Mom's bed. Ian didn't want me to have it and certainly wouldn't let me keep it. Fortunately, Mom wouldn't let him throw it out since GrandPops gave it to me and taught me to use it. I hacked the combo a long time ago. Mom suspected, but Ian never knew."

This was almost too much, not quite what he'd expected from his eighteen-year-old niece. Nate and Sarah had been close—he'd adored his big sister, and liked her husband, Anna's father. When Adrian hadn't made it home from his last tour in Afghanistan, he'd opened his home to let Sarah and Anna live with him in Charlotte. Anna had stolen his heart; he'd loved the shy, nerdy seven-year-old as if she were his own daughter. When Ian came into Sarah's life four years later, he'd reluctantly drifted away. He and Ian hadn't gotten along, and Nate didn't want to cause trouble for Sarah.

Anna went into the master bedroom, and a few minutes later came out with two guns. The smaller of the two was black with pink grips, which she placed into a small pack—also pink—and fastened around her waist. The larger one was all black and in a belt-clip holster. She held it out to him.

"GrandPops always said you carried too small a caliber. Here's Mom's nine-mil. Ammo's in a can in the closet under the stairs."

Nate realized he was still holding both sledgehammer and his .380. He awkwardly put down the hammer and switched hands so that he could put the gun back in its pocket holster. Taking the larger firearm, he clipped it to his belt and settled it in place. "Okay, your duffel, the ammo can, anything else? We need to be moving."

"Food? Water?"

"In the car." He reached for her duffel...*Damn! That's heavy!* Anna picked up the sledgehammer and followed him down, then reached into the small storage space under the stairway and pulled out a military surplus ammunition canister. *Someone* in this house hadn't forgotten all of the lessons Pops had taught his kids!

Anna took the sledge and prepared to knock the wedge out of the door.

"This was my idea. Of course then I couldn't get it out fast enough." She paused. "Oh, wait! One more thing." There was a coat closet next to the door, and she opened the door and pulled out a sky-blue athletic bag with red and white striping. It clanked and rattled as she pulled it out.

"What is that, body armor?" Nate asked.

She gave him a sour look. "It's my karate bag... and yeah, it's got protective gear."

"I've never known white pajamas to clank." He tried some levity, but Anna wasn't having it. She just continued to glare at him for a moment, then swung the sledge to knock the wedge out of the door frame. She looked out at the street, waited and listened, then preceded him outside.

"Let's blow this popsicle stand," she whispered, and chills ran up Nate's spine as he recognized not only his own father's words, but his demeanor in the young lady in front of him.

The drive up to the mountains had been uneventful mostly because Nate had avoided the biggest population areas. Anna had pulled earbuds out of her backpack and was listening to music... or something. She had her eyes closed, and at one point Nate could see tears on her cheeks. It was approaching dusk when they finally pulled up the road to the farm referred to in his father's directions. There was a fence and a speaker next to a heavy metal gate. The residents were reluctant to let anyone through the perimeter as night fell, so they spent the night in the car—a long restless, sleepless night. Fortunately, Nate's preparations had included food and water. There was an out-house nearby, and Nate stood guard while Anna used it—holding one of the many rifles he'd had packed in the back of the SUV—then she did the same for him.

After a meal of energy bars, peanut butter and dried fruit, they tried to sleep, but Anna started at every sound. Around midnight, she'd started to sob, and Nate held her like he had so many years ago. She cried for her mother, lost innocence, and the sheer horror she'd felt when she realized the necessity to take her mother's life to save her own. She admitted to some remorse for Ian, but it was distant and lacking real emotion. Her mother's boyfriend had never filled the void in her life, and he had actively driven away the one person who'd come closest to fulfilling a father's role. A couple hours later she fell asleep from sheer exhaustion, and Nate continued to hold her until the first light of dawn.

After they'd been checked out by the farm "security detail" and been recognized by Munro, they'd been shown to a brightly painted, two-bedroom cottage complete with their own flower and vegetable gardens. There were several of them, all built for members of Munro's extended family. At one time, all five of his sons had lived at the farm with their own families: farming, caring for animals, and participating in the family hobby of stock-car racing and tractor pulls. Only two out of five sons, three widowed daughters-in-law, and a few grandchildren were left, now, but the family was well known in the area for rescuing stranded motorists and "taking in strays," so serving as a gathering point for survivors was nothing new. They were all family now, so the original relationships no longer mattered.

Everyone took turns working the farm, repairing machinery and patrolling the fence line. For the first month, no one was allowed out of the core farm buildings in groups smaller than five. The measure was for protection against one of their own turning as much as proof against attacks. As the days wore on, the sound of gunshots became less frequent, fewer visitors arrived at the newly fortified gate, and life settled into a routine of working during daylight, taking a turn on the stationary bikes that had been set up to recharge batteries and listening to the multiband radio by candlelight. Munro called them the "Voices of the Fall" and it was unfortunately all too true.

*"...The wrath of God. Brothers and sisters, repent of your sins and be saved. The cities of Satan have fallen and only those who repent can find safety..."*

The amateur radio broadcast from Lowgap ran from six to eight every evening. There was a brief news program immediately before the man everyone called The Reverend started ranting. Mostly it was news of the small town of Lowgap, about fifteen miles north of Munro's farm. It was always upbeat. Lowgap had fuel, they had shelter, and they had food. All you had to do was repent, and they'd take you in.

There were other voices in the night. Radio Free Texas was one; apparently the Texicans had managed to clear whole towns and were even talking about electing a Governor! The comical

King of Florida and the Dominion of CubaFloraTamp was always good for a laugh. There were brief hints of ships at sea.

One cold winter day, a new voice came from the radio:

*"Listen up! This is Devil Dog Radio..."*

Nate sat in the kitchen stirring the food around on his plate. He'd been up most of the night insulating the new bunkhouse they'd built for the single men, so he was eating later than most. They might have to make do for some of the materials, but they had shelter, food, ammunition. All able-bodied—men, women and kids alike—worked the farm. The kids collected eggs, slopped the hogs and pulled weeds in the garden while the adults built additional shelters, repaired fences, and hand-cultivated the bean, cabbage and corn fields.

As Nate picked at the remains of breakfast, he could see Anna outside on the lawn practicing martial arts. She had just started karate when Sarah had moved her to High Point, seven years ago. Anna confided that she was a bit out of practice, but had resumed her exercises after they'd arrived at the farm. Two young men had joined her this morning, and they were sparring, breath steaming in the cold air.

She managed to knock the legs out from one, but the other had her in a bear hug. Nate knew better than to intervene—he knew what was coming next. Anna's blond hair was pulled back in a ponytail, but she suddenly became a whirl of blond hair, pink skin and white karate uniform, and broke free of the grip. She spun and lashed out with a kick, putting the second male on the ground. All three were panting puffs of white, while flecks of frost gathered on their clothing.

Anna was almost nineteen and the oldest of the "kids," but was much more likely to be found with the males her age and a little older—such as right now. She wanted to join the scouting and scavenging parties, but so far, none of the women had been assigned those duties. Of course the fact that only one in five adult women *wasn't* pregnant might have something to do with that.

Anna could certainly shoot and defend herself, and she wasn't limited to karate or the .22 rifles carried routinely by anyone over the age of thirteen. She'd been trained by the same person who'd trained Nate, his father—her grandfather—Abraham Kelvin, and had done pretty well when tested on the farm's hunting rifles. Munro's youngest son, Zeke, had tested her on everything available when she'd bragged that "GrandPops even trusted her with the M-16 he'd conveniently forgotten to tell the Army that he still possessed." Anna, Zeke, and Chuck—an old Army buddy of Zeke's who'd arrived soon after Nate and Anna—had become good friends and trained during their off time, just like today.

The three were an odd match-up. At twenty-four, Zeke was five years older than Anna, and Chuck was another two years older than Zeke. Anna was usually energetic and talkative, Zeke was morose—he came back from the Army that way, according to Munro—and Chuck was somewhere between the two. Nate had been worried for Anna at first, but of course Zeke was a Munro, and Chuck was the medic who'd pulled Zeke out of an ambush in the Sandbox. He was confident that she was in good company, even as he worried about unwanted attention she might receive from some of the other single men (boys!) that found their way to the farm.

Anna listened to the radio with the other adults each evening. The Tales of Shewolf really got to her, Nate could tell. It was pretty clear to him that Anna saw a bit of herself in the near mythical character of Faith Smith and idolized her. It didn't matter if the stories were real or made up for morale purposes, Anna wanted to be the Munro Clan equivalent if only they'd give her a chance.

That chance came with the next change in weather, and a new voice on the radio.

"...Anyone in the vicinity of Pinnacle, Pilot Mountain and Mount Airy. This is Yadkin sporting camp broadcasting from the top of pilot mountain. Snow slows down the zeds, and we're sending a team to Mount Airy to look for survivors, food, and medicine. Meet us at the intersection of I-74 and U.S. 601 tomorrow morning at ten am. Repeating...we have snow!"

"So why should we risk our lives trying to raid 'Mayberry' when there's Winston-Salem and Greensboro to the south? Not that I want to try fighting my way in and out of the cities! That's a job for the young." Cyrus was Munro's oldest surviving son, yet still too young to remember the old black-and-white TV show from whence the town received its nickname, but it was impossible not to have heard the story of the program based on an actor's childhood memories of quaint, old-fashioned Mount Airy.

His nephew, Gideon, jumped into the brief silence. "Why not hit those cities? There's at least a National Guard Armory down in Winston, not to mention all of those stores just barely inside the city limits!" Gideon was the eldest grandchild, son of Munro's oldest son, Aaron. He'd been living in Winston-Salem since college, and had come home as the Pacific Flu hit, just in time to witness his father become the first infected in the valley. He had become the voice of the younger generation, even though at twenty-four, he was only a year younger than his Uncle Zeke.

"Actually, Armories don't have as much as you'd think. We'd need to get to a training site like Fort Pickett in Virginia if we wanted to find a good source of ammo. No, for now we just have to recycle and reload." Chuck had made that argument before—frequently with Gideon, and usually when trying to dissuade him from planning a highly dangerous raid on the larger cities fifty miles away.

"Even that is running low. I need smokeless powder, lead and copper or we're completely out of ammo in a month." Julio Cabral had been a neighbor before the Fall. The fifty-ish Portuguese farmer had property directly adjacent to Munro, and had joined forces with the Munro family when the last of his children succumbed to the plague. He served as the de facto armorer for the farm and extended family.

"What about the range in Elkin? Has anyone tried to see if the gun store is still intact? Maybe head down to the big ones in Rural Hall? Charlotte? They're on the edges of urban areas and close enough to the Interstate that we could get in and out at night?" Jessie Munro was twenty years old and six months pregnant. The father had died several weeks after the initial outbreak, so she'd retreated to her grandfather's farm to stay with family.

"We should be looking at the Scout Camp north of here, but I'm sure it's firmly under The Reverend's control!" added Julio.

The discussion broke down into muttering, small group conversations, and some rather pointed gestures. "People, stop! Focus here. The question is 'Why Mount Airy? What do we gain?'" Cyrus brought the group back on topic.

"Would you like to take a hot shower or bath again? There's a company that makes outdoor wood-fired and solar boilers that can make hot water for washing, cleaning and sanitation, without using generators or burning fuel." Zeke stood up and walked to the middle of the room. He was known for being quiet and reserved. The fact that he was speaking up in this group caught everyone's attention and the crowd quieted down.

"We need tools and we need raw materials." Zeke continued quietly. "There's a tool company with the largest selection of metal bar stock and rods in the area. Copper? Refrigeration units. Lead? Car batteries—there's *seven* car dealerships." He stopped and took a sip of clear liquid from a mason jar.

"We need more wire and a hell of a lot more fence materials if we are going to expand out of this valley. With gravel from the quarry, concrete, cement and rebar mesh, we can build *real* fences and barriers to keep the infected out." He looked down then looked back up at the group with a challenging expression. "And before any of you shitheads protest that this crap is all too heavy for us to handle, there's cranes, derricks and heavy equipment companies. Clothes at the department stores just as long as they weren't looted too badly . . . think about it. Clean clothes. Warm clothes. Clothes without holes, rips or patches. But the only way to be *certain* is to go in there and find out!"

"That's presuming that Lowgap didn't get it all." Gideon interjected. "The word is that The Reverend sent out a lot of scavenging parties before he went"—he pointed a finger at his temple, twisted it back and forth and whistled—"off his rocker."

"We also have to face the fact that sooner or later we'll have to open trade with Lowgap," Chuck said. "I know Munro said he'd met him once, and he wasn't a *bad* person, but frankly we don't know what The Reverend's terms will be. We need something to bargain with."

"So we need to have something he doesn't. The water systems are a good start. A foothold in Mount Airy would be even better. We'll check the hospital for supplies, maybe even find a doctor. Failing that, we check the vet offices. Antibiotics are antibiotics." Zeke sat back down.

"Fair enough. A vote then." Cyrus thumped the table with his fist. "All in favor? Ah, yes, Munro?"

"We need to do this for the right reason. Food? Supplies? Materials? Those would be nice, but there are many ways to get them." Munro's voice was quiet, much like Zeke's. Again, as with Zeke, he had everyone's attention. "Every single one of you came here from somewhere else. Cyrus, Zeke, and I are the only natives in this valley. Remember that. You were running for your lives and we took you in, because it was the *right* thing to do.

"We do this—we do it for the same reason. There are people out there, cowering in their homes in Mayberry. Alone, hurt, starving, and hoping for help that *has* not come. We do it for them, no matter what it takes."

There was a moment of silence, then Cyrus called for the vote.

"Wait. Why do they call it 'Mayberry' again?" One of the young people asked.

Everyone laughed and Munro explained the name *again*, and how it had come to mean not just the town, but the whole region around it.

Following the interruption, Cyrus again spoke up and called for a decision.

It was unanimous.

They were going to Mayberry.


After the meeting, Nate went back to his room in the bunkhouse and started putting together gear for the next morning. He would volunteer, of course. He owed it to Munro, and he owed it to every single person he worked, ate and slept beside on this farm.

There was a knock on the thin door. *That will be Anna. I knew this was coming. There's a search and salvage mission, and she wants in on it. She's an adult, she doesn't need my permission, but she's going to ask anyway, and I ... I'll have to decide on an answer.*

To his surprise, Anna wasn't standing there when he opened the door. Zeke was.

Nate opened the door wide, and offered Zeke the chair as he sat on the bed. The other man was usually quiet and reserved, but Nate had seen a fire in the younger man's eyes tonight as he spoke. That fire was still there.

"Forgive my bluntness; I'll get to the point." It still surprised Nate to hear Zeke speaking so much at one time. "Anna is afraid to ask your permission; afraid you'll say no. But I want her in my crew tomorrow morning."

"Wait...what?" Not Nate's most intelligent response, but Zeke's tone had taken him aback.

"She's *good*, Mr. Kelvin." Zeke paused for a moment, then leaned back and motioned through the doorway. Chuck and Anna were waiting outside, and Zeke waved them closer, then continued. "She's not just good, she has good judgment. We need that. *I* need that."

"We've trained together, shot together, stood watch together. Everything except hunted together, but I have no doubts," Chuck added his own voice to the appeal. "I know you think she idolizes 'Shewolf' Smith too much, but Anna is an adult. She would work well on the team."

Anna stood silently, but her thoughts were written all over her face. She wanted to go, but she wanted his approval just as much.

"One other thing, Mr. Kelvin, and this might help." Zeke spoke again. "We want you on our crew, as well. Dad and Cyrus figured we'd organize in four or five-person teams. I'm thinking the four of us plus Frank Cicero, my Cousin Betsy's boy. Frank's come up with an idea that should give us a bit more protection when the shit starts to fall."

Nate sat in the silence and looked at the others. Zeke still had that passionate look, Chuck seemed calm and placid, and Anna's eyes were pleading.

"Okay. I'm in." He gestured to the backpack on the bed and the open gun case against the wall. "I was going to volunteer anyway, but I'm with you."

"Good." Zeke smiled. "We've still got a lot to do tonight, so meet us in the barn at oh-four-thirty, Nate."

Anna hugged him, and the men shook hands. It was only after they'd left that Nate realized that Zeke had called him by his first name for the first time since they'd met.

It was still dark when Nate met the others to gear-up for the trip. Ten individuals had volunteered and been selected. Anna was the only female joining the group—not for lack of volunteers, but the fact that too many were pregnant. Waiting to take the teams into town were two off-road modified pickup trucks. One was hitched to a short flat-bed holding what appeared to be a highly modified Jeep. The second truck was towing a long, enclosed trailer commonly used to transport race cars. It had been heavily modified with what appeared to be additional steel plates, and narrow horizontal slit windows down the length of the sides. The pickup was likewise modified with armor over the windows, and an enclosed bed.

"What's this?" Nate asked Zeke as the teams gathered in the frosty pre-dawn air.

"That's our bolt hole. If everything goes tits-up, we pile into the trailer." Zeke abruptly stopped and looked embarrassed as Anna walked up, realizing that she had heard his comment.

"Julio and Munro have been working on it." Chuck was grinning at Zeke's discomfiture, but continued in his place. "If the zeds or our new friends from Pilot Mountain try to overwhelm us, we can fort up—there's food and water stocks, plus lots of ammo. The truck's been armored, so we should stay mobile as long as we have diesel. We can transport goods, and we can protect people. Consider it our version of an Armored Personnel Carrier."

"*O-kay*, I can see that." Nate responded. "Then what's with the Jeep?"

"That was Dad's pride and joy," said Gideon, walking up to the group. "Nine-hundred horsepower engine, or so he claimed. He built it for tractor-pulls. Runs on gasoline and alcohol, even has an attachment for a nitrous bottle. If we need to break, drag or tow—or even just to haul ass—we've got the vehicle for the job." He pointed to the fifty-gallon drums lashed to the flat-bed in front of the Jeep. "But we'd better be sure, because she's a fuel whore and will deplete most of our reserves."

Zeke was turning red and trying to signal his nephew to watch his language in front of Anna, but she just laughed at his antics. "Don't worry, Zeke. I've heard you guys talking before. You don't have to protect my virgin ears!"

That only caused Zeke to splutter and turn even redder. The others all laughed, but Nate took note of Zeke's discomfort. He was a soldier, and they'd all heard worse from him—but not around Anna. Nate was beginning to think that the younger man had other feelings as well.

*Shame on me that I didn't pick up on that last night, he thought. I know Sarah had The Talk with Anna, and God knows she's an adult and can make her own decisions in this world, but given that she's stated that the last thing she wants is to end up like the other pregnant women, we may need to have a chat when we get back.*

Not that Nate had any objection to Zeke. He was a fine young man, but Nate had been getting used to being *in loco parentis* again.

∽ ⊖ ∾

It was snowing when they left the valley, just a few flakes, but it picked up as they drove on. Snow in North Carolina was fickle. Most years saw two to three snowfalls, most less than an inch. Accumulations were heavier to the northwest into the mountains near Boone and Asheville. In the center of the state you could get a few inches of snow in Mount Airy, ice in Charlotte and Winston-Salem, with nothing but rain to the south and east. Then again, you could also get two feet of snow from Charlotte to Raleigh with only a dusting in the rest of the state.

This close to Virginia, though, about six inches a year was normal. This year was shaping up to be unusual—temps had been below freezing for two weeks, and they'd had one light and one heavy snowfall already. Munro had looked at various almanacs and records and proclaimed that this would be one of the snowy years, so this morning's snow was not unexpected.

The sun was coming up, but with heavy clouds and snow the air took on a bluish-gray tint. Nate had always loved the effect— cold, damp air, large flakes falling silently, distant objects blurred into shades of blue. Today, however, the lack of visibility had people on alert even though the muffling effect of the snowfall meant that they'd have to be awfully close to attract infected. Zeds were still human, even though they had no sense of pain, emotion or discomfort. Like any mammal, they didn't function well in freezing weather. An infected could die from exposure just the same as an uninfected human. That knowledge took the edge off of their nervousness, with the added bonus that their warm clothing provided further protection from bites. On the other hand, there was also the risk of someone deciding to do a little raiding on the salvage parties, so it was with mixed tension and wariness that the party approached the rendezvous.

It was a good location to meet, since U.S. Highway 601 was the shortest route into Mount Airy from the highway. There were several other pickup trucks waiting in the parking lot, all with various types of improvised armor. One vehicle stood out, a military-style Humvee, complete with pintle mounting for a machine gun—but no gun. It looked strange, though, not military. It was painted a glossy black, had bright chrome and tinted windows. As Nate and the teams circled back from the campground entrance to the parking lot, they noticed several men on horseback approaching from the south. Once the mounted party arrived, everyone dismounted, with most people taking up a guard position around their vehicles.

Zeke and Gideon spoke briefly to their respective teams and set most of them up in Watch position, facing out. Zeke put Anna up top in the Munro Farm's armored pickup—she didn't have a pintle-mount, but there was a roof hatch in the armored box over the bed of the truck, so she could stand up and have a height advantage over the dismounted men. Zeke walked over and tapped Nate on the shoulder, then motioned for him to follow.

Once everyone was in place, the various groups sent leaders to the center of the ring of vehicles and introduced themselves. The men on horseback were the ones who had sent the radio message the previous evening. They had sheltered at the state park riding stable next to the Yadkin Sporting Club in Pinnacle. The fancy Humvee was from Lowgap; the vehicle had been recovered from a home used by the Witness Protection Program—the protectee was long dead, and the lone remaining security guard had joined forces with the townsfolk. Pinnacle and Lowgap had each sent four men, with several other farms and hold-outs in the region each contributing one or two persons. In all, there were thirty men and four women gathered in the parking lot.

The plan was to organize into three large groups and target medical, clothing and shooting supplies as first priority. The people from Munro Farm formed the nucleus of two teams, while the folks from Lowgap organized the third. Personnel from the other groups were added to round out the teams. They would all head inward on 601 and set up a forward base in the parking lot at the D-I-Y store at the intersection of Route 601 and U.S. 52. Zeke's team would drop the armored trailer at that site as a fallback, and four people—including two of the women and one of the horsemen—would remain on guard. Zeke would then move north to the vicinity of the Mall, Gideon's team would head south toward the airport and industrial area, and the Lowgap team would head northeast into the city center. The plan was to not spend too much time checking the stores along the inbound route for the time being, since it was clear that many were burned-out and already looted. If they were able to extract without issue, they would double check likely candidates when they left.

The larger teams had handheld radios, but most of the two- and three-person teams did not. Fortunately, the Farm had a stock of walkie-talkies, and had collected and charged sufficient batteries to allow each team to have multiple communication devices. Each of the mounted men from Pinnacle had a radio and the additional mobility to act as an individual scout loosely attached to the vehicular teams. The heavy snow continued as they all moved forward into the town. In one sense, it meant that the sounds of their advance were muffled, and were less likely to attract infected. On the other hand, it meant that infected and potential survivors were now in their rear areas. It wasn't ideal, but the Pinnacle scouts spread out and checked for signs of both infected and survivors along their route.

It would be at least mid-afternoon by the time most of the teams reached their "target" locations. For Nate and his fellows, that would be the "Mayberry Mall" after first dropping the armored "fort" trailer and a guard at the D-I-Y store and making their way to the northern part of town paralleling Highway 52. Munro had suggested a few alternate targets, such as an auto parts store and tractor supply stores for batteries, air and fuel filters, plus spare parts to keep the farm vehicles running. The route also took them through several residential areas to sweep for survivors. Zeke's team had encountered infected, of course, but only in small groups of one to five, nothing they couldn't handle. They'd also mostly encountered looted and empty businesses. Both situations changed up on West Pine Street, when they had not only encountered the first "pack" of zeds, about twenty, but also mostly intact stores. Once they dealt with the infected, they started figuring out the best way to salvage the badly needed heavy construction equipment, engine parts, tools and supplies for the farm.

They'd also passed five churches along South Franklin Street as they made their way up to Pine. The story those churches told was the story of the Fall in a nutshell: The Christian Church and one of the Baptist Churches were wrecked and looted; the second Baptist church was burned. The Presbyterian Church showed evidence of shelters and barricades, but clearly hadn't helped, as witnessed by the months'-dried blood.

The radios reported isolated survivors in ones and twos along the various teams' routes. The Lowgappers found five people—mixed employees and customers—barricaded in the kitchen of one of the restaurants, living off of the stocks and retro-classic foods of the country store. One of the survivors was a nurse, and had been immediately drafted to check the other survivors. While passing through the neighborhoods around the churches, Chuck heard a faint call on the radio, and followed instructions to a small house a block away from the burnt-out Baptist church. Zeke, Chuck and Frank had carefully approached the door, with Nate and Anna on overwatch. They'd broken down the barricaded door and found the homeowner, a retired physician, in the kitchen. The man was thin and weak; he said he'd been out of food for a week, and would run out of water in a few more days. He had an expensive luxury-model pickup truck—fully fueled—and a considerable stock of first aid and medical/surgical supplies that he offered to the team in exchange for his rescue, so Zeke had sent Nate and Anna to drive the doctor in his own vehicle back to the gathering point at the D-I-Y center.

Nate and Anna were headed back up South Franklin to rejoin their team at the auto parts store. The snow had finally stopped falling and visibility was increasing, as was the distance from which their vehicles could be heard, which probably explained why they couldn't tell that there were survivors at the United Methodist Church. An American Flag was hanging from a second story window facing the road, and a road flare was burning in the snow directly beneath the window. Nate radioed his status to Zeke, and pulled into the parking area next to the sanctuary building.

Several figures could be seen at the window with the flag. The glass pane was raised, and a terribly thin man of about fifty stuck his head out.

"Sister? Are you from the Fleet?" he said. He had that drawl that Nate always associated with Southern Pastors.

"The Fleet? No, we're from Thurmond. The Munro Farm." Anna called back.

"You're not with the Navy? Wolf Squadron?" The man seemed somewhat disappointed.

"No, sorry. There's a group from Lowgap, Pinnacle, Cana, all locals," Anna replied.

"Ah. Okay. I'm Minister Neal. Please, let's talk inside." He disappeared inside the window, then returned in a moment with a ladder of the sort used as an emergency exit from upper-story windows. "I'm sorry about the ladder, but we have the lower doors and windows sealed shut. Please come on up and we can talk."

"Uncle—" Anna began.

"Hold it, kiddo." Nate interrupted. "You're not going up there by yourself. I don't care if you're the dry-land Shewolf." He checked the 9mm on his belt, and stepped out of the truck cab, slinging his rifle across his back. He grabbed a long knife off the console between the seats and placed it in the sheath on the hip opposite the pistol.

After getting—and giving—reassurances that neither party were brigands about to rob and kill the others, the minister sent down a young boy, Tevin, to stand guard with Anna while Nate went up to see to evacuating the other members of the church. Nate called his team leader and gave a report, then had Anna get into the truck and stay in the driver's seat with orders to take off if anything seemed wrong. Making sure Tevin was out of earshot, Nate also promised to come to the window and wave within five minutes if everything was okay, and then again every ten minutes thereafter. If he gave her the "thumbs-up" or any signal other than a wave, she was to leave him and get back to Zeke or Gideon. Left unsaid was that if things went "tits up" as Zeke had said that morning, she was to leave him and not come back. He could see the emotion on her face, so he reached out and lightly tousled her hair, touched her cheek, then headed toward the building.

After five minutes, Nate stuck his head out of the window and waved. Ten minutes later, he did the same again. It was almost time for the next check, and Anna was starting to get bored when her attention was caught by movement across the street. "Oh, fuck!" She turned to speak to Tevin through the window. "Heads up. We've got company!"

Anna had turned the key and was raising the electric windows in the luxury truck. When that was done, she pocketed the keys, and crawled back onto the rear bench seat herself. Two large black nylon bags were on the floor, and she lifted them with effort and tossed them into the truck bed.

It was not yet time for the next check-in. She needed to get Uncle Nate's attention. Unzipping one of the bags, Anna saw an

AK-47 rifle and an AR-15 lower with an AK-47-like upper. *Ah, Zeke's Franken-gun. At least it's not a "Barbie gun."* Unfortunately, neither of those weapons, nor the two dozen loaded magazines were what she needed.

The other bag contained an AR-15, for a total of three, counting the ones Anna and Nate both wore on slings, and another twenty or so magazines. It also contained a shotgun, with five box magazines, and one of the .22 rifles used for shooting varmints and small game.

*Hate to waste a Barbie round. That should do nicely.* She took out the small rifle, chambered a round, and sighted in on the window next to the one with the ladder. *Hmmm. Angle's good, someone'd have to be standing right at the window for me to hit them, and we won't have broken glass all over the ladder.* She took aim and fired a single shot. There was a crack from the small caliber round, not a lot of echo, due to the snow, so she could clearly hear the breaking glass.

As intended, Nate had heard it, too, and was at the window with his AR-15 pointed out. Anna looked up at him long enough to ensure that he saw her. She then dropped the smaller rifle, picked up the AK-47 and several magazines, then stood up and turned away, facing the figures moving between the buildings on the opposite side of the street.

"Zombies. I hate these guys," she muttered to herself as she seated one of the banana-shaped magazines, yanked back the charging handle and released it, chambering the first round of 7.62x39mm ammunition. She waited for a clear target; the range wasn't too far, but she hadn't shot this particular rifle. She knew that Zeke's AR-AK hybrid had excellent accuracy, and even had a red-dot reflex sight, but without batteries, it was useless to her. Better the less accurate iron sights of the AK. The larger caliber rounds would do more damage than Barbie rounds, anyway.

There was a crack from behind her, and she saw one of the lead zombies fall. They were still well across the road and would need to cross it and most of the parking lot to get to her. That had to be Uncle Nate, though. He had a hunting scope on his AR, making it pretty damned accurate at that distance. She also heard the rattling of the ladder chains behind her. She did a quick sweep of the area. GrandPops and Zeke always stressed maintaining situational awareness; for that matter, so did her karate instructor. The sweep had revealed that Tevin was approaching the truck, a small rifle shouldered, and fortunately, pointing toward the other side of the street. He dropped his guard only momentarily, to climb into the bed of the truck.

"Miss Anna? Minister said I was to 'back you up' if needed." He seemed pretty nervous, but the way he held the rifle showed that he'd at least had good training.

"You can shoot, right?"

"I shot Distinguished Expert up at Raven Knob," he grinned.

"That's the Boy Scout Camp, right?" In response to his nod, Anna continued. "Good. What did you shoot?"

"Twenty-two." He held up his bolt-action target rifle. "Shotgun. Bow and arrow."

"Ugh. Bolt action, this isn't Sporting Clays, and pretty useless right now. Your popgun's not much use right now. You ever shoot an AR?"

"Once, with my dad. He was one of the camp instructors." The kid's expression had fallen at her earlier remarks, and Anna took pity on him.

"Okay, good enough. There's an AR in there, plenty of magazines, and if you have trouble and they're *close*, you might as well pull out the shotgun. Besides, a Barbie round's .223, not much different than .22!" ... *and about as effective,* she thought.

Anna pointed with her chin toward the second nylon bag, and Tevin pulled out the remaining AR-15 and several magazines. She was impressed that he managed to do so while keeping the rifle pointed in a safe direction. Clearly he'd had a teacher almost as compulsive as GrandPops.

"What's this?" Tevin reached down and picked up an object that had dropped out of one of the bags onto the bed of the truck. He held it up, two cylinders joined by a rectangular section the size of one of the magazines. The way he held it reminded her of mouse ears made famous by the theme parks...

"Oh!" Anna exclaimed as she reached for the object. "Oh, come to Mama!" She took the double drum and popped one round out of the magazine. "Yes! Seven-six-two. Oh Baby!" She remembered Tevin's question and replied: "It's a one-hundred-round drum magazine for the AK-47. The things are finicky as hell and prone to jam, but I'm pretty sure this is Zeke's and he wouldn't have one of those crappy knock-offs. I'm sure he won't mind if I borrow it!"

She safed her own weapon, released the magazine, ejected the unfired round, then seated the drum magazine and chambered a fresh round. There was a satisfying *ssshhh-click* from the drum, and Anna was grinning from ear to ear. She thumbed the ejected round back into the standard magazine and laid it beside the others she'd stacked on the roof of the truck cab.

"Saddle up, Hoss." Anna took aim at the closest infected just as she heard the regular fire begin from behind and beside her. "Time to rock an' roll!"

Tevin soon had to switch to the shotgun. He just wasn't as accurate with the AR-15. Without being able to guarantee head-shots, the smaller caliber just didn't have as much effect as the twenty-gauge shotgun slugs.

Anna had gone through the entire double-drum magazine, plus three thirty-round magazines before the AK jammed. Something hadn't sounded right on the last round, and then the next one wouldn't chamber, something was blocking the barrel. She didn't take time at that moment to analyze, she'd simply dropped the rifle, pulled her own slung AR-15 to the front, and started using the magazines Tevin had abandoned when he switched to the shotgun.

Toward the end, shots from the window had become fewer and fewer, eventually stopping while there were still a half-dozen infected crowding the truck. Either Uncle Nate had run out, or he'd decided there was too much risk of hitting Anna and Tevin. As Anna shot the second to last infected right between the eyes, she heard a shot from her far left, saw the remaining infected jerk to the side, and heard a *ping* off of the truck nearly simultaneously.

"What the fuck?" she shouted at the man on horseback rapidly approaching from the south "You fucking bandit!" She turned and took aim at the man. "Don't come any closer, fucker, or you'll be sporting a third nostril."

She heard Tevin gasp beside her as the man pulled his mount to a halt and raised his hands. "Sorry, it's just that..." he seemed at a loss. "The blood, I couldn't tell."

Anna looked down at herself and the vehicle, which was covered with blood spatter. There didn't seem to be any on her skin, but there was definitely a lot. The formerly white truck was now a pinkish brown, as was most of the surrounding snow.

"I've still got my CLOTHES ON, you nitwit!" she shouted back, then muttered under her breath. "Trigger-happy hicks don't know that ZOMBIES DON'T SHOOT GUNS!" she ended in a shout.

"Sorry," the man apologized. "It's just that your team leader said you missed a check-in, and we had reports of heavy gunfire in the area."

"Well, the radio's locked inside the truck!" Anna pointed at the cab of the truck. "Not to mention we were KIND OF BUSY!"

"Easy, kiddo," said a voice behind her. Anna whirled to see her uncle approaching with his own weapon held at ready, although not pointed directly at the stranger. He addressed the man, "I believe there's a call-sign you're supposed to give?"

"Um. Yeah, sure." The man lowered one hand and slowly reached into sleeve pocket on his ski-type jacket. Pulling out a sheet of paper he read off "'Barney Fife is only allowed one bullet.' Who thinks up this shit?"

"Okay, that's good. Countersign is 'Floyd's Barbershop only has one chair.' Oh, and it was your own boss who came up with the phrases. I guess he figured we were returning to Mayberry, so we should have Mayberry references." Nate put his own sheet of paper back in his pocket. "Anna? Radio?"

"In there." She pointed to the radio visible on the dash.

"...and the key?"

"Oh!" Anna ducked her head and looked down, then reached into her jeans pocket and pulled out the key fob. A quick chirp and click signaled the doors unlocking.

"Good. I'm going to radio this in. We're going to need some transport and help getting people moved. I have no idea how they managed to have the supplies to survive, but they almost didn't make it." Nate turned to Tevin. "Hey, son, where'd they get all of those supplies?"

"That was..." He coughed and sat down in the bed of the truck. "That was my Eagle project. It was supposed to be a homeless shelter for the winter months." He began to shake with the released tension. Anna slid over and put a hand on his shoulder. He reached up and grabbed it, clearly trying to fight back tears.

"Well, then, Tevin. I'd say you really earned your Eagle rank. Good job." Nate turned to the man on horseback. "You got any rope? We're going to have to lower some of those folks out of the window."

"Sir? Mr. Kelvin? We don't need to do that."

"Oh?" Nate turned and looked back at the teen. "What have you got in mind? I thought the doors and windows were barricaded against getting in or out?"

"There's a basement door. We broke something off in the inside lock, but I have the key for the outside. Minister Neal told me to take it the first time I came out."

"All right! Always Be Prepared Eagle Scout Tevin!" Nate grinned. "Okay, Mountie, off the horse and come with me. Anna, call this in, and stay here. Play with the horse, keep the young mom in there company, whatever. You do *not* want to see or smell the mess in there."

Anna just rolled her eyes at her uncle.

Once everyone was down and out of the building, Anna called Zeke to reassure him about the missing radio check-in, and see about arranging transport. Unfortunately, none was available. Gideon's team had found survivors near the airport, and the Lowgap Team was busily shuttling them back to the gathering point. Everyone had encountered infected, but mercifully in small groups. Ammo was running low for all of the point teams though, and some of the rescues were busily sorting through scavenged supplies to send ammo forward to the teams.

Tevin surprised them all again by producing the keys to a church van. Everyone could fit inside it as long as they could get it to start.

The doctor had kept his truck operational by running the engine a few times per week then topping off the fuel. He ran it just long enough to recharge batteries for his radio and flashlights. The church van, on the other hand, had not been run since a few weeks after the Fall. It took a jumpstart and several tries to convince the engine to run. The tires were almost flat, but it would be okay for a mile or two, so Nate slowly drove the van full of people while Anna followed with Tevin, in the truck. Turner, the cowboy, went on ahead, sticking to the road with a clear avenue of escape in case any more infected were attracted to the engine sounds.

Back at the D-I-Y store, the parking lot looked totally different from when Zeke's truck had dropped off the armored trailer this morning. There was a large canopy set up next to the trailer, and several cabin-style tents. There were guards on horseback and

armed men standing on abandoned vehicles to cover all directions. There was even a guard sitting atop the armored trailer.

Dr. Jackson was still awfully weak, but he'd insisted on attempting to care for some of the new refugees. The nurse from the
restaurant was assisting him, and even from a distance it was
clear that she was insistent that he sit back down in the wheelchair someone had found for him.

As a Refugee Center, the area was booming, but it likely
wouldn't last once the temperatures started to rise. There was
a faint hint of blue sky on the northwestern horizon—the snow
was ending and the storm system was moving out—and they'd
soon need a more sheltered location, or to transport people back
to the Farm, Lowgap or Pinnacle.

Someone had a cookstove going. Nate wasn't sure that was
wise, since zeds oriented on sound, light and smell, but he had
to admit that he himself couldn't tell that anything was cook-
ing until he was handed a hot mug of soup. He tried to pass
it along to Anna, but she already had her own. He reached
into a pocket and pulled out a homemade protein bar—dried,
coarsely ground soybeans, molasses and dried cherries from the
farm, mixed with a small amount of the increasingly scarce
peanut butter. It was messy, but filling. After finishing the soup,
he checked again on the doctor and the recent rescues, then
headed back to the truck.

Anna was in the cab of the truck and Tevin was in the truck
bed. He appeared to be sorting through the remaining magazines
and reloading what he could. Nate climbed in behind the wheel,
and looked over at Anna. Her head was down and her shoulders were shaking, even though she wasn't making a sound. He
reached over and put his hand around her shoulders and pulled
her close. She sobbed a few times, then straightened up.

"It's okay, kiddo, you did good. You're safe, I'm safe, and the
people we rescued are safe." Nate tried to reassure her.

"For now," she sniffed. "I just…" her voice cracked and she
sniffed again. "I just miss Mom, and I miss Dad. Not Ian, he
was indifferent at best, never actually mean, but I didn't really
matter to him. I miss my real dad."

"I know Anna; I miss them too. I miss Sarah and Adrian and
Pops. I mean, I have no idea if Pops is still alive! He's an ornery
old coot and I know he had friends in Texas he could hole-up

with. Some nights we hear the reports from Hamlin and I wonder if he's there fighting zombies, kicking ass and taking names."

Anna sniffed at that, then reached over and hugged him. "You're as ornery as GrandPops, you know that, right, Uncle Nate? I think maybe we all have to be, just to be here, now." She straightened up, pulled down a visor to look in the mirror, snorted, and pushed it back up. "Well, we'd better get up to Mayberry Mall. Zeke's expecting us, and I am *not* missing out on a shopping trip!"

They took the direct route up U.S. 52 this time. Zeke had already radioed that they had reached the mall and were starting into the big department store.

"Look for winter clothing. We need warm stuff." Nate and Anna didn't recognize the voice, it had to be someone from another team.

"You idiot, they don't stock winter clothing in the spring and summer." That was probably Frank Cicero. "It was summer when they evacuated Mayberry."

"Tell them not to worry about heavy stuff, but we need T-shirts, jeans, and the ladies want fresh underwear," Anna radioed to Frank. She looked over at Nate. "Unc, ETA?"

"Five minutes. Ask them which end they want us to meet them."

Anna radioed the question to Frank, but didn't wait for his reply before adding, "Oh! Tell them look for a bath and body store."

"What, do you need makeup?" Frank asked derisively.

"No, asshole. I need soap, unless you like bathing with that harsh lye your Great Aunt made for the barn."

"Language," reminded Nate. "Open mic and all that."

"Well, he is," Anna retorted, but she hadn't keyed the microphone.

"Uh, roger that. Okay, Zeke says to bypass the department store on the south end and go in the southeast mall entrance next to the Chinese restaurant. They're in the interior." Frank broke off suddenly, then came back with more urgency. "Zeke says to hurry, they've got company."

"Pulling into the parking lot now." Anna could see the farm pickup, with Frank standing up through the large hatch in the roof of the armored bed. He saw them and gestured wildly toward the door he'd mentioned.

They could hear gunshots as they unassed their own vehicle. Zeke's team could be heard on the radio now that they were close. There were additional voices. Nate had heard that several Lowgappers and a representative from Cana had reinforced Zeke when Nate and Anna had been detached to take Dr. Jackson back to the Trailer.

"Zeke, behind you!"

"Where are they coming from?"

"How could they survive in here?"

"Water from the fountains, food from the Food Court, what do you think?"

"Damn, there's too many, they're in all of the stores. Send the kids out, they can take the supplies, but we have to cover them." The Lowgap addition to Zeke's team had found two teens sheltered in a paint store next to the mall. They survived by raiding supplies at night from the many restaurants along this stretch of road.

"I'm clocking out!"

"Nate! Where are you?" Zeke's voice was insistent.

Nate and Anna were each carrying slung AR-15's and pouches filled with loaded magazines. Nate also had Zeke's AK-47 "Franken-gun" and Anna had the shotgun she'd given Tevin earlier; it was only birdshot, but it would do for close quarters. Tevin was given instructions to stay with the truck. He'd been given a radio and they might need him to move the truck.

The two teenagers from the paint store ran out pushing shopping baskets filled with clothing and supplies. If the team was lucky, they wouldn't pay too high a price for those precious luxuries. Nate and Anna pushed past them into a nightmare scene.

A dozen or more infected attempted to chase the teens out of the building, and ran straight into the reinforcements. Anna immediately shot the two nearest her in the face with the shotgun, then she dropped it to use her AR-15 on targets more distant than arm's length. Nate was shooting his AR-15 exclusively, choosing to save the AK-AR hybrid for Zeke. They each managed to drop two or three zeds per magazine, but they didn't have enough ammo to keep that up for very long.

A shot from the interior took out the last zed coming at them, but they'd had to pass several store fronts to get to the central corridor of the mall, and Zeke's team. Nate could hear shuffling sounds behind and to the sides, so the path they'd cleared wouldn't last long. The main party was coming toward them, firing both behind and to the sides. They met halfway, handed over the spare firearms and ammo, and then turned to clear the path back to the entrance, only to be met by more zeds pouring out of the cafeteria they'd passed on the way in.

"This way!" Nate pointed toward a hallway leading to restrooms and the mall offices.

"It's a dead end." Someone yelled back.

"No, I used to draw blueprints for these places," Nate countered. "That door leads to corridors behind the stores." He switched on the bright flashlight attached to the fore-end of his rifle, and led the way down the short hallway, and through the double steel doors.

The back corridor was rough and dirty, the walls were bare plywood, and the accumulated trash from the days before the Fall was still present. The air smelled of wood and dust, and he had to resist the urge to sneeze. There didn't appear to be any infected in the back corridor, but the doors opened from the other side, meaning that they'd have to barricade them to keep the zeds from following. There was a distinct lack of materials to do so: several large elastic bands, some old plastic straps still attached to a wooden pallet, a discarded set of clothing.

Zeke was firing at the pursuing infected, the shots deafening in the enclosed space if not for the earplugs they'd inserted prior to entering the mall. The Lowgappers held the doors shut while Chuck worked with the available materials to tie the handles shut. While zeds were unable to consciously operate the door-latch bars, their sheer number would ensure that the bars were pressed and the door latches released. Thus, Chuck used the straps, bands and a pair of blue jeans to tie the door handles while Nate and Anna scouted ahead.

Stenciled names on the plywood walls indicated the stores behind each steel door. Thankfully the doors were all closed so far, the fire alarm latches on the opposite sides were probably still engaged. Ahead and around the next corner should be the doors to the outside, just so long as the doors behind them held for a few minutes and they weren't too far from the trucks they should be okay. Nate heard Tevin and Frank talking on the radios, reporting that they were starting to see zeds exiting the main mall doors.

Two turns brought them headed almost back to where they'd started, and there was a triple door ahead that should bring them out, but it was going to be awfully close to the mall entrance and the leakers from inside. Doubly unfortunate, the last interior door was open, into the kitchen of a cafeteria. There were sounds in the darkened interior, and Nate hoped that the gun-light flashes didn't attract more zeds than they already had. He paused a moment just inside the door to the outside and removed the magazine of his rifle, checking it and replacing it with a full one.

"Wait." Anna held up a flashlight. "It's bright out there. Look at me."

She filtered the light through her fingers, then shined it in his eyes, moving her fingers out of the way after a brief pause. He waited a moment for his pupils to adjust and then leaned into the door and opened it as quietly as possible. Anna's trick worked, and he could see in the bright light, but he didn't like what he saw: The trucks were about twenty-five yards away, but there were zeds between them and their current position.

There was nothing to do but move out and clear a path, so he eased the door open the rest of the way, took aim at the nearest zeds and went for headshots. Anna was right beside him, blinking, but firing at other targets.

"Not the trucks, shoot away from the trucks," Nate yelled over the punctuated blasts. Anna corrected her stance, still shooting at the figures between them and the vehicles, but now her shots were aimed well clear of their transportation and the two young men standing in the beds of those trucks, shooting back at the ones exiting the mall entrance several yards to their left.

"Uncle Nate, we need to provide cover. You go for the trucks and cover back to the entrance, I'll get up on that dumpster and cover back to the door." Anna moved immediately to the six-foot-tall trash container and scrambled up using the handles and projections on its side. Once she was up, Nate sprinted for the trucks. He stumbled once, but limped his way back to join Tevin in the bed of the truck. It was unarmored and might have to be abandoned, so he ordered Tevin to start transferring gear and cargo to the armored pickup while Nate took up position to provide cover fire as the rest of the team exited the mall. They were firing behind and through the doorways, so the temporary barricade had to have given way.

Zeke was holding the doorway, firing back through after each person exited. Chuck sprinted for the trucks as soon as he cleared the doors, his rifle slung, and no magazine in the well.

"I'm out!" Chuck yelled as he approached. "Frank, give me your rifle and get in the driver's seat." With Chuck and Nate both providing aimed fire, the rest of the team began to move away from the corridor doors, but more infected started exiting through the mall doors.

"Tevin!" Nate yelled. "Forget that for now, get behind the wheel and back us over toward Anna. We need to get her out of there." As the truck started to move, Nate lost his balance and almost fell out of the pickup, barely catching himself against the raised side. He had trouble standing back up and decided to just sit on the pallet of ammo. He could still shoot, but the moving truck messed up his aim. It also seemed to make his vision blurry.

They reached the dumpster and Anna hopped down into the bed of the truck. She gave Nate a quick look of concern, then moved up to the cab to shout to Tevin.

"Back us toward the doors, we have to get to Zeke and the others." There was a muffled protest from the cab, and she immediately shouted back. "Don't worry about them. Run over them if you have to."

The truck jerked as it reversed direction several times in quick succession. Even seated, Nate was having trouble staying upright. Anna moved over, helped him straighten back up and then gasped, "You're bleeding!"

"I think he got shot!" Tevin shouted from the cab. "I saw something spark off the pavement and he stumbled, but he seemed okay when he got in the truck."

"Ornery, stubborn old coot just like GrandPops. Hang on, let's get these guys and Blow this Popsicle Stand!" She began muttering to herself as she moved him to sit lower in the truck bed. Nate thought he heard her say something to him, calling him "Natty" the way she had when she was younger, but he was feeling disoriented and couldn't be sure what he heard.

She reached out and helped the two Lowgappers into the bed, then Zeke. All three were clearly out of ammunition and using butts of their weapons to fight off the infected. One of them had affixed a bayonet to an old Russian rifle and was using it as a spear.

"Here hold this." She handed her rifle to Zeke, then reached down and pulled out her karate bag. She'd made sure it was transferred from Zeke's truck to their own when they'd left the doctor's house. She reached in and started pulling out various items.

"Nope, not that." She rejected two short wooden dowels connected by a short chain. Next was a three-pronged metal Sai that looked just like a short pitchfork.

"What are you going to do with that? Pitch hay?" one of the Lowgappers mocked.

"Nope, gonna do this." Anna held the Sai with her thumb looped around one of the tines, the heavy handle pointed downward, then in a rapid motion extended her arm with hand outward, while the Sai performed a complicated rotation to end up points outward, buried in the eye of an infected that was trying to climb up the side of the truck. Yanking it back, she flipped the Sai back over and clubbed the zed over the head with the heavy handle. When it dropped off the side of the truck she dropped the weapon and dug back into the bag, pulling out a pair of two-and-a-half-foot, one-inch-diameter Escrima sticks and handed them to the person who'd mocked her just moments before.

"Use these, they're more your style. Or the Tonfas, there." She pointed to a pair of short clubs with side handles, similar to a policeman's club.

"What are you going to use?" The Lowgapper with the bayonetted rifle asked.

"This one's mine," she said with reverence as she pulled out the decorated scabbard and extracted the gleaming blade of the katana that her grandfather had "acquired" many years ago. "Ki-ah!" she shouted as she began a complicated swirl of the sword, resulting in sliced and splattered zeds.

"Lowgap's finally admitted they need help," Zeke had announced after supper several weeks later. "I'm heading up with a team to help them finally clear that old witness protection neighborhood. Some drug lord was there under constant security and a few of his old buddies decided it would make a nice, heavily armed fort. I'm taking a fire team up tomorrow. Minister Neal wants to go with us and have a 'little talk' with Brother Leonard."

There were more than enough raised hands; the influx of people from Mount Airy had swelled their numbers to the point that the outer fence line was being extended to include the farms in the next valley. They'd start clearing land this week; they now had enough capable adults—even with the pregnant women—to work the farm, provide defense, and support Zeke's and Gideon's rotating search-and-salvage teams.

"No, Nate, sorry. Doc Jackson says you need another couple of weeks' recovery." Zeke knew how much Nate would hate staying home, particularly since he also knew that Anna was going, no matter what. Still it couldn't be helped.

The morning was cool, but with a clear sky; it was sure to warm up, much as it had the past week. "Have you got everything?" Nate leaned his cane against the side of the truck as he helped Anna fasten the straps on her body armor.

"Yeah, Zeke built me a Franken-AK like his and trained me on it. I've got a Barbie gun, and a Saiga, just like Faith. I've got her 'backup plan'..." She patted the knives strapped to her legs. "...and I've got my own backup plan." She lifted the stained karate bag.

"Well then, be careful, be safe, and bring these guys—and—yourself, back safe, kiddo." He watched as she stepped over to the truck, tossed her bag into the back and climbed in with the rest of the team headed to Lowgap.

She leaned over and gave him a kiss on the forehead and gestured at his cane. "You get off that hip. Doc's orders." She straightened up and gave him a smile. A smile that made him proud and melted his heart all at the same time. "Don't worry, Pops. We've got this!"

*"...This is the voice of Mayberry. The town of Lowgap is now a member of Free Northwest Carolina. We have a low yellow clear zone from the Blue Ridge to Mount Airy to Elkin. Infected numbers are manageable to armed parties. We have food and we have shelter. If you can self-extract, come join us! If you can't, hold on, we'll come for you!"*

# It Just Might Matter in the End

## TRAVIS S. TAYLOR

"Roger that, Huntsville," Lyons said with a long slow exhale. He'd been EVA for well over six hours—the maximum permitted under normal circumstances—and Stephanie knew that from the mission timeline, they were pushing him to the physical limits. She also knew that the way things were looking, there was little hope that there would be another resupply mission for the International Space Station, well, probably ever. That was as in, ever again, period.

"Good work, Troy! For an astronaut, you'd make a pretty good Navy SEAL," Stephanie joked. She'd met all the astronauts during training courses. Hell, she'd trained all of them at one point or another, but she'd made friends with U.S. Navy Lieutenant Troy Lyons, a former SEAL, and Dr. Rizwana "Doc Riz" Shelley. She wasn't sure there was any way on Earth, or in space for that matter, to bring them home safely. She wasn't even sure there was going to be an Earth, or at least a place on Earth, to safely come back to. While nobody had officially come out and said there was a "zombie apocalypse" going on, the handwriting was on the wall, the sidewalks, the floor, the ceilings, and pretty much any damned where else one could look. People were turning into zombies and attacking other people, who in turn were turning into zombies. Granted it took days to weeks for them to turn, but they were turning nonetheless. Normally a person from the Timelines team wouldn't be talking to the crew directly, but the situation had gotten dire enough that the people left were starting to have to double up flight control positions. Her friendship with the crew made Stephanie a likely candidate for the Crew Interface Coordinator position.

Stephanie had played enough video games, watched enough "D" movies, and read enough science fiction in her life to know a freakin' "zombie apocalypse" when she saw one. The fact that the Garrison Commander of the U.S. Army's Redstone Arsenal, where the NASA George C. Marshall Space Flight Center was colocated, had lifted the "no personal firearms on base" rule was a loud and clear testament to the unofficially recognized fall of mankind. But Stephanie had also been accused of being the eternal pessimist most of her life, which wasn't true.

She was a pragmatist, a realist, and an oracle of Murphy's Law...which had always seemed appropriate, given there were Murphys in her family tree. For that reason alone she had excelled at manned space mission operations for more than two decades. She could anticipate the shit hitting the fan long before the fan was ever turned on or anyone had taken a shit. And in her mind, the fan was smelling pretty rotten at the moment. Like shit even.

"Thanks, Huntsville. Might look into that someday. Being a SEAL, that is." The astronaut on the other end knew exactly who he was talking to and continued the joke as somber as the current mood on Earth or in space was. "Done on the propulsion module fix. I'm sure Commander Daniels will be happy to get those burn packages uploaded ASAP. Moving to Russian habitat leak kit protocols."

"Roger that, ISS. The EVA is starting to go a little long here. If you need to call it, that is your decision, of course. But I need to point out that the Dragon will be ready for capture in six hours, and without that leak stopped, you will not be able to run the arm unless you're in a suit. Again, which I feel obliged to remind you, would be a bit...um, complicated and difficult." Stephanie looked at the timeline again and whistled to herself. He'd been out there going on eight and a half hours and still had at least another hour of work to do. She didn't have to type into Google or look up into any book to know that the longest spacewalk was performed on March 11, 2001, when STS-102 crew members Susan J. Helms and James S. Voss conducted an EVA that lasted a total time of eight hours and fifty-six minutes. She had been an entry-level console jockey then, not a senior engineer, but she was there on console when it happened. And now it was about to happen again, on her watch, and there would likely be nobody left to give a damn.

A tear rolled down her cheek, bringing her attention back to the work that had to get done. She wiped her eyes and face on the sleeve of her NASA polo shirt and readjusted her headset. She leaned back into her seat a bit, but the Kimber America 1911 .45 Automatic Colt Pistol in her hip holster pushed uncomfortably into the chair, causing her to squirm to a different position. She looked about to make certain the console watch supervisor hadn't seen her crying and that nobody had noticed the firearm. While the ban on the federal base had been lifted, Stephanie was of the Robert Heinlein philosophy that a "secret weapon must be just that, a secret," and so she didn't like to advertise that she was packing. But then again, this was North Alabama, and most likely ninety-nine point nine percent of the people still capable of working console were packing.

She scanned the control room for the payload ops director but then she remembered that he had turned several days prior, and one of the guards had put him down. Stephanie instinctively grabbed the bottle of hand sanitizer she kept by her coffee mug and habitually squirted some into her hands and rubbed it in. She paused and readjusted the picture of Darrell at the edge of the console by her mug that read, "YES IT IS ROCKET SCIENCE!" across it. She took a swig of the now very cold and bitter coffee, made a screwed-up face at the taste, and then wiped the tears from her cheeks.

"We're good to go here, Huntsville. Let's get that patch protocol going." Lyons was a trooper. No, he was a NASA astronaut and a former Navy SEAL. Steph knew he had to have been through much harder shit during BUD/S but she didn't really understand what that meant. In fact, she wasn't even sure what the acronym BUD/S stood for and why it had a forward slash in the middle of it. She just knew it was some serious shit. She looked about the nearly empty operations center and muttered to herself, "Serious shit indeed."

"Are we good to go, Huntsville? Do you copy?" the astronaut repeated in her ear as an instant message popped up on the computer screen in front of her almost simultaneously. It was from the flight surgeon. The surgeon was one of the few people still operating from Houston's Mission Control Center. The rumors Steph had been getting from there were that they had boarded themselves into the building and had been trapped in there for more than two weeks now. The Texas National Guard had been sent there by the governor but for some reason they had never shown up. Or at least that was the story the flight surgeon had given her during one of the late night shifts while the astronauts were on a sleep cycle.

"Uh, roger that, ISS. Sorry Troy, I was checking something. I need to let you know that medical has just reminded me to tell you to hydrate."

"Hydrating. Roger that." Lyons paused. Stephanie could hear him swigging at his hydration tube. "So, good to go on leak protocol?"

"Good to go on leak protocol, affirmative."

The EVA had gone on for another two hours, putting the longest one in history at ten hours twenty-three minutes and eight seconds. Nobody would ever give a shit except maybe the astronauts on board the ISS who needed the EVA work done in order to survive.

Once the astronauts were buttoned up for the night, Stephanie was exhausted. Going home though, wasn't really an option. The Garrison Commander of the Redstone Arsenal, a full bird colonel now that the two star had succumbed to H7D3, the ARSTRAT three star had disappeared, the MDA three star had committed suicide, and the AMC Brigadier had been relocated to, well, somewhere else with the rumor being Utah, had closed the base to all but essential personnel. And since the Marshall Space Flight Center was inside the gates, it was locked down. The essential NASA mission personnel were all locked inside NASA Building 4663, a.k.a. the ISS Payload Operations Center. Most NASA folks who spoke "NASAese" called it the POC, pronounced like it rhymed with clock.

So many console jockeys and mission ops engineers had succumbed to the H7D3 virus that it was taking as many operators still, uh, functional from both Houston and Huntsville as they could manage, to keep the station operations going in such a way that it was not overwhelming to the astronauts. Especially since the majority of the Russians and the Europeans had bailed with the remaining Soyuz capsule before there was a replacement. Nobody ever heard from them again either. That was a shame. So Steph wasn't going to bail on the remaining astronauts no matter what. The astronauts were the only family she had left. She did need to refill her coffee mug though. She "tagged out" from her console for a much overdue break.

On any other "typical" NASA day there would be a person at every console and four or five backups waiting in the wings. There would also be management, administrative support, and even janitorial personnel wandering about. Since the H7D3 the POC was a ghost town. There were seven people total in the entire building as far as Stephanie could surmise. In Houston, they had started with fifty-three. There were eight still communicating with Huntsville. They had to go through Huntsville, as for whatever reason, the uplink to the ISS through the Space Network, the Transmission and Data Relay Satellites, and even the "NASA Satern" computer network was acting funny there. E-mail and instant messages and video messaging were still working from Houston to Huntsville, but not into space.

So Huntsville had become a serial link in the logistics and command chain to the ISS. While the people in Houston could have communicated to them with amateur radio, none of the survivors were even licensed amateur radio operators. Where the ISS got lucky was that the Huntsville POC was inside, deep inside, an Army base. It was a base that was surrounded by fences, guard shack entry points, and vast farm land. Houston's Mission Control, on the other hand, was near Clear Lake in Texas and one of the biggest cities in the country. Houston had apparently been much easier to fall to the H7D3 impact on security.

At least the astronauts were safe from the virus. They were her friends and Stephanie took it as her responsibility to keep them alive as long as she could manage. What efforts she could put in just might matter in the end, maybe. She wasn't sure, but she also wasn't going to just quit on them. Besides, there was nobody else left for her to care about except the astronauts.

Two Russians, Colonel Nikofor Kuznetsov and Lieutenant

Colonel Varfolomei Matveev, had drawn the short straws and had to stay behind. The Americans, Troy and Dr. Gordie Price; Commander Daniels, who was Canadian; and Dr. Rizwana Shelley, who was a British citizen, were, well, shit out of luck since they didn't have a spacecraft of their own and had been buying rides from the Russians for almost a decade. The astronauts were in a bad situation. As far as most of the ground teams were concerned, they were going to hang in there and keep things going until SpaceX got them a backup plan—a backup plan that had not been fully tested and had yet to be man-rated.

Even if the new Dragon system worked, after being rushed into service and launched during a "zombie apocalypse," if it actually managed to be captured and mated to the airlock, who knew if there would be a place to bring it down. While the Dragon had been tested in a cargo configuration and unmanned, it had yet to be used to bring back astronauts.

And on top of that, it would be the last supply mission they would have in a long, long time—if ever again. They were going to run out of fuel, oxygen, food, water, and everything else eventually. The question was which critical item would go first...if they survived that long.

Most people in the general public had no idea how hard it was to keep the ISS afloat in space. There were solar flares to worry about. Leaks to deal with. Repairs and breakdowns. Personal interactions. And there was the occasional debris cloud that had to be avoided and this required a push from the engines on the Zvezda Service Module. Astronauts on board the ISS had no data about orbital debris. That data came from radars on Earth. Astronauts on board the ISS also didn't have the simulation tools to calculate orbital debris mitigation burns. That required smart folks on the ground like Stephanie and her colleagues.

"Steph, you look awful," Andy Freeman said as he fed change into the soft drink machine and then stared at it as if he didn't know what he was intending to get. Stephanie rubbed at her eyes and then propped her face in her hands with her elbows on the round gray government breakroom table. "I mean, not, H7 awful, but awful. When was the last time you slept?"

"I haven't slept since they took my husband to the recovery center and he never recovered." She started crying again. That had been days, maybe weeks ago. Time had sort of lost meaning to her outside of the astronaut's mission timelining efforts. "They're gonna die, aren't they?"

"Who? The people in the recovery centers. I think once they're there, they are already...oh, sorry, I, Hell. Steph, I'm sorry. You need to get some sleep." Andy told her. She couldn't sleep.

"It's okay. We're scientists. We know what happens when things occur. Doesn't make us feel any better about it. I'll miss him forever, you know. But, that wasn't who I was talking about." Stephanie flipped the lever up on the single-serving coffee machine, removed the old cup, and then dropped in a new one. She chose the cup marked "Ultimate Caffeine." After snapping the lever back in place and pressing the button, she sighed in anticipation as the familiar buzzing and hissing of the machine began dripping coffee into her rocket science mug.

"You mean the crew?" Andy seemed shocked. Nobody ever talked about losing a crew. "Steph, no. We have a job to do. We'll keep them alive. Somehow, we'll get through this. We'll get *them* through this. The Dragon is on approach in a few hours and they will have an evacuation option then. It's simple. The capsule matches orbital velocity and approaches closely enough for Captain Daniels to grab it with the arm and then they lock it in place. You know the drill, Steph. We'll get them down."

"Right. A job to do. But..." Stephanie turned from her mug briefly and shook her head at her colleague. She stopped herself from finishing the thought that wouldn't have been helpful. Telling him that she didn't think there would be anything left to come down to was probably going through his mind as well.

Andy continued to stare annoyingly at the machine selections. Steph just shook her head at his idiosyncrasy. She stepped closer and pushed a button on the soda machine for him. Andy always got the same thing and everybody on the shift knew it. He just had a hard time making decisions for himself. He would stand there for ten minutes sometimes, trying to figure out what to get, but in the end he'd always get the same thing. That was why he was backroom and not on console.

"Are you going to try and go home at all?" She asked him as the machine went *cachunk,* depositing a soft drink at the bottom.

"No way. I heard that there were more zombies at Bridge Street than you could shake a stick at. At least here on the base there are fences and soldiers." Andy sounded truly frightened. Everybody was. Stephanie had sort of gone through being frightened and had come out on the other side of it. She wasn't sure where she was at the moment.

She sat there for a couple of hours, staring off into space, drinking coffee and ignoring the vending machine as best she could. The refrigerators in the kitchen area were filled with lunches and leftovers that nobody was coming back for. There was even three-fourths of an uneaten birthday cake in one of them, along with about five pizza boxes filled with various mixes of pizzas from a party they'd had a week before. It was the last "good time" any of them had before people started not showing up in large numbers. Stephanie suspected most of them had turned like Darrell had.

After Darrell had turned, she had gone numb for a long while. Fortunately for her she was a police officer on the local Indian reservation and had been trained in self-defense, carried a firearm, and had handcuffs. While she and her husband had joked about using the handcuffs for, uh, other means, she had ended up using them in the end to restrain him after things had gone bad. She couldn't bring herself to shoot him. Seeing him get sick and then turn was bad enough.

Darrell was a magician, a good one. He did parties for side money, but not really because they needed the money, more because he enjoyed doing it. He enjoyed bringing smiles and that sense of wonder to people as they saw his antics and tricks. She'd pleaded with him not to go, literally begged him. But as long as they'd been married he'd never missed a "gig," as he called them, even once. That time when he had caught the flu and another time when a tornado had torn through town and blocked most of the roads he didn't miss his gigs. He was going to keep the promise to the family he'd booked.

"Some kid will be heartbroken," he'd argued with her. So he went and one of the children turned in the middle of the party and Darrell had gotten bitten in the process. It was only about thirty-six hours later when he turned. She couldn't bring herself to put him down, but she had already cuffed him just in case. The two of them said their goodbyes and cried and then he started getting angry. And then, then he wasn't Darrell anymore. She called 911 and eventually, they came for him. Steph had sat on the sofa gently rocking back and forth, near catatonic for hours until her alarm had gone off. It was time for her shift and nobody missed their turn at the console. Nobody.

"Roger that, Flight. We have the Dragon in visual range now." Commander Daniels announced over the astronauts' open channel. "It all looks good."

"Be advised that we only have Dragon flight control on a landline talking us through this. The SpaceX facility is on lockdown and is on a minimum crew at present time." The flight director sounded as calm and commonplace as usual, even though Houston had pretty much fallen to the virus and Johnson Space Center was locked down. Nobody wanted the astronauts to know just how bad things were on Earth.

"Understood, Flight." Commander Daniels replied.

"Houston, this is Huntsville," Stephanie said on a back channel not open to the astronauts.

"Go Huntsville."

"Flight, we are go for main arm warm up sequence."

"Roger that, Huntsville," Flight replied and then changed channels. "ISS, we are go for Mobile Servicing System boot sequence as practiced."

"Copy that, Houston. Go for boot sequence."

Stephanie watched the video feeds that fortunately were still functioning. The ISS and the Dragon were within two kilometers of each other and were currently over Asia. The ground stations there were autonomously functioning and would do so as long as something didn't go haywire, like a zombie getting loose in the control room or power feeds. Half of her big screen was exterior ISS view and the other half was split into two sections. The upper section showed Houston, and the bottom, the inside of the ISS. Troy and Commander Daniels were floating almost motionlessly while staring out the window at the approaching capsule and tapping at controls occasionally.

Originally Stephanie had two other monitors at her console station that showed data from the environment systems and the astronaut workflow and timeline. Since they were so shorthanded due to the H7D3 virus, she and Andy had moved as many of the consoles around one station, hers, as they could manage. She sat at that seat while Andy monitored the lesser function ones. The seven other people who had managed to get locked into the POC

with them were management and custodial and weren't much
use with mission control. It looked like Houston was faring a bit
better as there were four bodies on consoles, including Flight and
Medical, and what looked to be one security guard in full body
armor in the background. Steph made a mental note to ask one
of the other seven on lockdown with them to take up a guard
position outside the door.

"Steph, does Flight look, I dunno, more agitated than usual?"
Andy asked as he turned to her, palms up.

"Why wouldn't he?" She shrugged. "There are zombies beating
down the doors and he's trying his best not to crash a spacecraft
into the ISS. And I might add that the controllers for the spacecraft can only be reached by voice on a landline. Not optimum
for a stress-free environment."

"Yeah, but..."

"Yeah, but...just pay attention so we don't kill anyone today,"
she snapped, maybe a bit harshly. Stephanie had to admit that
Flight did look a bit haggard.

"Flight, we see the Dragon on approach. Lidar shows closing
range at zero point seven five kilometers. Closing rate is three
point six kilometers per hour. ETA to capture point is twelve
point five minutes," Commander Daniels said. "Advise on burn
sequence?"

"Roger that. Be advised that SpaceX informs us that all telemetry looks normal and we are go for braking burn in ten minutes
twenty seconds."

"Copy that, Houston."

Stephanie studied the many monitors about her station, looking for anything that might be an anomaly or an issue. Radar and
lidar data looked good and coincided with what the astronauts
were saying. She also noted that heart rates and other vitals on the
astronauts were good, even though that wasn't her job to monitor.
The Zvezda module showed environment control was functioning
appropriately and the telemetry showed no scheduled orbit correction burns. It was pretty much a waiting game now, and then
at the last second, SpaceX software would kick in, firing thrusters
to reduce the relative velocity between the capsule and the station.
Then Commander Daniels would use the CanadaArm2 and reach
out and grab the Dragon. At that point, the two cosmonauts would
go out and help guide it into the docking ring.

Steph took a moment to sip from her coffee mug and then looked at the video of the astronauts and from Houston. The astronauts, her friends, looked no worse for the wear. But the four people in the Mission Control Room in Houston looked as frazzled as she felt. Then she noticed something familiar. The flight director started scratching at his left arm unconsciously. Perhaps he just had an itch. Then she noticed that he squirmed a bit, rubbing his back against his chair as if he were scratching an itch there. He started to rub at his right shin with the heel of his left foot.

*Medical this is Huntsville.* She typed into an instant message for the medical officer in Houston.

*Hi Steph. What's up?*

*Connie, is Flight okay?*

*Sure. Why?*

*I'm not sure but he looks unsettled. What d'ya think? Connie? What's happening?*

The messages stopped promptly and Steph could tell from the video monitor that Dr. Constance Amir had been startled. Severely. Startled. The video of the control room still played but it looked like Flight had cut the sound to keep everyone from listening. Or maybe he cut it accidentally. He was clearly angry about something and was scratching at his face and arms so hard that blood was showing. It looked to Stephanie like Connie was trying to calm him down, but then he did the unthinkable and hit her square on the jaw, knocking her backwards and to the ground. The other console riders at Houston stood up, startled, and as far as Steph could tell, not sure what to do.

"Oh my God!" Stephanie said in horror. "No no no! Not now! He's turning!"

"What!?" Andy jumped from his seat and ran behind her to watch the monitor.

"Houston, this is Huntsville! Copy?" Steph said urgently into her headset. "Houston! Copy?"

The flight director grabbed a chair and started smashing it against his monitor clearly screaming all the while. Just as suddenly as he had started going nuts, he dropped the chair and stood still for a brief second. The scratching and twitching stopped. It looked as if he had gained control of himself, but Stephanie had seen it. She knew better. The H7D3 had gotten control of him. The flight director was now turned. He was a zombie.

The rest of the console jockeys started to spread about the room and one of them cowered behind his monitor. Then like a wild predator, Flight was moving fast and deliberately after a prey. He jumped at Dr. Amir, clawing and gnashing his teeth, biting her. His teeth tore into her flesh and he must have hit her jugular, as blood began to squirt from her neck in pulsating red blobs onto the floor. Stephanie felt as if she were going to be sick.

One of the others picked up a chair and swung it at Flight but only managed to gain his attention. Flight rose with bright red blood spattered across his forehead and face and drooling from the corners of his mouth. He twitched unnaturally, and then he moved so quickly onto the man with the chair that it was over in an instant. The man's body fell backwards right beside the other controller hiding behind his console monitor. Flight lurched and clawed at the man crouching there and they fell out of view behind the console. All Stephanie could see were the two men's feet and Flight's head occasionally rising above the monitors.

Flight rose slowly now, completely covered in blood and with what looked like a government issued ballpoint ink pen sticking out of one eye. Then he jerked violently, falling backwards, and quickly struggled to his feet while turning to the opposite direction. He was bleeding from his chest but it didn't seem to slow him much. Steph could see the guard in body armor firing his pistol again and again as Flight rushed him. He had been too slow on the draw to help anyone but himself. Perhaps he'd panicked. Who knew?

The guard continued to pump what Stephanie surmised to be nine-millimeter rounds into the turned flight director but it didn't stop him. Flight leapt onto the guard, taking yet another round as he bit at the man's face. There was a struggle and the two of them rolled on the ground until the side of Flight's head exploded and then he rolled over limp. The guard made his way to his feet and instinctively and in a panic started wiping blood from his face and arms. Then he ran away out of camera view and Steph watched the video from Houston's Mission Control Room with her jaw dropped, and tears formed in her eyes.

"Oh Jesus! Jesus!" Andy cried. "Oh my God!"

"Andy," Stephanie said calmly.

"Oh shit! Oh Hell! Oh my God!" Andy continued. "Flight killed them! Oh God, we're gonna die in here!"

"Andy, return to your console, please." Stephanie forced all of her emotions as deeply down inside her as she could.

"But, Steph! Oh my God!" He cried uncontrollably. "Didn't you see that? He turned into a zombie and killed them!"

"Andy, in four minutes and seventeen seconds the Dragon capsule is going to make a burn. We need to be able to monitor that burn and flow that telemetry back to the astronauts. I have to get SpaceX on the line. As far as I can tell, we are all that is left of ISS Mission Control. Do you understand that?"

"Oh Jesus," he whimpered, but noticeably calmed himself. "I do, Steph. I do understand that."

"Houston. ISS. Over?

"Houston, this is ISS, do you copy?"

"What do you tell them? I mean..."

"Don't worry. I'll talk to them. Now get over there and see if you can get any of the consoles from Houston up here," she ordered him.

"Houston. ISS. Over?"

"Uh, hello ISS, this is Huntsville. Do you copy?" Stephanie could see the reaction on the astronauts' faces when they heard her.

"Roger, Huntsville. We are waiting for go or no-go on capture from Flight. Any word?"

"ISS, be advised that until further notice Huntsville is now Mission Control and I am acting as flight director for now. Do you copy that?" Stephanie talked while typing e-mails to the telemetry team at SpaceX hoping that somebody there was still alive and answering e-mails.

*Houston has been compromised by the virus. Huntsville is now Flight. Please direct flight data here via the NASA Satern datalink.* She typed and sent.

"Uh, Huntsville, Steph, is that you?" Troy asked her.

"Roger that, Troy. Stephanie here."

"Give it to us straight, Steph," Commander Daniels added.

"We are not in contact with SpaceX just yet and communication with Houston has been compromised for the time being. We might be on our own here, fellas. Can you give me a continuous update on your short-range lidar? I will update you in turn from our long-range radar if needed. But I suspect your range data will be way more accurate." She explained as little as possible.

*Dr. Malcolm Story here, Huntsville. Sorry to hear about Houston. We're having difficulties ourselves. I am currently unable to log into Satern. E-mail is working. Please advise.*

*Dr. Story, Stephanie Osborn here. Houston is down. We are trying to guide the astronauts from Huntsville. Please advise on status of Dragon telemetry as real-time as possible with e-mail.*

*Understood. Burn in T-minus two minutes and forty-one seconds. Be advised that we are no longer receiving ranging data and fear our downlink has been compromised.*

*Copy. Will feed back from ISS as best we can.*

Stephanie had been afraid of that. SpaceX was having their own zombie apocalypse problems, it appeared.

"ISS, T-minus two minutes forty seconds to burn. I need a continuous range report at ten-second intervals." Stephanie kept an eye on her clock. "Andy, get over here."

"Roger, Huntsville, range at five hundred seventy-three meters and still closing at three point six kilometers per hour."

"Copy, ISS. Three point six." Stephanie quickly typed *573 meters* and hit send.

"What do you need me to do, Steph?" Andy stumbled over a monitor power cable and nearly fell on his face. He caught himself on a chair at the last second.

"Five hundred fifty meters...five hundred forty..." Commander Daniels continued.

"Get your cell phone out, quickly!" she said.

"Got it. Now what?"

"Set a timer for two minutes, quickly." She paused to check her e-mail. Nothing yet, so she typed, *Please advise at T-minus two minutes and five seconds.*

Almost as soon as she clicked Send, her e-mail dinged. She clicked it open.

*T-minus two minutes and five seconds.*

"Start the time, Andy!"

"Okay, got it."

"Five hundred ten meters."

She typed the distance and sent it to Dr. Story.

"We are less than two minutes from braking burn, ISS. You can hold on range report for now, but as soon as you see the burn initiated, tell me the range data and go back to continuous updates. I would also like delta-vee updates as available."

"Copy that, Flight."

"Steph, what if the burn is too short?" Andy asked, but he already knew.

"Anything faster than a one kilometer per hour or so delta-vee with that much mass might collapse the arm and then we have a collision on our hands," she said, and then pointed at the monitor displaying the astronauts. "Then *they* have trouble."

"Oh my God. Oh my God. Oh my God!" Andy repeated nervously and in rapid fire succession.

"I know, Andy. Do your best to calm down. Panicking will only get them killed. We are safe in here," she reminded him. It was just her luck to get stuck with the only engineer at NASA that handled stress so poorly that he couldn't manage to choose what soft drink button to push. Now they were for all intents and purposes pushing *all* the buttons on the International Space Station. The timer on Andy's phone sounded almost simultaneously with audio from ISS.

"Dragon burns have initiated, Flight."

"Roger that, ISS," Stephanie said, then recalled the arm had a camera on it for just such purposes. She wasn't trained as Flight. She was a mission timeline expert. Now she *was* Flight and had to remember such things.

"Andy, find me the channel for the arm camera video and bring it up fast!" she said.

"Oh yeah, that is over here. I just saw it on one of these..." he said almost nonchalantly as he sat down at a console and calmly set to work sending her the feed. Stephanie suddenly realized what calmed him. Work. She had to keep him working.

*Dr. Story, we have burns starting.* Steph sent to SpaceX.

"Got it, Steph." Andy jumped up from where he was and set a monitor on a chair next to her. "Don't want to mess with any of the ones you already have up."

"Good work, Andy."

"...one zero nine meters at two point one kilometers per hour..."

"Look! It's firing again." Andy pointed at the Dragon in the video.

The camera on the CanadaArm2 was pointed directly at the nose of the Dragon capsule and retro rockets fired out of several locations in short bursts in what to the uninitiated would appear a random fashion. But Steph knew that the guidance, navigation, and control (GNC) algorithm was taking its own range data from lidar, radar, and camera images and was making precise corrections to the spacecraft's trajectory and velocity vectors.

"...eight zero meters at one point seven kilometers per hour..." Commander Daniels reported.

"Come on baby, figure it out." Steph sat with her fingers crossed. There was little she could do until the burns stopped. She also knew that if SpaceX had done the software inputs correctly that the algorithm in the GNC would, as it had in the past, work flawlessly.

"More burns!" Andy pointed again.

"...five six meters at one point five kilometers per hour..."

Stephanie looked at the trajectory lines of the station and the capsule on one of her monitors and at the current pace, the capsule was too far off axis for the arm to reach it. But on the upside the velocities were closing.

*Dr. Story, orthogonal vectors have yet to close.*
*Flight, sorry to hear that. How far off?*
*Nineteen meters at fifty meters out.*
*That's too far.*

"Flight to ISS. Troy, we're gonna miss! Get Matveev and Kuznetsov out of the airlock now and prepared to freefly! Now!" Steph ordered them. Instantly she could see the two astronauts reacting. Daniels remained at his post while Troy pushed back toward the airlock.

"We heard you, Flight. The colonel and I are already in the airlock. Cycling now," Matveev responded. "Soyuz would not miss."

"Not the time, comrade," Kuznetsov added.

"More burns, Steph!" Andy remained riveted to the monitor.

"...three one meters at one point one kilometers per hour..."

"Be ready, fellas. Worst case, we'll need to slow it down with the jets in the EVA unit," Stephanie explained. The trajectory and position vectors were still not closing but were to within ten meters of the arm's reach.

"We will lasso it like you cowboy Americans."

"Never ridden a horse, Varf," Troy Lyons, Navy SEAL turned astronaut, replied. "But if you snap a tether on it, it just might slam into us."

"Either that or let our ride go," Kuznetsov replied.

"Flight to ISS. Do not tether the Dragon to ISS," Stephanie warned them.

"...one nine meters at zero point seven kilometers per hour..." Commander Daniels announced. "With this delta-vee, guys, we could catch it with the Zvezda if you can't with a suit."

*Dr. Story, we are still 9 m too far. But at 0.7 kmh.*
*Understood. Burn shut-off is at 2m.*

"Look, Steph, the Russians are almost to the arm." Andy toggled the interior viewscreen to a split screen showing the interior and exterior. Every view was up somewhere in the room, but they simply hadn't had time to fix that for one person to watch.

"Great, Andy. As long as we don't get much more to the burns from here, I think we'll make it."

"Hey Steph, what happens to the GNC if the cosmonauts attach to the capsule before the routine is finished?"

"Oh shit!" Stephanie wasn't one hundred percent certain but she was also one hundred percent certain she didn't want to test that. "ISS. Flight. Do not make contact with the Dragon until given the all-clear. Understood?"

"Roger, Flight, uh, we copy," Kuznetsov replied.

"...ten meters...nine...another burn there...six meters..." Steph and Andy sat quiet as several burns fired.

*Huntsville? Status?*

"...four meters...three meters at zero point three kilometers per hour...two point five meters..."

"Come on," Steph said through clenched teeth.

"...two point nine meters...another burn..."

"Wrong way!" Andy replied.

"It's okay, Andy, as long as it stays slow."

Several burns fired and the ship moved almost two meters away and then back. It was clear the algorithm was confused and was trapped in an oscillatory mode about the location vector it was trying to reach. It would never reach it.

*Dr. Story, can you send an approach shutdown sequence to the Dragon now!?*

*Understood. Yes.*

They all waited. There were several tens of seconds with no burns.

"... one point two meters and holding at zero point zero one kilometers per hour," Daniels said, breathing a sigh that was audible over the comms. "Not close enough to grab but close enough."

"That is great news, ISS!" Stephanie cheered. "I recommend we let our cosmonaut friends bring it in the rest of the way to the arm and then we dock it in place."

"Roger that, Huntsville!" Troy replied out of protocol.

"Flight. ISS. We are initiating capture sequence," Daniels said.

"Just turn it off, Andy. It sickens me to watch it any longer." Stephanie pointed at the monitor for Houston Mission Control Room. Several infected had started using the room for what Steph could only guess was a nest. One of the infected wore a guard uniform and was clearly the guard that had been in the room three weeks prior during the Dragon capture sequence.

"Okay," Andy said robotically. "I wonder if anyone is left in Houston at all. At least they still have power, it looks like."

"Yeah. I suspect we won't for much longer. While this building and most of Redstone Arsenal have backup systems and all of our power comes from the solar power array down on Redstone Road, who knows when weather or even zombies will cause some sort of mechanical problem for us," Stephanie added. "But we have to keep being smart and keep only interior room lights on."

"Yeah, we don't want to be the only bug light left on in town," Andy agreed. "Been difficult explaining that to Janice and Mr. Mason."

Stephanie only nodded and almost cringed at the thought of an upper manager and his administrative assistant being the last of the original seven left in the building not to have turned. Hell, Dennis, the janitorial service contractor, had been helpful and useful. He knew where things were and he was a hard worker. It was a shame the virus had taken him. It also had taken the two others that Stephanie never really knew. In the end, there were four of them left in the entire building. She and Andy were the only ones that were qualified in any way to help the astronauts.

"The astronauts are on a sleep cycle right now and don't need much watching. Besides, they're about to pass over the Atlantic and we'll lose them for the next several hours. We need to see if we can figure out why our TDRSS links aren't working." Steph frowned. "But before that, we should check on Janice and Mr. Mason and see if they filled up all the water jugs and bottles like we decided."

"I bet they waited until we went to work and started, uh, you know," Andy said sheepishly.

"Uh, yeah, I know."

"Huntsville Flight Director. Please respond." An unknown voice sounded over the loudspeaker. "Huntsville Flight Director, do you copy?"

"What the hell?" Andy looked startled out of his mind. He literally ducked as if he were going to hide behind something.

"Easy, Andy. What channel is that on?" Stephanie looked at the receiver spectrum on one of the consoles that they had rigged up near her station. It was on the open amateur band that the astronauts used sometimes to talk to people around the world for fun and public relations.

"Huntsville, do you copy?"

"Flight Director Stephanie Osborn here. Who's speaking?" Steph said reluctantly, then keyed off the microphone and shrugged at Andy. "What the—"

"Director Osborn, stand by for General Brice."

"Well, we knew it would happen at some point, Andy. I just can't believe it lasted for more than three months. Quit worrying about it and keep your eyes on the road." Stephanie looked out the rear passenger-side window of the Ford F250 "dually" that Thomas Mason had driven into work pretty much every day for the last four years that he'd been in the supernumerary manage-ment position. He was a bean counter and not much use to Steph from the point of view of saving the astronauts.

On the other hand, he was an upper middle class, very upper middle class, single man from north Alabama who had an affinity for hunting and fishing, along with all the toys. He didn't have a family to spend his time and money on, so he found expensive hob-bies. Although it was his truck, he rode shotgun, literally. He had a Remington 1100 autoloading twelve-gauge propped out the window. He'd removed the plug so it held four double-ought buckshot shells in the magazine and one in the chamber. He was wearing a hunting vest with a bandolier filled with shells. At least he'd come prepared for the zombie apocalypse when he decided to come into the office.

"So, Steph, you think you can actually fix it?" asked Janice Farley, Mason's "admin assistant." "I mean, what will we do without power?"

"Fix is probably the wrong word, Janice. Rig is more likely what we'll end up doing. I'm just surprised the water is still running. I expected it to stop by now. We'll cross that bridge someday soon probably. At least the river is just right down the road." Steph scanned the road for zombies but there were none. Not at least like the ham radio and Internet folks had been talking about and there was certainly nothing like the last bits of news from the big cities falling showed.

The Redstone Arsenal was a very large Alabama wilderness base. It was bordered by the half mile wide Tennessee River on the south and was completely surrounded by eight foot high fences topped with barbed and sometimes concertina wire. There were gates that had been all blocked and closed. And there were buildings with other fences and such scattered about the roadways which were separated by pastureland, two mountains, and forestry.

The only zombies that would be inside the Arsenal would have been ones who were locked in with them once the base had been closed to "non-mission-critical personnel" or from those personnel who turned, and that was a two- to maybe a three-digit number at max. They had actually only seen thirty-seven personal cars in parking lots so far which sort of gave them a number to work with. The Redstone Arsenal was actually not a bad place to be during a zombie apocalypse.

"Go on down to Redstone Road by the fire station light and hang a left. Then you'll see it," Thomas told Andy. "The solar farm is there. I killed a nine point buck right over there on the back side of it last year."

"I never drive this far down here. I had no idea all this Army stuff was here," Andy said.

"Seriously?" Steph asked. "You've worked for NASA for as long as I have and you've never driven around the Arsenal?"

"Not really. Come to think of it, I've only been in a few of the NASA buildings. I've never even been in the SLS building," Andy replied. "I should've gotten out more."

"It's a little late now," Steph drawled, dry as dust.

"See them up there?" Thomas pointed as they rounded a slow curve and the solar farm stretched out for a mile almost.

"I've never been here. Wow!" Andy seemed amazed. "I mean, I read about it and saw pictures on the news but, just, wow."

"Take that little gravel work road there." Steph leaned over the seat and pointed. She fingered the safety of the thirty-ought-six hunting rifle that Thomas had given her and leaned back against her .45 just to feel that it was there in the holster. She was ready.

"We might make a run to the SLS building next, Andy. They had some really nice vending machines. We could restock sodas, water bottles, and snack foods," Thomas suggested. "It should be sealed and might not have any infected inside it."

"I'd vote for the Sparkman Center or the Von Braun Center, Tom," Stephanie added. "They're bigger, have cafeterias, and a lot more vending machines. Maybe more chance of running into baddies inside them, though. And on the way back I want us to stop by the RV and Boat rental place. They rented campers and generators and stuff. We might find a genie there we can use until I get this solar thing figured out."

"Good idea, Steph." Tom agreed with her. As managers went, Steph didn't think he was half bad. "I rented a fifth wheel there for Memorial Day one time and it was loaded and had a genie in it. They also have gas pumps there. We could refuel the truck."

"Okay Andy, pull up as close as you can get between these two panels here without getting us stuck. It rained yesterday and you know Alabama red mud."

"Stuck? My truck? Not likely." Thomas grunted as if he were offended by the notion.

Stephanie and the others stepped out of the big "4x4" six-wheel-drive truck apprehensively, constantly scanning about for zombies running out of nowhere. Fortunately, the solar panel farm was in the middle of a long field and right beside Redstone Road. It was in the open and easily accessible.

"I'd suggest, Janice, you stay behind the wheel with the engine off. Shouldn't make more sound than we need to. And the rest of us up in the back until Steph needs a third hand," Thomas suggested. His outdoorsman and leadership qualities were shining through his bean counting.

"Just keep an eye out for me, please," Steph said. "Now, where is that toolbox of yours, Tom?"

Tom slid the tailgate down and dragged a big metal "carry-on suitcase" style toolbox to the edge of the truck. He slipped a key in the lock and popped it open for her.

"It has everything in it you might want in a zombie apocalypse. I added stuff the day before I decided to camp out in the office."

"Looks heavy," Andy noted.

"Let's leave it in the truck in case we have to make a quick getaway," he said. "What d'ya need, Steph?"

"Right. Voltmeter and leather gloves are what I need first."

It had taken the better part of three hours to disconnect three panels electrically and mechanically and then load them into the back of the truck. Then Stephanie had them collect as much cabling as they could, as well as several regulators. There were emergency backup batteries aplenty back at the POC, they just needed twelve volts on them to recharge. The solar panels should do the trick. It was just going to take several days to rig everything up, and in that time they only had ham radio communications with the ISS...and Stephanie didn't like that.

The panels were strapped in the back of the truck and looked as if they were taking the ride just fine as they traveled north back up Patton Road and then they took the off-ramp to the recreational vehicle rental facility. That place was a treasure trove. Almost everything was still in place. There were full sized RVs, pontoon boats, fifth wheels, campers, barbecue grills ranging from back porch to pull behind size, bass boats, and best of all, generators. It took all four of them to figure out how to load the truck but they decided to go with four small to medium size generators rather than the larger pull behinds, their thoughts being that the small ones could be brought inside somewhere to limit the noise. There was also camping gear, extension cords, rope, and power tools.

"We'll have to come back to this place for more stuff," Tom said.

"We could load up an RV and just drive it over," Janice offered.

"Not today. We have to get the power up and check on the ISS orbit," Steph told them. As flight director, and from the power given her by the General at "The Hole," whatever that was, Stephanie was, as far as she could tell, in charge of NASA. Hell, the four of them and the ISS astronauts most likely *were* NASA. "Let's load this up and go."

"Moo."

"Holy shit! That cow scared me to death." Steph's heart skipped a beat as a cow passed across the road to greener grass on the other side. She shrugged and pointed west. "How'd the cow get over here? The pasture is four hundred yards that way."

*Bang!* The sound of the 30.06 echoed three times and Steph nearly soiled her pants. She reached for her pistol and turned as Tom lowered the rifle.

"Shotgun would have messed up more of the meat." He shrugged. "Sorry if I startled you. I didn't want a good chance at steak to get away from us. Get me some coolers out of the rental center and I'll start field dressing her."

Brandishing his scabbard knife, Tom turned toward the cow as a figure burst from the trees. The zombie had likely been tracking the cow. Steph quickly reached into her back holster and drew down on the infected, releasing two rounds into his chest and then one in his head.

"There might be more from the noise. We should get a move on it before dark sets in," she said. "Andy, take the shotgun and stand guard over us while we finish up."

"Why don't you do it, Steph. You've been at it all day." Andy handed her the Remington 1100 and went back to loading the truck.

"You mean they're finding survivors all over the Atlantic!?" Tom responded to the video conference image of the general and the national continuity coordinator. "That's amazing! We haven't found a single survivor here on base yet. But there are radio broadcasts from Monte Sano Mountain State Park. We hear there is a survival group up there, holding out."

"We need satellite imagery real-time. While there are still some functional national assets giving us imagery, we are losing capabilities daily. ISS video is our best bet." General Brice said. "Can we get video real-time still?"

"Only when they pass overhead. We, um, commandeered a few of the satellite dishes around the Arsenal and relocated them here but for the most part, there's nothing to see. We still get a signal from Dish Network but all it shows is the empty guide channel and a view of the Earth from way out at geosynchronous orbit. There are a few repeaters up there that are still working and we're tapping into them, trying to create a makeshift relay system, but it's slow going. We'd be best off to have them take the data we want and then start downloading it on every pass. I'm not sure why the Transmission and Data Relay Satellite System is nonfunctional but we're getting nothing from it."

"How long would that take?" the NCC asked.

"Single pass downloads?" Steph asked for clarification.

"Yes, that."

"Days to weeks depending on the passes. We'll work it out," Stephanie said. "The next pass is in an hour and we'll talk with them then. I'm also working out a way to do Moon bounce communications with the amateur radio setup they have up there. That way we could at least talk to them for half of every orbit."

"Great news, Director. We'll send you what we want."

"Uh, there's one more thing General, ehr, maybe it is actually several things causing one big thing. Call it death by a thousand cuts," Stephanie added reluctantly.

"That doesn't sound good," General Brice replied.

"No ma'am, it isn't." Stephanie pulled up the bulletized list she'd made in preparation for the video conference and started at the top. "We've had seven leaks in the past three weeks, each requiring patches from external surfaces. We had three of those seven occur simultaneously. The EVAs used up precious LOX as well as our patch kit materials. Also, about the same time as the three simultaneous leaks occurred, we had total failure on two heat exchangers. There is one functioning heat exchanger left and we haven't been able to come up with a fix on the others yet."

"I get it. Space things wear out and need repaired." General Brice looked solemn in her response.

"Well, yes, but no ma'am." Stephanie realized that very few

people truly understood all that was required to keep the ISS afloat. "Ma'am, the reason the leaks occurred at the same time the heat exchangers failed was because of orbital debris."

"You mean the ISS was hit by something?"

"Not just something, a cloud of somethings." Stephanie raised her eyes from her bulletized screen. "We haven't had orbital debris radar data in months and I've been running a model off the last data to do orbital debris cloud mitigation maneuvers with the Zvezda propulsion system . . . but without new radar data, the model is no longer any good."

"So what are you saying, Stephanie?"

"Ma'am, if we don't get them out of there, it's just a matter of time before they are all hit by micrometeorites, paint flecks, nuts, bolts, you name it, moving at a relative velocity of about twenty thousand miles per hour."

"Jesus!"

"Yes ma'am, I pray to him on an hourly basis that our astronauts are safe." Stephanie nodded. "We need to bring them down."

"Stephanie, we've been working this as best we can with our limited resources and I haven't wanted to task you with this because I needed you keeping them alive. But now I think it's time we come together on this. So, that said, it is now your full time and sole mission at this point to figure out how to get our astronauts down alive and well. Is that understood?"

"Yes, ma'am."

"They want to land where?" Stephanie asked Andy to repeat what the astronaut Doc Riz was telling her on the ham rig. She bumped her head on the underside of the console panel she was rigging with a C band transceiver they had found on the test range at the south end of the Arsenal. "Shit! That will leave a mark."

"Somewhere in the Atlantic. An island down there called—uh, I wrote it down—Anguilla in the British Leeward Islands."

"Oh yeah, Darrell and I went on a cruise there once," she replied.

"Well, they need, and I quote, 'NASA to verify the orbital calculations for reentry and landing and to generate timelining and Dragon return procedures for the safe return' unquote." Andy shrugged. "Can you do that, Steph? I can't."

"Sure you can. We did it in training. I did it in college. And there are textbooks all over this building showing how to do it. Plus, we have software for that. We just have to brush up on it. And, um, find it. We can't let NASA look like they can't even bring their astronauts home, can we? And I'm pretty sure that Dr. Story can help us on the SpaceX side of things."

"Hey, you two," a now several months pregnant Janice poked her head in the Control Room. "Tom says the last of the steaks are ready. We should eat now while they're hot. I'm sure he'll want to go hunting tomorrow."

"Okay, be there soon, Janice. Besides, I can't wait to listen to the latest antics of Wolf Squadron on the radio," Steph said, taking the hand up Andy offered her. She set her small tool pouch on the table next to the most bizarre array of equipment laid out and connected through what appeared to be every randomly colored cable they could find.

There were walkie-talkies, CB radios taken from campers and boats, radio transceivers they had removed from single-engine planes at the flying club, three Army SINCGARS radios they had found in a radio lab off Buxton Road, and they had even found several small satellite ground stations in the Von Braun Complex with full-spectrum analyzers and software defined radios. They were pretty much set up at the POC to receive any radio broadcast mankind had ever made. They had spent months setting up dishes, Yagi-Uda antennas, bowties, dipoles, whips, and helical antennas all about the building. The roof was one big solar panel and antenna farm and so was the parking lot. More than twenty solar panels were simply laid out on the ground with cables leading back into the building.

"I guess we need to get some space imagery of this island then. You'd think some of the people at the NRO or CIA would have survived, but I guess those places were in big cities. We were so lucky here to be isolated like this. So, it's on us," Stephanie said. She didn't think she was lucky. Her husband hadn't been lucky, but that was nearly a year ago. She was still grieving but not as much. "But let's eat first."

"Dragon. Flight."
"Go Flight."
"You are clear for release of the docking clamps and initiation of reverse retro burn."

"Copy Flight. Releasing docking clamps. Initiating retro burn in three, two, one, mark."

"Flight. Dragon."

"We copy, Dragon."

"Are we clear for reentry initiation burns yet?"

"Hold on that, Dragon." Stephanie watched as the numbers scrolled by in front of her. The models in Matlab, Satellite Tool Kit, Xcel, Mathcad, Chebytop, and two others that she'd managed to put together in Fortran were all running in front of her and updating based on GPS data coming from the Dragon itself. Had they been able to use radar to create real two-line element sets to calculate proper orbital quarternions, this would have been a cinch. But as it was, they'd be damn lucky to hit the Atlantic, much less a little island in it.

"Flight, our window is closing quickly."

"Understood, Dragon. We are going to hold on this opportunity and go for the next window." Stephanie's heart sank. Five of the seven models she had running showed they would miss the island by an extreme margin.

"Come on, Flight. That's twice now." Commander Daniels sounded frustrated.

"Dragon, we're sorry, but the error was just too large and we can't risk losing you. There is another pass and window in..." she tapped at her computer and pulled down some menus in Satellite Tool Kit. "Looks like in six hours. I'm so sorry guys. Hang in there. We'll get you home."

"Dragon. Flight."

"Go, Flight."

"This is as good as it is going to get, guys. There's an eighty-nine percent probability of hitting our target. We will be go for a full reentry burn in three minutes on my mark in ten, nine, eight, seven, six, five, four, three, two, one, mark!"

"Mark! Copy, Flight. We are go for full burn in T-minus two minutes fifty-four seconds and counting."

"They're in the reentry blackout, General. We'll know in about four minutes if they survived reentry. Following that, we should be getting their GPS signals and telemetry through the subs. The algorithms here will update and in a minute or so following that we'll start getting trajectory predictions."

"Understood. Standing by, Steph."

"Dragon. Flight."

"Go, Flight! We're taking a hell of a beating in here."

"Telemetry shows you are off trajectory slightly but the automated course-correction systems are functional. What type of beating?"

"Extreme vibrations. Accelerometers are showing around four hundred Hertz. Teeth are getting rattled out of my head."

"Hang in there, Dragon!"

"Flight. Correction burns kicking in. Buffeting reduced dramatically. Something gave way and flew off the top of the capsule. Not sure what."

"Any pressure changes or temperature anomalies?"

"Negative, Flight. She's riding smooth as a whistle now!"

"General, your package will be delivered in seven minutes and counting."

"Dragon. Flight. Do you copy?"

"Dragon. Flight. Do you copy?" Stephanie held her breath for what seemed like forever.

"Dragon. Flight. Copy?"

"Flight, this is Dragon. We are down and all occupants are alive and well!"

"Copy that, Dragon! Welcome home! You've got a bunch of guys turning blue down here. We're breathing again finally. Sit tight and some Marines are supposed to be there to get you soon. It's great to have you back, guys!"

"Dragon for Steph. Great job and thank you."

"Pleasure was all mine, guys!" Stephanie sat back in her chair and for the first time in a year let herself cry like a baby. She had never been sure why she'd made it through the H7D3 virus outbreak, and why she'd survived when her husband hadn't. Whether it was fate or luck or divine intervention, she didn't care. She'd done her job. *She* had done *her* job *and* if humanity was lucky enough...it just might matter in the end.

# Inhale to the King, Baby!

## MICHAEL Z. WILLIAMSON

Eric Magnus Lamont was heading south on the Dixie Highway in a red Charger convertible. The road was mostly clear at this point. It looked as if dozers and other equipment had bashed their way through the abandoned and wrecked cars, leaving a clear, if somewhat meandering route across the lanes. The sky was bright, a few puffy tendrils of cloud shining in the afternoon sun. The temperature was just right for top down and draft.

Eric Magnus Lamont. That was a great name for a king. He was the Warlord of the Wasteland and the Sultan of Funk.

Magnus was a musician, playing whatever anyone needed—studio, stage, bass, keys, drums, horns. He had not gotten famous outside of the musician community, but he had gotten sort of rich.

He gunned the engine on the Charger and zoned along, shifting lanes around the crashed Yellow semi, the tumbled Pacifica, the battered and smashed Mercedes. He took the ramp down to the surface streets.

At the dead traffic lights, there was a small cluster of zeds, chasing after who knew what. Possibly a feral cat or dog. Possibly a feral gator.

He stood on the brakes, unsnapped his seatbelt, rose on the

pedals while racking the bolt on the M76, then twisted out the side and ran off a burst.

"SCOOORE!" he shouted and cackled, as he literally busted caps in the ass of the zombies. Two sprawled in the road, unmoving. He gassed it and ran, not wanting to stop for long.

The Charger would do for now, but he really needed a 1970 Mustang convertible to do this properly. Also, it should be in L.A.

He wouldn't go back to L.A. even if he could.

For one thing, he couldn't have owned the M76 in California. He'd bought it on a whim with a large royalty check, but it was paying off now.

He'd try to find a baby blue Mustang, though.

He couldn't remember what song had been played in that movie, either. Instead, he was listening to Charlie Daniels while tokin' on a number. For a white dude, Charlie understood things. His music didn't funk, but it did have character.

Really, there was no reason for him to be out here, except it helped him clear his brain. Being a king was work, of the dull, administrative kind.

He turned back toward the Village and the Palace. Just like in the movies, he needed to reach it well before nightfall. It was currently two in the afternoon. That was enough before dark for safety. He hadn't got where he was by taking pointless risks. Only ones with a payoff.

At the bridge his guard detail stopped him, checked under the car and in the trunk, then waved him through with a bow. He reciprocated with a forefinger salute to his right eyebrow.

Outside the Palace he put the beast in park, let the valets take it, and imperiously strode inside.

"Welcome back, Your Majesty," announced some underling, and everyone turned to bow to him.

"Please, do continue," he replied. They always bowed. He always made it brief. Respect worked both ways. He'd learned that in the Army. Respect, organization, planning, supply, communication were all as important as fighting.

He let the elevator operator take him to the penthouse, his home and center of operations. As he entered, Antone handed him a fat Cuban blunt, just lit.

He accepted it, took a huge drag and felt nicotine and THC fight for territory in his brain.

What he hadn't learned to do in the Army was ganj. Or rather, learned not to do.

He posed for just a moment, the cigar extended in his right hand, and swept his gaze around the room.

He announced, "Here in Florida, on the Rocket Coast, with a huge hit of weed, I am Spaceman Spliff!"

Everyone laughed, but he had to admit it was pretty funny.

"Summarize!" he commanded as he slumped into a deep chair. He never bothered with a throne, though perhaps he should. He shifted the S&W around under his left arm, muzzle pointed back and down.

The carpet was a bit ratty, but hell, he had a carpeted penthouse, and most of the world didn't.

The glass of rum Vivaldi brought him, though, was in fine cut crystal salvaged from somewhere. It was from a complete set.

"A taste all around," he ordered, and the butler buttled for more glasses.

Garius, the biologist, started the reports. "Your Majesty, the fishing boats have brought in their catch, and added another boat to the flotilla. It needs some hull and engine work but is sound. We have a dried surplus of about fifteen days at this point."

"Good," he replied. More food was better. "We need more chicken and beef, though. Even goat. Fish gets boring."

"Your Majesty, the gardens are progressing. Oranges are coming into season. I've allocated some for eating, some for juice and storage, and brought some fresh for you."

He took a sip of the offered sample. Delicious. "Gracious, my man. Can booze be made from OJ?"

"I did follow up on that. It can make a wine or a distilled liquor."

He grinned and said, "Then you know what my next order is."

"How much, Your Majesty?"

"Enough for a bottle each for Christmas. Or less if you must."

"At once, sire." Garius nodded and went to the desk to make notes.

They went through grain and vegetables and fruit. Scavenging inventories. All stuff to keep his populace alive and loyal. The hotel was his, but there were some formerly choice lodgings on the island, and easy waste disposal. Rain catchment was working well enough for drinking water. They had ongoing reinforcements against intrusion. It wasn't a beach resort, but it was a livable home.

Posh the botanist stepped forward. "The new strain is excellent. I have a sample if you'd like to smoke it."

"Well, I would if I wasn't already yellow mellow. Schedule that for breakfast. Will there be enough for church?" He remembered he had the cigar and took another long, tasty drag.

"Enough for two joints or a good rip each on Sundays, Sire."

"Excellent," he replied. Food, booze, weed. Keep people happy and they didn't care how much the world sucked.

General Kertz said, "The defense news is that we've acquired another cement mixer, and plenty of aggregate. The second wall will commence at once. We were running low on nine millimeter, but we found a good stock of forty and some thirty-eight special. Inside patrols are carrying that. The entry checks are one hundred percent—"

He interrupted with, "Indeed they were, even for me. I approve. Continue."

"We do have a trade delegation from the Bahamas wanting to meet you."

"I am so cool with that, I could chill beer. Message them a go-ahead. But we still need alliance with Cuba." He waved the cigar in emphasis.

"We are still attempting radio contact before trying a boat."

Dr. Nik said, "Three citizens showed symptoms of turning. They are in quarantine at the wall."

"And once you know, you'll open the appropriate door."

"Yes, Sire."

The briefing was interrupted by one of the balcony guards shouting, "Zeds in the wire!"

Lamont ran to the north side balcony while holding his right hand out. Someone slapped a rifle into his grasp. He pulled it around, checked the load and raised it as he reached the French door. His people understood the drill.

There were in fact zeds in the wire, doing the Neutron Dance, as 110,000 volts zapped them repeatedly. That and the coils of razor wire turned them into live entertainment. They'd come along the pilings under the bridge, it appeared, and tried to climb through what he'd named the Tarantula's Web. Now they twitched like spastic acrobats.

"No need to waste ammo," he said. "If they're not sliced, diced and tangled in an hour, send some newbs out for clubbing practice." He required all the new hires to demonstrate their willingness to kill by personally clubbing, slitting or crushing a zombie. If you wanted to find out if a man could pull the trigger, you made him prove he didn't need one.

"We need to back that up better, though," he said. "No telling how long the power will last, and our generators are limited. And do find out why the watch didn't see anything earlier. We may need to sanitize more underneath."

"Yes, sire."

He handed the rifle back, and someone took it for him. He realized he still had the M76 slung on his chest, but he'd put down the blunt. That was a good one, too. He went to retrieve it.

He hung onto the subgun because he liked it. He didn't really need a weapon or a bodyguard. The folks enjoyed how he ran things and knew he was at the front of any zed defense. The king led, the people followed. Someone had tried to dispute his reign once.

Once.

He'd physically tossed that clown into the wire and left him until he begged for a bullet. Something he'd learned from Kipling. Mercy was relative.

Most saw him as the doping king, the man who ran this hood, and assumed he was some gangbanger or other with some punks to back him up.

A handful knew he'd learned a lot in the Army.

Only a few dozen knew he'd been a sergeant in the 75th Ranger Regiment before he pissed hot on a test. He enjoyed his weed. He let people think it controlled him. Then he showed them where they were wrong. He never boasted. Or rather, he boasted about the things they thought were important to him, not the things they didn't need to know.

The next day, he woke, enjoyed a cool shower, dressed in a crisp gray suit, and sat at the large desk in what had been the hotel manager's office. One of the windows didn't close, or rather, was broken and cleared. Otherwise, it was quite nice digs. The breeze was gentle and warm for now. They'd need to replace or board that window before it got chill.

The pleasant location did make administration easier. Slightly.

Food levels, personnel, ammo, all the things he'd been briefed on, and then fuel and their limited power options. The scavenger teams brought back diesel and gas, but the radius to recover the dregs from the tanks got larger every day.

He nibbled on mini cucumbers and avoided the shrimp. He'd had far too much shrimp of late. For a moment, he rested his head in his hands and let his eyes stare at phosphenes.

Dolores, his secretary, entered and said, "Sire, there is an element requesting entry. They seem to be safe."

"Who are they?"

"It's a contingent from farther south, Sire. From the north Keys. They wish to become part of Your realm."

"Send them in."

Once again his lands were increasing, his people fruitful.

He opened a drawer and withdrew his Shark Crown.

The crown had been some rich bitch's necklace of linked cavorting dolphins. He'd had a jeweler solder it solid and upright, then carve the silver dolphins into sharks. It was modest compared to most real crowns. He liked it. He still wanted one of coconut and palm leaves, just to fuck with people, though.

With a sharp suit, a rolled tie and a silver crown, he looked official without being pompous in a robe. It also meant he could reach the Glock in the shoulder rig if he needed to.

Dolores showed them in, escorted by five of his best goons with rifles.

"Greetings, visitors."

"Uh, greetings, uh, Your Majesty," one said. "I am Roger Valenti, Representative of the Key Survivors Co-op."

He nodded just barely to indicate they should bow next time. That would be a test.

"I am Magnus the First. Please sit. I understand you wish to speak of alliancing?"

The man and two of his three companions took seats on the couches.

The third stood, holding what was clearly an official gift.

Magnus pointed, and one of the goons took the box and brought it to his desk.

Well, damn. A humidor of Cristos, and about three pounds of Italian chocolate. That was a serious presentation.

"I am graced by your gift. I thank you. You mentioned alliance."

Valenti replied, "Yes, Your Majesty. We understand you have a respectable fishing fleet, and good defensive support."

"I see. And what do you offer?" He took a sip of orange juice, then drew from the bong on the table.

"Our island is defensible, but not self-supporting. We can offer a section of it."

"That's possible. What else?"

"Uh, we have a solar and wind power system, Your Majesty."

"That's very interesting. Do you have any engineers to maintain it?"

"Your Majesty, we have two engineers from NASA who do maintain them, and a number of spare components."

"Well then, we may come to a deal, once the finer points are elaborated. It seems we both may prosper."

"Thank you, Your Majesty. I am certain we can discuss details of mutual benefit."

"I can make that happen," he said with a nod. "First, you must swear allegiance. I am the King of TaMiamHamas."

The man's eyebrows flared slightly. "You control all the way to the Bahamas?"

"I do, even if they are not yet aware of it. We shall agree to a pact, whereby we join in the love of national confluence, a mystical binding of seeds."

That made the dude look nervous. "Uh, we're still talking about the treaty, right? Your Majesty?"

He grinned. "Indeed I am. And we must smoke. It is how we seal the deal, which shall be written in the holy blood of Bic."

Magnus took a huge rip from the bong.

"This is the pure shit," he said as he passed it over. "Grown fresh, roasted instead of dried. We will smoke until we are doobious, or bongious, as this is not a doobie."

"Are you well buzzed, er, Your Majesty?"

"I am one toke over the line, Little Brother."

The man raised the pipe and took a cautious draw.

"No, you must trust and share, and forget your delicate senses. Breathe deep of the gathering gloom."

Valenti seemed to shrug, and took a hearty heave on the

pipe, fuller and more until he turned white and it seemed his chest might bust. Then he held it, held it, and burst out in a dry, abrasive cough.

"Ooooh, shit, that's some strong...shit."

"Indeed. Be welcome for the night, and partake of our bounty of the sea. My people will hammer out details, and we shall sign a pact. If it is worthy, we will escort you back to my expanded realm with gifts in return."

"That is most generous, Your Majesty."

Valenti stood and bowed his head. The others followed suit. Perfect.

"I believe our union will be fruitful."

One of the guards arrived at the man's shoulder and said, "I can escort you to your suite now, sir."

After they left, he told Dolores, "Get me Rawson."

Jocko Rawson was his engineer. He arrived moments later, while Magnus rolled one of the Cristos in his fingers and tested the aroma.

"Jocko, my man. Business first, of course."

"Thank you, Sire. I do like my wits for discussion."

"The last contingent spoke of a solar and wind setup. How useful is that to us here?"

"Well, we should be able to run through existing cables. I suppose we'd need to ensure it was cut elsewhere to avoid line drainage."

"We and they would be the sole users?"

"Unless someone in between spliced in. Is there anyone?"

"I don't think so. If so, they must become of the Kingdom."

"Then yes, it's workable."

"It's also a bargaining point for others if they track down the splice. The power they were stealing, my power, can be earned through alliance."

"I am impressed by how you gain favor with people. I'm not sure if you're batshit insane or fucking brilliant."

The king fixed him with a gaze until Jocko added, "Your Majesty."

Then Magnus grinned hugely and said, "Embrace the power of 'and,' my friend."

"You do realize dope doesn't stop or prevent the infection, right, Your Majesty?"

"I know, my man. You aren't immune, but you don't care. That also is important. A mellow buzz makes for a steady nerve."

King Magnus I of TaMiamKey took another hit.

He said, "You join the discussion tomorrow. Is it within your schedule?"

Jocko replied, "There are no pressing matters elsewhere."

"Perfect. You handle your end. Rasta Roger can handle fish and trade. We'll make this a thing. Ganj?"

"Only a small puff, Sire. You know how it affects me."

"It is a gift that you need so little for so much euphoria."

"Something like that."

Jocko took a puff, almost coughed as his eyes bulged, then sat back. He grinned, stood, bowed and left.


The islanders joined his realm, and the available power increased slightly. Lamont designated a portion for searchlights and radio for security, some for the fencing, ensured a positive supply to the greenhouse growing the Florida Gold, then split the rest between the lighting block and entertainment. His people loved him. He declared a rave for the evening, and even walked in personally to blow some sax in the middle of a techno trance. Rhythm and beat and soft horn and pot and rum made it just about a perfect evening.

Just about.

"Tyressa, would you and Loren join me at the Palace in about an hour?"

"Are you asking as Magnus the First or just as Magnus?"

"Magnus requests your glorious presence."

The two women smiled at each other, and nodded.

"Then we accept."

He ordered grapes to be brought up to his suite. It wasn't properly an orgy without grapes.

It would be a perfect night. It was good to be the king. The King of Jacksamalando.


He awoke to the alarm. That alarm was reserved for one thing, and it had only been rung twice. A banging on the door was his assigned bodyguard. His ears rang from liquor and pot.

The women were gone. He never trusted anyone to sleep with him, only to stay awake.

"I am unharmed," he said specifically. "You may enter."

It was Sergeant Jack Beaumont.

"Sire, we are under attack."

"So I gather."

Lamont was wearing underwear. For now, that was enough.

At the window, he looked out and saw movement beyond the wall. A moment later, the duty crew turned spotlights out.

Where had that mob come from? There were hundreds of them. They shrieked, tried to climb the walls and the fence, and beat at the gate. He didn't see any way they could actually penetrate, but he had to take the threat seriously. One inside, or even just some of an infected's fluids, and it could be disastrous.

He ran to the rack on the wall for a rifle. He pulled down the FAL with the Starlight and grabbed the mag pouch below it.

The night vision scope showed little with the glare. He swore. Down below he had a day/night scope that would be perfect for this. But he couldn't see the crowd in the spotlights.

How far back did it go?

Quite a bit. There was no rational way for a mob this size to form. They had to have been herded across the bridge.

Was that someone with a weapon?

A lot of someones. They were using the zeds as cover and distraction, and hoping for a breakthrough.

That was stupid. You never risked contaminating your target. Unless all you planned was loot. Was this the Cubans being Commies again, or some petty tribalist, or what?

Sneaky, sneaky.

And how had they managed to round up that many zeds all at once? Must have been bait.

First, secure against the zeds. Inpolice and second string could do that. It would give them valuable experience.

Second, get a force behind those invaders, who were to the North, where his new Holdings were. It might take time, but it would hinder their retreat.

Finally, flank them from the sea and inland.

He grabbed the Motorola and shouted orders.

"General, there is a hostile force behind the zeds. Send out an element in vehicles. As many as you can spare, but at least fifteen. I will follow up when you are en route. Admiral, get three boats out, armed, ready to interdict anything leaving or arriving. Chief, the zeds are numerous but manageable. Rifles, then protective suits and clubs. I want experience for our new boys."

"Yes, Sire!" "At once, Sire!" "I'm on it, King."

There were other marksmen at work, but he wasn't going to let them have all the fun. He picked out a dense cluster with iron sights, put two rounds into it, and watched them frenzy like sharks, ripping into each other for the meat they thought was there. Or something. Who the fuck knew how a zombie thought?

It had been less than a minute, when five more of his guard arrived, and took station on the balconies and against the door behind him.

He said, "I assume the following force is hostile. Prepare to return fire and engage if they shoot, but only if they do. If they retreat, I'll decide our response. Dig?"

The LT in charge, Zimmerman, said, "Yes, Sire. I'll relay that."

The zeds were dispersing around the perimeter, with occasional ones wandering off in confusion. The traps had worked, as had the limited outgoing fire.

Now, on to those motherfuckers driving them.

They'd formed two components. One west near the gate to I-95, the other north on the tidal spit. Given the angles, that would let them secure the industrial quarter of the town.

Well, fuck it. He couldn't just be a defensive. They weren't here for a jazz concert.

By phone, he buzzed, "Branson, Courtland, Adams, how's your angle on that hostile element?"

All three reported a good field of fire.

"General Kertz, are you positioned where I asked?"

"Yes, sire."

"Drive 'em. We'll snipe from here."

If Kertz drove them, the rest could gun them down.

"Marlon, if that group up north starts to move anywhere except away, waste them. Admiral Ortiz, stand by in case of incoming support craft, or to provide cross fire."

"Aye, sir."

"Got it."

Kertz's men played Bumper Zeds with their trucks, supplemented with potshots. He watched two F-350's and a limousine buzz the outside of the cluster, herding the shambling bodies into a tighter mass. Through firing ports in the door of the limo, someone gutshot a couple. That kept the others busy with the smell of fresh meat.

"Sire, the element to the north is now approaching our gate." That report was punctuated with short bursts of automatic weapon fire.

"Be frugal, but shoot those fucks," he reiterated. "Kertz, see if you can bring that flock around from the west."

"I think we can, Sire."

The trucks and limo coaxed the zeds bit by bit around the northwest corner and toward their probable captors. Some of them splashed into the shallows by the bridge. The concertina and stakes should hold them for the time being.

A herd of non-sentient creatures doesn't change direction easily. They had to be pressed and encouraged until ripples moved through the mass, and individuals decided to change direction. Once enough did, the rest reluctantly took the hint and the whole mass wandered eastward, now as a long, vertical line rather than a clump. That was fine.

When that armed element, and it was possibly fifty men, realized the zeds were moving in on them, they panicked and started shooting. The northern end tried to run south, the southern tried to run north, and shortly they were a round gaggle surrounded by gawping, biting former people.

There were volleys of fire and distant shouts, and someone with capacity for leadership got the element moving south, killing zombies as they advanced.

"Shall we exterminate them, sire?" Kertz asked.

"Not yet. They can take care of the zeds for us, then we'll see what the rest have for intel."

"Roger that." He was a veteran, too. Air Force. For a wing wiper, he was pretty good.

That cluster at the northwest, though. They were climbing over each other. Then they were climbing the wall. Beyond that was a pit, but...

"Someone get on that deadpile of motherfuckers, fast," he ordered.

"We're on it, Sire."

They were, but the fuckers were inside and chasing people down.

He leaned over and added some support fire.

*What's the difference between fresh zeds and those who've been around a while? You have to lead them more.*

His shot was perfect, high on the chest of some cheerleader grade chick.

*And you couldn't have any hesitation at all.*

He hoped to shit this didn't jump the species barrier to other animals, or it might all be over, not just most of it.

One of his own got swarmed and bitten. Someone else put a bullet in the poor bastard's brain, and then more shots into the three piled on him.

His people were back in control, with precious flammables atop the wall, keeping that area controlled.

At this point, the trucks were simply smashing zombies and grinding them underwheel. The influx were all beaten to literal pulp, except a handful in the wire who'd just been brained. The remains of the attacking element numbered about twenty, and were surrendering, arms raised.

"Bring them to the north containment," he ordered.

Lamont took the elevator down, wearing his rolling wave crown. It was twisted from silver wire, in long, beautiful curves that were tasteful, but showed the workmanship. At some point, he might have some made in gold, but the silver contrasted well with his skin tones.

Image first. One of the staff—Posh—carried his rainbow titanium hitter on a cushion. He took a huge puff from the anodized pipe. Someone else had his chair and his communication console dolly.

Oh, yeah, that was sweet stuff. One of his best decisions was finding Posh and asking him to breed this wunderpot.

"I am King Magnus the First. Who speaks for you?"

There was lots of nudging and eying each other, but no one spoke. He waited, patient on the outside, while inside he counted down seconds until he'd shoot one as an example.

Or better yet...

"Ahmed, Cletus, take those two to the cage." He pointed at two near the front.

Ahmed and Cletus were in protective suits, and came forward. It was obvious that the indicated chosen grasped what that meant.

The pair shied back but their own buddies slunk away. Lamont grimaced. They were scum with no cohesion, no identity.

The cage at the north center was easily visible from where the group hunkered under his men's rifles.

The two started shrieking.

"Nooo! God have mercy, no! Please! I beg you! Show some decency!"

He replied, "Perhaps you should have done so first."

The two were shoved into the outer cage, just within scratching range of the enraged, imprisoned zeds, who went ballistic at the taunt.

Turning to the rest of the prisoners, Lamont told them, "In ten minutes, they will be brought back in with you. How you deal with it is up to you. What weapons you have depends on how you respond to me."

From the middle of the pack, one of them hissed, "You're a monster."

"Incorrect, my man. I am a king, doing what is best for my people. You are the monsters who disturbed our peace."

He added, "And who are you? With that braid on your collar?"

The man glanced around and realized his entire contingent had abandoned him. They'd withdrawn as if he were infected.

"Bernard Lyndon Kennedy."

"You will address me as 'Your Majesty,'" Lamont said.

"Whatever," Kennedy said with a shrug.

"There is no 'whatever,'" he replied. "You must acknowledge me, or you will not return."

"You're not a real king."

"I am king here. I will be when I get there. In the meantime, you will show respect. I am 'Your Majesty.'"

Kennedy shook his head and almost smirked. "That is not going to happen."

"Higgs, show him how to respect me, please."

"At once, Sire."

Higgs pulled out two syringes and started poking. The yelps and curses turned to outright squeals. It wasn't fifteen seconds before the man said, "Okay, goddammit, you're 'your majesty.'"

"Say it like you mean it," Higgs said with viperlike viciousness, while holding the syringes about an inch from the dude's eyeballs.

"I am most humbly sorry, Your Majesty."

Higgs put on an almost gay accent and mockingly said, "Muuuch better! I knew you could do it."

Lamont asked, "And where are you from, Mr. Kennedy?"

The man shuffled, looked around, seemed to realize he was on his own, and considered.

Finally he said, "Cuba."

"You're American."

"Yeah. A lot of us went there, thinking they might be quarantined enough."

"And what happened?"

"They were, until someone brought the infection with them."

"Ironic. American boat people going to Cuba."

He continued, "That was easy, wasn't it? Now, why are you here?"

"We were going...to secure a beach head to reconquer the mainland."

"Ah, but it is conquered. I am the King of Miami, much as it is, and soon all of Florida and beyond."

"As you say," Kennedy acknowledged. He seemed to have no fight left.

"Cletus, please put those two poor bastards out of their misery."

"Yes, Sire," Cletus replied, clearly now his mask was off. He raised his rifle and shot. The first one panicked and struggled, taking a shot to the shoulder and screaming until the second one burst his heart.

The other one understood, and came to attention like a man. He closed his eyes, straightened his shoulders, and only a shiver gave away his panic, ending when Cletus blew his brains out. The body dropped to join his companion, and the zeds again entered shrieking frenzy, as suited newbs came up with harpoons to stab them to death.

Lamont ordered, "Fetch a large enough skiff to hold these men, and a large enough spliff to work my buzz."

Then he turned back to Kennedy.

"Now run," he ordered. "Run, and paddle, and tell your bosses they can join my kingdom, or be slaves. It might take a year. It might take twenty. But you will not fuck with me again, or I'll air drop zeds all over your city and whatever you use for a palace."

Kennedy nodded, looked both ways, then bowed. "I understand...Your Majesty."

"Excellent."

Lamont sprawled back on the Royal Lawn Recliner that was not a throne, and drew deeply.

He had more than he'd ever dreamed of before the Fall. A palace. His choice of women. *Beau coup* pot. A huge army of doping, gunning homies of all colors, prepared to take the world.

It would be a glorious future.

It deserved a radio broadcast to His people, and others.

Today it was the East Coast of Florida. Soon, Cuba. The Bahamas. Then possibly, the world.

With a massive hit of the pipe, he gestured for the commo, raised the microphone and shouted to all.

*"...King of Miami and the Kingdom of Florcubatamp! All shall bow before my magnificence...!"*

# Ham Sandwich

## JODY LYNN NYE

"Whiskey Edward Seven Foxtrot Foxtrot Yankee, anybody?" Billy Marx said into the fat, steel-rimmed condenser mic. He pressed one can of the oversized earphones to cup his ear as tightly as he could to shut out noise leaking into the storeroom from the Foresight Genetics lab. "Anyone on? Over."

The teen had been clinging to the ham radio unit for almost two hours, shifting all over the allowable frequencies, straining his ears to hear even the faintest reply. Before the Fall, he had talked to thousands of fellow radio fans all over the world. Getting back on the air felt like coming home, as much home as he ever would again, maybe. If only he could find anybody out there.

A burst of static came out of the eight-inch speaker on the makeshift table beside Billy's radio. Billy jumped.

"Whiskey Edward Seven Foxtrot Foxtrot Yankee," a lilting, deep male voice said. "Golf Whiskey Four Echo Hotel India here. Good lord! You still alive, Effy, *bach*? It's been months!"

Billy sat back in the metal folding chair. His hands sweated so much he thought he would drop the mic. Only his old ham friends called him Effy, after his registered call sign, WE7FFY.

"Geraint, I don't believe it! Are you okay? Where are you?"

A long sigh almost overpowered the underlying static.

137

"Son, I'm at the far end of everything-eh. Out on Holyhead, a long way from Gwynedd, I must tell you. There's five souls living-eh here in Ynys Lawd. That's a lighthouse, my boy, down and across from the island on the South Stacks. Any hope you're close enough to bring us something to eat? We're all getting tired of fish and bara brith." The electrician's musical accent extended one-syllable words into two or more. Where Billy might clip off the final "g" in a word, Geraint's exaggerated diction overemphasized it.

"Only you Welsh would try and make bread out of seaweed," Billy said, relaxing against the back of the cold, metal folding chair. The easy bantering made his chest swell with nostalgia. He almost felt guilty for enjoying the laugh. Geraint, at least twenty years his senior, was one of his oldest friends. Where Facebook had been new, until the Fall, he had been talking to Geraint and his other correspondents in the ham community since he was a boy throwing in a shy word or two over his dad's and grandpa's shoulders. He glanced at the volt-ohm meter on the old metal case, watching the silver needle ping into the red zone. "Look, I only got permission to connect the radio yesterday, until we were sure that I wasn't taking power away from necessary functions. We got plenty of electricity here, but the current's really uneven. I'm running on Q, very low power."

"*Ach y fi*, bureaucracy is alive and well, though millions died. Billions?" the Welshman's voice cracked, but he kept his tone light. "I can't tell you how good it is to hear you. There's powerful few of us left. Are you safe, boy?"

"Yeah," Billy said, shifting in his seat, eager to tell everything to a new listener. "Remember the lab my mother works at? Up in the Tennessee hills? It's secure—at least, we're doing everything we can to stay secure. We're working on vaccines. I mean, *they're* working on vaccines. I'm helping run errands and clearing the area of zombies—infecteds, the bosses call 'em."

"Nightmares, we call them," Geraint said. "They've about eaten each other, and the rest of them we have had to take a shotgun to. Curses on the British for not allowing the ordinary folk to have anything with stopping power. Lucky for us it's impossible to get to this stony little outcropping-eh, and we blew the bridge with dynamite from the stone-clearing. But, it's been thin times here. I have to pull my belt around my belly twice to fasten it.

How's your girl, then? Still with you, I hope? Though it seems to me she sounded far too good for you."

Self-consciously, Billy tugged at the loose waistband of his own jeans. Although he was kind of tall, his body was pear-shaped—or had been. He *used* to be on the fat side around his belly and rear end, with narrow shoulders, but months without his favorite junk food, or much in the way of real food, had pared him until he was just plain out of shape, and none of his clothes fit right. His girlfriend had liked him anyhow. He never understood why a girl that pretty and smart cared about a homely nerd. The only things he saw that they had in common was the amateur radio club at school.

"Cindy sure was—I mean, is," Billy said, and another wave of worry swelled up fresh in his stomach. "I hope. I pray every day she's not dead. Her parents took her on this fantastic trip to Asia, just before everything went to hell, and all the phone lines and the Internet went down. You haven't heard anything from her, have you?"

"Not a sound. Ah, God, it's good to hear from you! I've been bending-eh the ears of my friends up here, and they're ready to throw me to the walking-eh dead, should any of them make it across the causeway."

"Mine, too," Billy said, a grin lifting the corners of his mouth. "We've got the building Wi-Fi working again, but it's not like social media." He tried to sound more positive than he felt. Like in the old black-and-white movies, they were *under siege* in the compound. What would happen when the day came that they ran out of ammunition scared the piss out of him. He hoped what the bosses said was true about working on a cure for the zombies. Vaccinations didn't help if you got eaten alive. So far, though, the only cure was bullets.

"Ah, you kids and your social Facebook and Insty-gram. This is where the real staying power is, my *bach*."

"Breaking in," came a clipped female voice. "Hotel Lima Eight Whiskey Oscar November here. Geraint Jones?"

"Ubon Park!" the Welshman cried, in delight. "It's been days! How the hell are things in Antarctica, Doctor my dearling?"

"Cold," Ubon said, briefly. "Dire. We will starve slowly to death if no one brings us supplies. We lack vitamins, especially. But we are afraid to admit anyone to the research stations in case they are infected."

"Same here," Billy said. "We're all vaccinated, but that don't mean they can't try to eat us. I've got a bunch of bite marks. The whole world is crazy."

"Breaker, Oscar Juliet Niner Quebec Uniform Echo. Effy, glad to hear your voice! I'm getting tired of these old bores!"

Billy's heart swelled with joy. One after another, ham friends checked in from all over the globe, until eight of them were cutting in, talking over one another. He had turned eighteen during the beginning of the zombie apocalypse. He, his mother, and his sister had been running for their lives and had no time or thought to devote to celebrating it then. This felt like the party he missed out on having.

"How'd you get away?" he kept asking them. "Where are you living?"

Everyone had their own stories about running away from the infecteds. They tried to top one another, but Geraint won, hands down. He told them, with breathless detail, all about running over the bridge between Holyhead and the South Stacks, then blowing it up, then seeing his BMX-racer friend lead one final group of zombies off the end of the broken span with a twelve-foot jump. It was a yarn nobody was going to be able to beat. With each fresh success against the shuffling horde following them, his fellow ham operators laughed, all saving up their own stories for after. Billy leaned into the small speaker, rapt at the sound of Geraint's lilting voice, clenching his hands, hoping the racer would get away.

"...And then, would you believe it, the boy spun around on his front wheel, and gave them two fingers up...!"

A burst of static erupted from the speaker, obliterating all of the voices.

"Nooo! Goddammit!" a voice yelled from the corridor.

The room went dark, and something very close to him went *BANG!*

Billy leaped up. Smelling smoke, he snatched the radio's cord out of the wall. The vintage radio gave off an acrid, metallic odor he knew only too well. One of the ancient capacitors—that took the place of the tubes that had run it in his grandpa's day—had blown inside the case. He dragged the scavenged table lamp over and pulled a screwdriver out of the loop on the leg of his jeans to undo the case. The smoke made his eyes burn. He dashed the mist away with the back of his hand and examined the inner working. Just like he'd feared, the big, square blue capacitor next to the chip in the middle of the breadboard had burst apart, spraying pieces of ceramic into the guts of the radio.

Billy turned the case upside down and shook it. Pieces scattered, but he managed to retrieve the center section that had the capacitance rating on it, and his heart sank. He didn't have anything like that in the toolbox he had pulled out of their old house. Everything there had been trashed, turned over, pissed on, gnawed, bled all over, or just smashed to smithereens. His little radio cave in the basement had not escaped the zombie invasion. The miracle that the radio had been intact was the only one he had been granted by heaven. All of his other gear lay wrecked in a corner so disgusting he could hardly bring himself to handle it with heavy gloves.

Even with an escort of two National Guardsmen with high-powered rifles, Billy didn't dare take the time to hunt for all the scattered components. He'd taken the radio and the few tools that hadn't been stolen, and fled at the wailing and groaning noises coming from outside. You just didn't dare stay put after the infecteds heard you moving around.

Another bang, this one from the storeroom door. He spun around, and a wedge of light lanced into his eyes. Resentfully, Billy recognized the silhouette of Jud Tomkinson, the chief technician and founder of the Foresight Genetics corporation. The silver-haired man squinted into the dim room and located Billy by the light of the red and blue LEDs on the radio unit and the meager beam of the lamp.

"We've got a problem, son. Come and give me a hand."

Billy felt as if his stomach had been wrenched out of his body. He looked back at his radio unit. One last wisp of smoke rose from the grille on top of the steel box. He longed to take the whole thing apart and see if he could get it to work without the busted capacitor, but if the chief needed him on his break time, the emergency far exceeded the importance of reconnecting with his old friends. The old radio would have to wait. He flipped the screwdriver back into its loop.

Tomkinson glanced down at the youth and gave him a kindly smile. He had the broad face and long, dark eyes of his mother, who had been one of the Korean war brides who traveled home to the mountains of Tennessee with her serviceman groom when that war ended. Billy knew all about his family from Marissa Tomkinson, one of the chief's daughters he knew from high school. The chief's mom had been a wireless operator and phone technician in Seoul when she'd met Mr. Tomkinson senior, which is where their six kids had picked up the scientific knack. God only knew where Marissa was now. She had gone to college at MIT, and hadn't been heard from since . . . well, since. Same as Cindy. Same as lots of people's relatives and loved ones. Compared with the number of people who had been around before the disease hit, it felt like there was only a handful left.

"Sorry to pull you away, Billy, after we just let you boot up that radio. I need at least four hands for this job."

"No problem, Mr. Jud," Billy said, wiping his hands on the front of his baggy T-shirt. He hoped he didn't stink too much. Despite having all the water in the world piped up from the Columbus River, most of it was for the scientific folks to use in the labs. He wasn't scheduled for a shower until the next day.

Because of his hobby, Billy was the junior handyman on staff, second to Tomkinson, who had helped build the facility. Mr. Jud only came out of retirement as chief scientist again when the Fall happened and what was left of the government in the Hole in Nebraska heard he had made it up to the facility alive. He was a good leader, which was what the facility needed. Foresight might be the last place inhabited by uninfected human beings left in the whole state, maybe the whole Midwest.

They might not stay unzombified if they didn't get the power back up. All the labs and workshops they passed had no lights on. From the big lab where they analyzed tissue samples, a loud beeping indicated that its refrigeration unit was running on battery power.

"Is the fence working?" Billy asked, thinking horrible thoughts about infected coming over the strands of hot wire at the top of the hastily constructed eight-foot pickets.

"Not at the moment," Tomkinson said. "That's the big problem. Everyone who's not working with sensitive materials is out on the line, watching out for zombies. We've got to get the power back ASAP."

In the hallway near the stairs, Ms. Melanie Trimble, the current manager, and Neeta Patel, one of the genetic engineers, caught up with them.

"Hey, there, Billy," Ms. Melanie said. Her broad, dark face lit up when she saw him. "Saw you got your radio antenna built."

"Yes'm," Billy said. He felt deep pride for the metal spire. The hollow frame had a square cross-section with sides that looked like trellis. He'd done it all with the remains of his original antenna and scavenged materials, and it didn't take a single bite of food out of anyone's mouth.

"Thirty feet tall, is it?"

"Fifty, ma'am. It's turning out to have real good range, up here on the ridge. Much better than...than at home." Billy knew he had to get over feeling his stomach sink every time he thought about the house. This was home now, maybe for a long time. He and his mom and sister had a whole room to themselves, which used to be the office of the comptroller. The lavatories were down the hall, and the shower rooms were off the lab wing, but they'd made it comfortable enough.

"Well, just don't ask me to climb it!" She laughed and patted her midsection. Like Billy, she used to be fat, but now she was just what she called "well-covered." Pretty soon, they'd all look like walking skeletons, unless something better happened.

Tomkinson led them down into the basement, dug two stories down into the hilltop where Foresight overlooked the Columbus River, to the back wall where the facility's main fuse box lay. Red LEDs, set on a battery-operated motion-detector circuit, came on as they approached. The chief pried open the gray metal door.

"Aw, hell," he said.

Billy peered over his shoulder at the fuse box. Several switches were thrown, which meant a power surge.

"We got an overload somewhere," he said, reading the labels. "Most of these are on the north side of the building."

"Think the zombies got into the turbine again?" Ms. Melanie asked, her face stained blood-red by the lights. "We lost one of the centrifuges when the lights blew. I think it's salvageable. I hope. Can you fix the power?"

Tomkinson frowned.

"Maybe. We're gonna have to rig a transformer unit and install surge protectors on all the sensitive equipment. I never thought I'd say this, but I miss the TVA, bless their hearts. We might not have had much, but we had reliable power when they were on the job." Tomkinson shook his head. "Dammit. I was hoping we'd have enough juice to extend the building Wi-Fi to the outbuildings so we can run walkie-talkie apps off our smart phones. But this will need some rewiring just to get the basics covered. Billy, you and me've got a big undertaking ahead of us."

"What do we have to do?" Billy asked, fingering the tools hanging off his belt. He was all in favor of getting the Wi-Fi up and running, although he was afraid the job was beyond him. The Internet, and all those manuals that described how to make things work, had died with most of civilization.

The chief shook his head.

"I'll send a detachment of Guards down the bank to take a look at the turbine. You've got a special assignment. You're gonna have to go shopping."

The battered green Toyota Prius hardly made a sound creeping down the gravel-lined road as it eased out of the barricaded parking lot, but every crunch terrified Billy into gazing around him for zombies. He clutched the pump-action shotgun on his lap and patted the pockets on his pants legs stuffed full of shells.

"Goin' ta Walmart," Ms. Nora Fulton told him with a gleeful grin. She was dressed in the same yellow plastic hazmat suits as the others, to defend against contamination. The hood bobbed on her shoulders. Around her neck hung the filter mask all of them had to deaden the stink of almost every building everywhere, thanks to the zombies.

The little part-Choctaw woman didn't mean an actual Walmart. Every one of the superstores had been looted or trashed in the early days of the plague. Whatever was left in the giant buildings had been soiled or destroyed by the zombies. Anything left intact was probably buried under a ton of wreckage. If you could get to it. If the store wasn't a nesting ground for infecteds.

Shopping meant scavenging, anywhere they could find raw materials or any food or clothing. Usually these days, it meant breaking into people's houses and taking their stuff. Billy always felt guilty about it. He carried a pad of paper and a pencil to write IOUs to the people who used to live there. They were never coming back, but it made Billy feel better.

Ahead and behind the Prius, four hunters rode two of the diesel pickups they had "shopped" from somewhere. Ms. Nora and her fiancé, Mr. Lou Hammond, sat in the front seat. Billy and lanky, big-nosed Orin Feldman jammed in the narrow rear seat with a pile of logo-printed tote bags from everywhere between them.

"Gotta bring your own bags these days," Orin joked. "Those plastic grocery bags are gonna be the death of the environment, you know."

Mr. Lou held tight to the wheel as they took the hairpin turns down the road at the rear of the ridge with only the running lights on. The big African-American man was almost comically large for the little car. Unlike usual, Ms. Nora was smiling. She patted Mr. Lou's arm.

"We just got engaged," she told Billy and Orin.

"Congratulations, ma'am!" they chorused. Any kind of good news was rare. Ms. Nora gave them a nod and turned her attention to the windows.

Zombies, more emaciated and thinner even than the people holed up in the facility, still shuffled into the valley in sickening hordes. When you had almost two million people living in and around Nashville, that meant a lot of naked not-really-people-anymore trying to kill you. The facility was trying to make not only quantities of vaccine for those who were still healthy, but a cure for the condition. So far, it had been a pretty fruitless undertaking. Mr. Jud said if they could only wait a while, the few healthy humans left could outlive every zombie out there, but it might take a year or two. In the meanwhile, no crops were being grown, except in the compound, and Billy hadn't seen any farm animals alive in months. Once in a while, they spotted a rabbit or a deer. If he had to live by himself through all this, it would get lonely.

Unless it was in drive, the Prius ran almost silent, meaning they could hear noises outside the car. Rustling in the bushes to the left alarmed Mr. Lou. He put down the window a couple of inches so Ms. Nora could stick her rifle barrel out. Billy's eyes almost started out of his head as a stag bounded out of the woods and leaped clear over the hood. Before any of them could move, it was gone.

"Dammit," Ms. Nora said. "We coulda had some meat for dinner!"

They weren't the only ones who had noticed the deer. More rustling, and a bunch of totally naked, skeletal humans staggered out from the same gap in the bushes. Their hollow eyes fixed on the car. Bone-thin arms held out in front of them like monsters in a movie, they shuffled toward the Prius, teeth bared.

"Step on it," Ms. Nora snapped. Mr. Lou jammed his big foot on the accelerator. She blasted the first one out of the woods. It dropped hard. She withdrew the barrel and held on tight to the Jesus strap. "You two, blast anything that gets close, but don't waste ammo."

"Yes'm!" Billy and Orin lowered their own windows and stuck their shotguns out. Billy was pretty sure they couldn't follow. The zombies looked almost completely dead, and bones showed through the skin of their feet. They couldn't run. As soon as the car was out of reach, they went back to eat the one Ms. Nora had shot. Billy's stomach turned. There but for the grace of God could've been him and everybody at Foresight.

In a quarter mile, they had outdistanced the infecteds.

"We can collect the spinal columns on the way back," Ms. Nora said, sounding dispassionate again, as they bumped over the neglected roadway. Business was business. The nerve bundles in the dead zombies went to make vaccine.

The jarring made Billy's stomach twist even more. He thought he ought to feel sick about infecteds eating their own, but he just couldn't anymore. Zombies were just like big rats, only rats took care of their babies.

They rode in tense silence, everyone immersed in their own thoughts. After a while, Billy couldn't take it any longer.

"I talked to my friends in Wales and Antarctica today," he blurted out. Ms. Nora relaxed a little.

"God in Heaven!" she said. "You mean someone's alive beside us?"

"Yes, Ms. Nora," Billy said, eagerly. He launched into a recitation of Geraint's story about the BMX biker. The three in the car hung on every word, until he got to the part where the biker had given the zombies the finger. Billy stammered a little, and fell silent.

"And then, what?" Mr. Lou asked, as they pulled out among the abandoned wrecks on the highway.

"And that's when the power surged, Mr. Lou," Billy said, sadly. "It knocked me off the air. A capacitor in my radio blew up."

"I wanna know how it ends!"

"Me, too," said his fiancée. "He jumped the bridge! Didn't the infecteds try to get him?"

"Well, that's when my radio stopped working," Billy admitted.

"But that's not important. We gotta get parts so we can stabilize the power in the facility."

"Hell, no," Mr. Lou said, with determination. "This is the first out-of-town news I've heard since everything went to hell. I want the rest of the story! And any others they got. What you need to fix that radio of yours, son?"

"Capacitors, diodes, resistors, maybe a soldering gun," Billy said, wishing he had had a chance to really examine the inside of the elderly unit. "I'd sure like a surge protector, too, in case we get more spikes."

The couple exchanged a firm look, almost grim.

"You'll get 'em," Ms. Nora said. "We ain't had no news from anywhere in months."

"I know where to go, if it's still there," the big man said. "I took my television to a place on Mount View Road. Lemme tell the others." He put an arm out of the window to signal the two security cars to a halt.

The National Guards and other protectors in the cars sounded as excited as Mr. Lou.

"We'll get you there, son," Sergeant Angel Velasquez said, with a decided nod of her helmeted head. She pointed ahead on the road. "Follow us."

"Lookie here, Walmart!" Ms. Nora declared, as they pulled up on the curb in front of the appliance repair store. Its gray sign had weathered in the months since the Fall. The front window had been broken out, leaving only a jagged edge of glass all the way around, and trash pulled from the interior out onto the sidewalk. They had no problem stepping over the frame into the gloom of the shop. "Now, what do you need?"

With a former recon scout at the head and a Tennessee state trooper at the rear, Billy picked his way around, scanning all the shelves.

Time was, he would have gone to the Radio Shack, but that was gone a long time before civilization fell.

The place had been trashed, and the zombies had used the floor for a toilet, like everywhere else. The Tyvek booties over Billy's shoes were the only thing that let him walk around the dusty room. His eye lit on a black box about a foot square and six inches deep with eight outlets in two lines on top. Shoving the shotgun in his arms around on its strap to his back, he picked up the box and pushed the TEST button. To his amazement and delight, it turned green.

"Anything that looks like this," he told the others. "These are surge protectors with battery backups. We can plug lab equipment into them. They'll keep it from frying when the power surges. Anything more heavy-duty would be better."

"Okay," Ms. Nora said. She swept a hand around the room. "Fan out. Billy, Orin, you see a zombie, you run back to the cars. Leave us to shoot it. Don't be a hero." She said that every time. No sense in arguing. To Billy, she was scarier than the zombies. He had never known anyone who was her equal as a shooter. She could put a bullet into a squirrel's eye at a thousand paces.

"Yes, ma'am."

Corporal Chaz Miller, the Tennessee state trooper, let out a whoop as he uncovered a bent and grayed cardboard box. Under a tangle of wires and cables was a pile of battery backups. Six of them still showed green. Billy poked at the others, but couldn't raise a response.

"They're probably dead," he said.

"Take 'em anyhow," Sergeant Velasquez said, shoving them clattering into a canvas holdall. "They might just need charging up." She gestured to the others to help her.

Screwed to the wall above the battered butcher-block table in the back room that had been the shop's main work surface Billy found a rack of tiny drawers. The ones that hadn't been yanked down and scattered by the zombies were neatly sorted by component type, resistance, and size. He pulled one after another open, looking for a replacement for the capacitor that had exploded, then realized he was wasting time. He shoveled all of the small pieces into a shopping bag, promising himself to sort them out later, and followed them up with every tool he could find on the floor. On his little pad of paper, he wrote, "IOU a whole bunch of components, wire strippers, soldering guns, pliers, a set of clippers, and one dozen battery backups, six working, six maybe. Thank you. Billy Marx."

"Still quiet?" Sergeant Velasquez asked Dieter Vance, the former recon scout, who had stationed himself at the door. Small and wiry, with hollow cheekbones and eyes, he looked like a tan skeleton. He scanned the street. The sun began to dip below the treetops, making the area more hazardous, as the infecteds liked to come out under cover of darkness.

"Nothing I can hear or smell," he said. "There's nothing left to eat on this whole road except us. Don't waste no more time."

"We're done," Ms. Nora said. She signed to each of them which bags to carry. "Long as it's still quiet, let's hit the Target, too."

Again, she didn't mean any of the three superstores in the city or the dozen or so in the outlying Nashville area. Those were as broken and empty as the Walmarts. Instead, they drove uphill into the rich neighborhoods, once owned by the stars who had sung at the Grand Old Opry and run the hotels down in town.

Billy shook his head ruefully as they drove up and down the nested avenues and cul-de-sacs of the Nashville suburbs. What with the riot of warm oranges and yellows of the autumn trees punctuated with tall, triangular pines in the light of the sunset, it ought to have looked as pretty as a postcard up there, but none of them could stop looking around in case they were attacked. Zombies would eat absolutely anything, and they could live anywhere they found a water source. The group from Foresight had cleaned out more than one nest that had been living on the scummy bilge that filled above-ground swimming pools behind a lot of these mansions.

Most of them had gates across the driveways, but that wouldn't stop either the desperate normals looking for food and shelter, or the zombies that had come after them, from climbing over. Half the doors of the huge, elegant, brick-fronted homes stood ajar, and practically every window at ground level had been busted out. The rooms inside lay dark.

But the zombies weren't likely to take toilet paper, or any kind of clothing, and the folks up at the facility needed anything they could get. The caravan had cleaned out one multilevel house after another, leaving white paint smeared on the mailbox to indicate it no longer had valuable items inside. After several months, it meant that they had to travel farther on the tree-lined streets to find one that might still yield treasure.

Once in a while, they found the corpses of both zombies and normals collapsed on one of the overgrown lawns, waiting for burial or cremation, whenever a crew had time and felt safe enough to take care of the dead. Billy flinched as he saw a rat run out of one of the piles of bodies.

∞ ⊖ ↝

"Yowie!" Ms. Nora cackled, digging through a pantry in the kitchen of a white-fronted mansion. The shelves had only escaped looting because the white-painted louvered doors were stuck tight from humidity so hard they had to use an axe to stove them in. "God in Heaven, coffee!"

"How much?" Mr. Lou asked, crowding over the small woman for a look.

She turned, her eyes shining, clutching the slick paper bag. "Enough for a cup or two for us, and trade the rest. This is a good day!"

Billy reached past her, earning a slap on the wrist, but he extracted a rolled-down paper bag of sugar from between two paper boxes of cereal.

"This is for my mom," he said. He stuffed it inside his shirt before the others could register a protest. Any kind of seasoning, food, sweeteners, or candy were more precious than gold. With the bag banging against his ribs, he collected all the linens out of the closets upstairs, including the fancy keeping closet, and threw pillows over the carved wooden balustrade to the tiled floor in the foyer. Once the goods were collected and loaded into the back of the pickups, Billy carefully wrote out his IOU and placed it on what was left of the white-tiled kitchen island. At the sound of Mr. Lou pounding on the Prius's horn, he ran outside.

To his horror, it wasn't a summons, but a warning. Three filthy, skeletal infecteds blocked his path, gnarled nails reaching for his face. He froze, wondering if he should run back inside or try to get to the car.

"Hit the dirt!" Sergeant Velasquez bellowed from beside the lead pickup. Billy threw himself to the ground, one hand protecting the precious bag of sugar. Rifle shots pinged over his head, some slamming into the door behind him.

A heavy weight fell across his back. Billy's heart pounded. Were they going to chew his spine out?

But the weight didn't move, at least until it shifted sideways and fell off. Billy sprang to his feet, panting. Mr. Lou gave him a hand.

"Get in the car, boy," Mr. Lou said, turning him away from the three bodies on the ground. "We need you alive to make that radio work."

"Got some toilet paper," Ms. Nora cackled, patting a bag at

her feet, as the caravan peeled out. "Paper towels, too! Even a bag of dog food. God bless Target."

The sound of gunshots would be bringing zombies from everywhere. Sergeant Velasquez lit out of the subdivision and out onto the main road, not stopping until they were miles away.

"No time to paint the mailbox," Orin complained.

"We'll remember," Mr. Lou said, gently. "Better not to let them trap us there."

Billy sat back and caught his breath. As the caravan veered back onto the mountain road, he spotted a familiar sight. He grabbed Mr. Lou's shoulder.

"Can you go up that way?" he asked. "I see a ham radio antenna!"

"Where?" Orin demanded. Billy pointed and kept pointing, fixing his eyes on it like it was an old friend.

They might be able to see only a couple of feet of crosshatched openwork weave of silver metal peeking above the thick autumn trees, but that fragment was enough to tell them it was the same as the one the boys had helped to construct in the middle of the Foresight Genetics facility.

"Think you'll find another radio up there, boy?" Mr. Lou asked.

"Even parts will help," Billy said. "My rig is really old. These rich people probably have fancy shortwave technology. I could tune it onto my frequency."

"If it ain't burned out or torn up," Ms. Nora said, darkly. "All right, turn. I'll signal to the others."

Billy could hardly contain his excitement as they wove their way into yet another set of tiny, leafy avenues. The scavengers followed their noses around corners until they were in front of a broad, gracious red-brick mansion three stories tall, in what must have been some really pretty gardens. The antenna, at least five yards taller than the one he had built, peeked up over the roof. Dieter Vance and Corporal Miller sprang out as they pulled into the semicircular driveway and ran around the back. They returned, scanning the bushes.

"Pool's empty," Dieter said. "Even if there's infecteds here, we got us a little time."

Vance led the way through what was left of a big carved oak door. On either side of the foyer, the fancy sitting rooms were lined with gold records on the walls and framed photographs, both black and white, a lot of them smashed on the floor, mixed in with a lot of the usual disgusting detritus. Billy scanned the pictures. He recognized a lot of country and western music stars, all of whom had appeared on the Opry stage over the years.

"Who lived here?" Ms. Nora asked. Her voice echoed off the lofty ceiling.

"Not a star," Orin said. "All these pictures have the same man in them, but I don't know who he is. Was."

"I bet he was a producer," Billy said, getting more excited with every step, trying to place the image of the burly, gray-haired man in the photographs in his memory. He hoped that one of the bodies he had seen wasn't the house's owner, but it stood to reason that it was. "I bet he had his own recording studio in here." His hands itched to get a hold of the equipment. Maybe there were a couple of good microphones, and a better speaker than the tinny little one he had.

"Chances are that it's in the cellar," Mr. Lou said. Cautiously, with the guardians standing by with weapons leveled, he threw open every door in the corridor until the last one near the kitchen revealed stairs leading down.

Scout Vance led the way, the pinpoint spotlight picking out dirt and excrement on the walls as he went. The noxious odor of one or more decaying bodies hit Billy in the face like a dead fish. He blinked hard to clear his eyes and raised the filter over his nose and mouth. It only cut the stench a little.

The bottom floor of the house was as big as the main floor. First thing they passed was a wet bar. Ms. Nora took a look, but not a single bottle of liquor remained behind it. The stainless steel tap was wide open, but nothing came out of it.

The opposite door led into a full-grown home theater, with about thirty seats, the kind that were in real movie houses. All of them were ripped up from the floor and piled haphazardly over the remains of bodies and piles of excrement. The big white screen had been torn down and defecated on, too. Big posters from classic movies used to be bolted to the walls, but they were all down, torn to shreds, and the glass glittering in the light of their torches. Billy flicked his light here and there. All the machinery that had been attached to the ceiling or the back wall, from the most expensive, best brands, was smashed and pissed on. Billy wished he could have seen the room in pristine condition, even come to see a film there.

"Man, the way rich people live is like a fantasy book," he said.

"But, they die same as us," Orin said, darkly.

"Pantry," Ms. Nora said, heading for a metal-banded door to the left of the ruined screen.

The food storage room was made to look old-fashioned. It had to be a custom build, like everything else in this neighborhood, but constructed more than half a century after the style of the root cellar in his granny's and every other old house in the part of town where Billy had grown up. The shelves were empty except for some broken jars on the floor. The word "blackberry" and a date three years old was on the label of one of the smashed jars. Billy felt a pang. Blackberry jam would have tasted mighty good. They didn't get much in the way of sweets.

"I could have eaten a whole jar with a spoon," he said ruefully.

"Me, too," said Orin, his long face disappointed.

The body of an infected male, stark naked, lay rotting in front of a door on the right, completely blocking access. From the look of it, death had claimed it at least a couple of months ago. Billy just tried to think of a prop from those *Creature Features* movies on television, and not associate it with a real human being.

Careful not to tear his protective suit, Trooper Miller shoved it out of the way with one foot and the butt of his rifle.

A rectangular sign next to the door said ON AIR—not lit up, of course—meant there must be real broadcast equipment inside.

"The studio door is gonna be soundproofed," Billy said. "Means it's going to be heavier than any regular door."

"All right," Mr. Lou said, picking up one of the theater seats. "Let's break it down. I want that there radio of yours working again."

Dieter Vance hefted another chair. He was a lot stronger than his small frame made him look. The two of them took turns smashing at the door with the chairs. It took about twenty tries, but the last big blow by Dieter broke the hinges and sent the heavy portal plunging down into the darkness on the other side of the frame. He threw the seat aside and bounded up over the fallen door.

"Let's see what we've . . . goddammit! Help!"

"What? What?" Gun up, Ms. Nora and Mr. Lou rushed after him. Billy had the impression of something big, dark, and shiny eating them alive. "There's one in here! Ow! Stop it! Kill it!"

Billy dragged the shotgun around from his back and hurried inside, leveling the weapon.

The three scavengers were enveloped in what looked like a giant black fishing net that slithered and rustled around them. At the sight of Billy, a small, wild-haired figure turned and swung a metal disk on a pole toward him. He jumped back just in time, but his heels caught on the broken door. He fell on his butt and the shotgun twirled across the floor. Sergeant Velasquez and Trooper Miller dashed in, guns at the ready.

"Kill it!" Ms. Nora screamed, trying to free herself from the mass. "One got trapped in here! Shoot it!"

"Don't shoot!" Billy yelled, staring at the phantom. "It's got *clothes* on!"

"What?" Miller asked, agog. He tried to fix his light on the figure, but he had to stay moving. Zombie or not, the survivor was determined to hit them with the sharp-edged disk of metal. "Miss? Whatever you are? We're here to help. You're safe, miss. Please, stop it. Drop the weapon. None of us want to shoot you, I swear."

The disk stopped moving and sank slowly to the floor.

"You're not... sick?" The person's filthy face almost looked like a zombie's, with hollow eyes and a narrow, pointed jaw. Her voice was so raspy Billy guessed it had been a long time since she had spoken aloud.

"No, ma'am. There's a few of us left. We're glad to see you. What's your name?"

Ms. Nora wriggled out of the net. Billy picked up the edge of it. It had been *knitted* out of recording tape, probably from the hundreds and hundreds of broken cassette and video cases stacked in the corner of the room.

"I'm sorry," she said. "I'm sorry I'm sorry I'm sorry..." The girl—or woman, none of them could guess which—collapsed into a heap on the floor and began weeping, but she was so dehydrated no tears came. Billy sprang forward with his bottle of water.

"That's okay," Ms. Nora said, cradling the skeletal female in her arms and rocking her. She took the bottle and held it to the girl's lips like she was feeding a baby. "You're safe now."

Now that he had a chance, Billy took a look around the recording studio. It was so fancy, he couldn't believe it. It stank, as every place they had found uninfected humans living, but apart from the masses of tape everywhere, it was tidy. The girl had taken care of herself as best she could.

"How'd she live down here for months?" Orin whispered, glancing back at the slight figure slumped against Ms. Nora.

With a grin, Billy pointed to more tidy stacks next to the piles of black VHS boxes.

"We solved the mystery of the empty pantry," he said. She had every single jar and box in the corner, all of them empty, licked absolutely clean. Only two still had food in them, a box of crackers with one half-eaten strip of saltines still in it, and one open jar of blackberry jam.

"This is all that's left," Orin said, picking up the jar. He stuck a finger in it.

"No! Mine!" Like a hornet, the girl rose up and ran at him, hitting him with her bony fists, shrieking incoherently. Shielding his face from her scratches, Orin pushed the jar at her.

"Okay, okay! We got other things to eat, ma'am!"

"You see what you need here, boy?" Mr. Lou asked.

Billy remembered why they were there, and looked around, almost breathlessly. This was a candy store for technophiles. Shure microphones, Blaupunkt speakers, even two Grass Valley switchers, one with slide pots, and the other pure digital.

"I'd take everything," he said.

Mr. Lou grinned. "Well, let's just start with the basics, all right?"

"Take the net, too," Ms. Nora said. "We can use that."

They blocked the door to protect the rest of the equipment until Billy could come back again with an empty truck, then got on the dark, empty road, with the girl jammed between Orin and Billy in the back seat of the Prius. Billy had written his IOU and put it on the broken projector in the home cinema.

"I can't believe you found me," the girl said, snuggling in tight. She clutched Billy's water bottle in both hands. Her name was Tee Figueroa, and she had met the producer in New York when she was on the crew at the Country Music Awards. He hired her away with a promise of an interesting career, but she hadn't a clue how interesting it would get. "When everything went crazy, there were three of us down there, my boss, another sound tech, and me. I don't know how my boss got infected, but he took off his clothes and started to attack us. I figured sooner or later he was going to make a pass at me, but not like that! We got him out the door, but he bit Tommy! Two days later, Tommy started doing the same things. He tore off all his clothes and came at me like a banshee. I..." Tee's voice faded away.

"It's okay," Ms. Nora said, soothingly.

"No, it's not okay," Tee said. "Dammit, we're human beings! I'm so ashamed. I...I hit him with that mic stand."

"That packs a wallop," Mr. Lou said. "Thing must weigh fif-teen pounds."

"I had to keep his body in there with me until it all went quiet. I only dared to sneak out of the room one time, to take the food out of that room because I was starving to death. I'm sorry about hitting you. The zombies never tried to get into the studio before. The door's too heavy, but you kept trying."

"No problem," Orin said. "You had no idea who we were."

"How'd you make that net?" Billy asked.

Tee grinned shyly. Her teeth were in good shape for someone left trapped in a cellar for months, but one broken bicuspid was going to need to be pulled.

"I started knitting to keep myself from going crazy. I made a giant set of round needles out of a pair of directional mics and six feet of cable. I made myself a hammock to start, then I got the idea to make a net in case the zombies got in. All those tapes were from his recording sessions with famous people. They're worth nothing now. There's no power."

"We got power," Billy assured her.

Underneath his feet was a beautiful radio, forty years younger than the one Billy had been using. The producer had been a hobbyist. She led him right to the dead producer's ham rig. Not only the radio was tucked into a niche in the studio, but tidy racks of components and other gear, plus modular padding on the walls that put the old quilts he used as sound baffles to shame. She was too weak to load any of that in the trucks, but she had pointed, and they got most of the valuable stuff, includ-ing a high-powered tuner that went all over the radio spectrum. They also got not only power backups from over the house, but a building generator that still had fuel in it. Billy wrote his IOU and put it on what was left of the hall table.

The folks at Foresight Genetics greeted Tee like a heroine, eager to hear all about her story. Once she had a good meal, a shower and some new clothes, Mr. Jud was happy to have her help Billy fix the electrics and stabilize the delicate equipment. She had a double degree from Columbia University in broadcasting and electrical engineering.

"No, hook up the generator right there," she said, directing both of them from a chair near the rear of the building where the heavy cables came in. Even with a day or two of good feeding, she was too weak to do the work herself. "We'll need to make a workaround before the fuse box, or it'll blow again the next time there's a power surge. We can use that to step down the current, and it'll act as a capacitor in case of power drops, too."

A whoop of joy came from the sharpshooters on the line as Mr. Jud yelled for them to back away from the fence so he could re-electrify it. Triumphant, the two men helped Tee back into the facility for a celebratory meal.

Billy felt like an uneducated hick listening to her reel off instructions like a pro, but she never looked down at him. She liked teaching.

The two of them got his old radio fixed in no time. He looked wistfully at the new rig. He really wanted to use it, but Tee warned him that they needed to be sure the transformer would hold before they risked blowing it out.

"You won't believe it, but yours is more stable than anything they're making now," she said. Billy agreed, feeling a little shy.

Once she started to get meat on her bones again, she was a really pretty lady, with wavy black hair, big brown eyes, and golden skin. Billy felt shy around her. While a couple of the men showed an interest in her, she stuck close to Billy. They had kind of bonded over geeky tech stuff.

As soon as he got permission from Mr. Jud, he booted up the radio and got on the horn to Geraint.

"Thought you were gone for good, *bach*," the Welshman said. "And welcome back to the world of the living, young Miss Tee!"

"Thank you, Geraint," the young woman said, into the headset mic she wore.

"We want to hear the rest of the story about your boy on the bike," Mr. Lou said. He and Ms. Nora sat in the storeroom with Billy and Tee.

"Ah, a new audience-eh!" Geraint's voice said. A crackle rose. Tee leaned forward and adjusted the controls a hair. The static died away. Billy felt almost as though he ought to feel jealous that she could use his equipment without having a lifetime of experience with it, but he was just grateful that it worked again. "Well, I'll tell you, I'd call it the adventure of a lifetime, but every day is one, now. I was working-eh as an electrician in Holyhead, and Mrs. Davies from down the way was sweatin' and screamin' outside the primary school next door..."

*School.* That word struck a chord in Billy's mind. He grabbed the mic. "Hold it a minute, Geraint."

"As you wish, Effy," the Welshman said, sounding a little hurt.

"Hey, son, I want to hear the story," Mr. Lou said, looking a little peeved.

"I know, but it just hit me," Billy said, apologetically. "Everybody here's going to want to hear his story, and everyone else in the compound will, too."

"So, what's your idea?" Ms. Nora asked, narrowing an eye at him.

"In my high school, we had a kind of radio station that broadcast over the in-house PA system. Mostly they just used it for announcements and the Pledge of Allegiance, but we played music during intramural events and broadcast basketball and football games to the classrooms. We've got enough equipment now. If Mr. Jud gives us permission, we can wire it so Geraint and my other friends can tell their stories to all of us. And we can play music in between. Like a real radio station."

"Now, that's a great idea," Mr. Lou said. "How hard will it be to set it up?"

"No problem at all," Tee said, with a smile that lit up her narrow face. "I *built* some of those systems. Now that the power's stabilized, it won't take much current. And there are enough speakers at my old boss's house to put one in almost every office here."

Tomkinson didn't take much convincing.

"News from outside? Music?" the tall man said, clapping Billy on the back. "That'll do wonders for morale," Mr. Jud said. "But I don't want days and nights of your caterwaulin' Top Forty."

"Nossir," Billy said. Tee held onto his arm, making him feel proud. "And we've got some other ideas. We can broadcast out to the rest of the world. There might be people out there who can't talk back to us, for some reason. It's not hard to build a primitive ham radio. We might find some other people who are alive."

"Like me," Tee put in. "For a while I listened to a crank-winding emergency shortwave radio, but no one was broadcasting after about a month. I've been a DJ at a couple of stations. I used to make public service announcement recordings when I worked at a station in south Georgia. I bet there are others out there who were listening to a shortwave like me. If any of them are still out there and trying. Billy remembered that she had given up listening. I'll do anything to help save even one more person like me. It'll help me feel more...normal."

"Me, too," Billy admitted. "If anyone's still alive out there, we'll teach them how. In between entertaining them. Geraint and my other friends are dying to tell their own stories of how they survived."

Tomkinson nodded. "That'll be as good as food to people. I'll check with the Hole, but I'm going to give you a tentative go-ahead. No one else is using those frequencies."

With Tee's old employer's tuner, Billy wrote up a rotation, varying the broadcast of their recordings from the storeroom from 1413 up to 17830 kilohertz. Using his grandpa's old radio as an example he described the schematics of putting together a working radio and powering it with a crank or batteries. Tee built a parallel system so the folks in Foresight could listen to everything going out over the shortwave signals as well as the internal "station." Billy fell back into his days as a teenage disc jockey, playing stuff from his personal music device and thousands of songs not only from everyone else's devices, but what unbroken disks they retrieved from the mansion and all the other "Targets" and "Walmarts."

The new radio was so much better than his old rig that he could put out a strong signal. Within a few weeks, it paid off. A few stragglers reported in, to cheers from his comrades on the ham circuit. A couple were marooned on a small island in the middle of the Pacific Ocean with a marine radio. A forest ranger called from the fire-jumping platform in a national park in Wyoming. He even heard from a couple who didn't want to say where they were, as if Billy might jump out through the radio and bite them.

The music proved popular, but not as popular as the stories of survival from around the world. Billy kept up descriptions of radio building every day on a different frequency. Broadcast instructions, to anyone hearing on any frequency that didn't belong to emergency responders. Billy knew he was breaking the law, but the BBC World Service frequencies were the ones that more people in the world listened to than any other. With Tee's help, he recorded his correspondents reciting the instructions in every language that they knew. Dr. Park in Antarctica spoke not only Korean and English, but Mandarin and French. Geraint also spoke Swedish. Sergeant Velasquez translated the instructions into Spanish and read them carefully off a piece of paper.

"I don't know what I'm saying," she said, "but if it helps, I'm glad."

"People are walking with more energy than they had when I came here," Tee said, as the two of them sat down for another show in the now well-padded corner of the storeroom. They had LED lights now, also low power to conserve electricity. The whole place was beginning to look actually professional. "It's all because of you." She gave him a hug.

Billy felt as if his heart might pound out of his chest.

"Uh, thanks," he said. "It couldn't have happened without you."

She smiled at him. Very shyly, he took her hand. She squeezed his fingers.

"Better get started," she said. She dialed the tuner to the main ham frequency. "Anyone out there? This is Tee and Billy in Nashville, Tennessee!"

With every passing week, Slowly, gradually, a few—so few!—more voices started coming in on the ham frequencies. It made everyone happy to be in touch. Geraint, the reigning grand old man of the airwaves, got them talking, gave them all their own call signs based on their locations, with an X designation for the two who were so cagey about their location.

Billy listened, happy to get news he could share with the others. He was the most popular person in the mess hall. He broadcast it live when one of the island operators in the Atlantic was rescued by the Wolf Squadron. Ms. Melanie organized a celebration.

"Thanks, everybody," Billy said into his mic, when the rescue was over. "You're all making this work amazingly!"

Geraint's plummy voice chuckled. "You're the one in between us all, *bach*. Shortwave, ham, public address disk jockey. A regular ham sandwich."

"God, I wish I had a ham sandwich!" Dr. Park burst out. "We are eating penguins and penguin eggs. It breaks my heart to do it, but we must survive. I hope someday Wolf Squadron will come down here and save us."

"Ham! I pretend this fish is ham, me, too," said Francois, in his lilting Jamaican voice. "Last can of Spam is gone months ago."

"Don't talk about ham sandwiches!" Tee said, draping her arm around Billy's shoulders. "But he's a treasure, for sure. He's my new boyfriend." Billy looked at her in shock. She smiled, and leaned in to kiss him. Her lips were warm and soft. Billy felt like he might explode with joy.

"Oh, no, he's not!" a new voice piped up for the first time. It sounded hoarse and far away, but Billy sat up straight in shock when he heard it. "He's mine!"

"N-no way," Billy stammered. "No way! *Cindy?*"

A sob broke over the speaker. "Oh, my God, Effy! I heard your voice over the shortwave. I couldn't believe it!"

He grabbed the mic. "Where are you?"

"In a monastery in Tibet! The nuns rescued us. They shot the, the *walking dead* with bows and arrows until they stopped coming. We've been living on rice and meditation. Dad's okay, but Mom..." Her voice trailed off.

Tee looked at him and sat back, raising her hands to her shoulders.

"I don't mind sharing," she said, with a wink.

"So, Cindy," Billy said, very casually, wishing he could leap through the radio and hug her, and die of embarrassment at the same time. "What's new?"

"Well," Cindy said, through a burst of static. "It's awful dry up here. But, you know, they had a pretty good appliance repair shop."

# The Downeasters

## BRENDAN DUBOIS

*"…this is WBLM, Portland, Maine, about to sign off. We've been running on diesel and it's gonna run dry in a couple of minutes. This is Gus Leighton, intern, and…well, if my parents are listening, Mom and Dad, I'll try to get home. The last news we got from Augusta is two weeks old, when the acting governor urged people to stay indoors and listen to local public safety officials…for God's sake, I don't know why, because nobody's got a good idea how this damn plague started or how to stop it…"*

From: *Collected Radio Transmissions of the Fall*
University of the South Press, 2053

When the knock came at daybreak at his home on Massabesic Island off the coast of Maine, Fred Paige rolled over in bed and picked up the always-loaded 9mm SIG Sauer P226 with one hand and grabbed a flashlight with the other. His wife Lori murmured from the other side of the bed and said, "What's up, hon?"

"Somebody's at the door," he said, grabbing a bathrobe from the bottom of the bed, shrugging it on. "I'll get Ken to back me up downstairs. You know the drill, babe."

Lori got up and took another flashlight in hand, switched it on, and then took a 12-gauge pump-action Remington shotgun from the near corner of the bedroom. "You be careful," she said, wearing a dark blue cotton nightgown that reached just above her knees.

Fred slid his feet into a pair of L.L. Bean moccasins. "Careful is my middle name."

"Liar," she said. "I know for fact it's Courtney."

He smiled. "That's why I married you. Because you're so smart."

She held the shotgun in the crook of her arm. "Liar again," she said, smiling in return. "You told me that you married me because I had the biggest knockers on the island."

"Shhh," he said. "You don't want Penny or Ken to hear that."

The knock came back, louder. "Go," she said. "And don't keep me guessing."

He went out the bedroom door, lit flashlight in one hand, pistol in the other. He went past their eight-year-old daughter Penny's room, and then went to their twelve-year-old Ken's bedroom door. He gave it a sharp rap and Ken quickly opened the door, yawning, bare chested, scratching at his thick brown hair, wearing a dark blue pair of sweatpants that said U-MAINE ORONO in white letters on the left leg.

"Yeah, Dad?"

"Somebody's at the door. Come along."

"Sure," he said. His son ducked in and came out with a .223 Ruger Mini-14, and he followed his father as the two of them went downstairs. Fred glanced up and saw his wife Lori—still shapely and beautiful after fifteen years of marriage and two kids—standing in front of their daughter's bedroom door, shotgun in her arms.

Just another typical morning on the island.

At the bolted heavy front door, Fred called out, "Who's out there?"

"It's me, Darryn," came the familiar voice. "Me and Paul are out here."

"Anybody else there?"

"Nope."

His twelve-year-old boy was standing partially hidden down the hallway, Ruger up to his shoulder. Fred turned and whispered, "Remember the drill, okay? Fire only if you see me drop to the floor. Otherwise, you're gonna have one pissed off mom if you shoot before that."

Ken just nodded.

Fred unbolted the door, then stepped back, flashlight illuminating the two men standing there, both with long rifles over their shoulders, pistols at the side. Nearly as one, Darryn Ghent, the head of the island's Public Works Department, and Paul Lucian, one of the other two selectmen that governed the town, lifted their hands to block the light.

"Christ," Darryn said, squinting his eyes above his full beard. "It's just us."

"Sorry," Fred said. "Habit." He turned and said, "Ken, back to bed. You tell your mother everything's just fine."

He stepped out into the fresh Maine air, thinking again of how lucky they were, that the prevailing winds seemed to keep "it"— whatever the hell "it" was—away from their island. One of the mainlanders, Dr. Tilly Wilson, who once worked for the government in some Army-related medical research field, told the islanders a few months ago that Massabesic and its folks should remain safe, if, and only if, they stayed put and didn't let anyone else in. She was a cheerful sort, until a month after that public meeting when she hung herself off the town bandstand, a note pinned to her blouse, saying, *My fault I was part of the system that allowed this to happen.*

Paul Lucian took off his black-rimmed glasses, rubbed the lenses with the tail of his old black-and-red-checked hunting jacket. "It's like this Fred, Janet says the generator, it's gonna crap out soon. Maybe today, maybe this week, but sure as hell within the month."

Fred said to his public works director, "That right?"

Darryn shuffled his big booted feet. "Yeah, it's been running rough the last two shifts. I mean, nearly shaking itself to pieces rough."

"What does Janet say?" Fred asked.

Both men kept quiet, and Fred felt the cold fear and just the hour-to-hour, day-to-day grind and heavy weight of responsibility on his shoulders for the sixty-one souls who were still alive on this sliced off piece of the Maine coastline.

"Okay," Fred said. "I get it. Later this morning...say, eleven, we'll have a town meeting to discuss it, all right? Ask the Chief to send couriers out, but only after the sun's been up for an hour. Don't want anybody get their head blown off 'cause someone startled a neighbor with a door banging."

"Thanks, Fred."

"Yeah, Fred, thanks."

Both men walked down the gravel path, off to the main road, where they climbed onto bicycles and made their way to the village. Fred looked at the sun rising over the fog-shrouded mainland, less than a half-mile away from the island.

He still could go back to bed, maybe catch a couple of more hours of sleep before breakfast, but he knew he wouldn't sleep, he'd just be restless in bed, thinking and thinking.

It was going to be one long hell of a day.

About ten minutes after eleven, Fred Paige walked up to the entrance of the Massabesic Town Hall, a two-hundred-year-old white clapboard building that was one-story with tall windows. It started off on the island as a barn, was converted into a meeting hall for the GAR, and then the Grange, and then it was donated to the town back in 1932 to serve as the town hall. No real business was conducted there—the town clerk was Rosie Cranston, and she kept the necessary files and paperwork in her spare bedroom—but it was the place where there were craft fairs, contra dances, church socials, and like now, meetings of all of the island residents.

No cars or trucks were parked in front. There were three horses, and a host of bicycles. Up the road a ways was the low white building that served as the town library, police station, and volunteer fire department.

Inside there was a low buzz of conversation and he walked across the wide wooden planks, until he got to the front, where there was a lectern and table. On the empty stage behind him were flagpoles holding up the State of Maine and American flags.

Rosie Cranston was there, ready to take notes, and at the table was the selectman from that morning, Paul Lucian, and next to him was Matilda Grant, the oldest woman on the island. She was in a wheelchair and defiantly smoked a cigarette about ten feet away from a bright NO SMOKING sign. Matilda didn't know it, but most people on the island had given up smoking so that she wouldn't go without her butts.

Fred went to the lectern and nodded to Rosie. "Mind leading us in the pledge?"

Rosie got up and so did the rest of the townspeople, and

facing the flag, each with hand over each heart, the residents and survivors said the Pledge of Allegiance, and like he had secretly done these past several months, Fred wondered if they were just mouthing empty words.

Was there a United States of America anymore?

With the words "under God..." drifting away, Fred turned to the lectern and said, "Well, I'll get right to it. It looks like the town generator is about to croak."

There was an audible sigh and a few groans from the residents, sitting calmly in folding wooden chairs. Fred said, "Darryn, you want to give us an update?"

In the front row that was reserved for town officials, Darryn Ghent stood up and said, "Fred, if you don't mind, I'll have Janet talk to us."

From behind Darryn's seat, Janet Wilmot, the assistant public works director and the best damn mechanic on the island, stood up from her own perch. She was a heavyset woman wearing black rubber Wellington boots, blue jean overalls, and a hooded white sweatshirt. Her hands were raw and always soiled with grease, she kept her hair in a crew-cut, and her "roommate" was Barb Zachary, a fisherwoman, and this being small-town Maine, nobody really gave a shit.

Janet said, "I wish I had better news, but the damn thing is running rougher and rougher. What it needs is a good overhaul but I don't think I got the right parts, and if I do an overhaul, some damn thing just might break and we'd be shit out of luck."

A voice from the townspeople. "Whaddya think we should do, Janet?"

She looked around, scared yet defiant. "Only one answer, much as I hate it. We need to get some parts, and get a spare generator, 'cause you know winter'll be here 'fore we know it. That means we gotta go over to the mainland."

With that, the entire hall went silent.

Janet sat down, her wooden chair squeaking on the floorboards.

In a few seconds the silence was broken, by lots of loud voices and questions.

"...not going over there, nossir..."

"...we go over there, we're dead, just like that..."

"...who the hell is dumb enough to go over there..."

Fred used the gavel—TOWN MODERATOR JOHN POPE MEMORIAL GAVEL 1998, it said on a gold seal on the handle—and called out, "Order, c'mon folks, order. We'll all get a chance to speak, don't you worry."

Buster Abrams stood up, hands pushed into his Patriots windbreaker. "I say, let the damn generator fail. We don't need it. Am I right? My granddad and grandma and most everyone else's grandma and granddad, they grew up without electricity here on the island. Am I right? I ain't gonna risk going over to the mainland to get eaten or infected. Nossir."

There was some applause at that, which made Fred feel uneasy. This wasn't going well. He had to save this before it went too far. More voices were raised, but he pointed his gavel at Doc Molly.

"Doc Molly? What do you think?"

Molly Templeton was a retired vet and since the suicide of Dr. Tilly Wilson, was the nearest thing to a medical expert on the island. She slowly stood up, wearing a dull floral dress with a heavy blue down vest around her shoulders and muddy boots. Her gray-white hair was pulled back in a simple ponytail and she said, "There are some vaccines and medicines that we need to keep refrigerated, or they're spoiled. With the generator running on the current schedule, we were able to keep enough to last us several months, if we're careful in using them. If we were to lose power . . . well, maybe some of you folks are ready for nineteenth century medicine, but I ain't."

She sat down and there were other calls and questions, and Fred did his job again, pointing to Chris Allain, who got up and licked his lips, nervous-like. He was skinny, with thick glasses, and he wiped his hands on his khaki slacks as he spoke.

"It's . . . well, it's like this . . . my radio's doing all right . . . I'm broadcasting every day at noon and at six p.m. . . . and when the conditions are okay . . . I can pick up some traffic out there . . . though most of it's confusing . . . and, er . . . scary . . . but there's other news . . . like I heard a couple of messages about a survivor fleet down off Florida and the Bahamas, called the Wolf Squadron . . ."

A voice: "For Christ's sake, Chris, talk about the goddamn generator!"

His face flushed. "Oh, right . . . well, I got a recharger to keep my batteries going . . . but without power, well, eventually we'll lose communications . . ."

A different voice this time, from a defiant woman: "What's to hear anyway? Probably most of the world is dead, anyway."

A younger woman—Jenny Smith, with her young girl in the crook of her arm—yelled back, "We don't know that! We don't know that! Suppose...suppose it works out, some...and there's relief...wouldn't you want to know?"

Now the crowd of people—his friends, his neighbors, his townspeople—talked and argued, and Fred thought, now, now was the time. He rapped the gavel on the lectern until everyone got quiet.

"Well, we could go on arguing for a while but time is wasting. Like Janet said, the generator could tear itself into pieces today or tomorrow. Best we take care of this now."

A voice from the back of the hall: "Aren't you gonna put it to a vote?"

Fred shook his head. "No need to. This is an informational session, not a regular town meeting. Public safety is part of the selectmen's duties, and as chairman, I deem that sending a volunteer party across the channel to the town of Gilbert to secure spare parts and a generator is in the town's best interest."

Buster Abrams stood up again, and before he spoke, he looked at all of the townspeople and said, "Did you hear that? Volunteers! Our government is asking for volunteers to go across the channel...get infected...bit...maybe even eaten by what's still alive over there. Volunteers! Hah! Who do you think you're gonna get to volunteer, Mister Chairman?"

Silence came over the hall interior, and Fred was struck with a bout of nostalgia about all the fun things that occurred in this same place over the years, from Christmas pageants to a church play to music and dancing.

Now?

He cleared his throat. "Me, for one. I intend to lead the party."

Minutes passed with a few more shouts and arguments, and then Janet Wilmot, the assistant director for Public Works, stood up and said, "I volunteer!"

Fred shook his head. "Ah, heck, Janet, we can't risk having you go across. It's gonna be too dangerous."

She said, "You need me to get what we need."

Matilda Grant, one of the other two selectmen, coughed and

said, "Can't you provide 'em with a list? Like Fred said, shit, hon, you're worth too much to the town for... for something bad to happen to you."

Janet said, "Yeah, I can make a list, but them hunting through Arjay's Hardware over there, trying to match a list, that'll take too much time. I can go in with a couple of guys to cover me, and I can get out fast. Same thing with the generator."

Murmurs and looks, and Fred said, "Okay, that's a good point."

A firm but quiet voice came from the end of the front row. "I'll volunteer, Fred."

The voice belonged to Gil Pachter, and Fred seriously considered that for a moment. Gil kept to himself, lived on the other side of the island with his Belgian Malinois dog Loki, who was sprawled on his back, his belly being rubbed by the three-year-old Fuller twins. Gil was regular size, with regular muscles, but his black eyes were sharp enough to cut steel and looked to be hiding lots of dark memories. Gil had been in the service but never talked much about it, but when... it began, his knowledge of weapons and tactics had saved the town.

Gil was sitting next to Police Chief Aaron Swinton, who sat slumped and didn't ever have much to say. After the crisis had begun, and not to insult the chief—who had been chief for fifteen years—Gil was named deputy chief and ran the island's defenses.

Fred spoke carefully, because Gil was known to have a temper and he didn't want to upset the man.

"Gil, there's nobody I'd want more at my back than you... but you're vital to protecting the island. I can accept taking the risk of bringing Janet over, but I'm sorry, the town needs to have you stay here." Fred had been about to say "stay behind," but he knew that would be an insult.

Gil just pursed his lips, nodded, and in a few minutes, two others had volunteered, both from the town's police force: Jack Tiller, age nineteen, and his uncle Brad Tiller, age seventy.

Fred said, "All right, I'll ask the party to meet at the town dock, with anybody else that wants to go along to wish us luck... and Patrick, Patrick Beecham, I'm sorry, but we're gonna have to requisition you and your boat."

Patrick was in the rear and hidden by other townspeople. He said, "Okay... but the town'll make good on the fuel I burn, right?"

"Of course."

"Would rather see a formal vote, Fred."

He looked to the other selectmen, and Paul Lucian made the motion, Matilda seconded it, and then it passed unanimously.

"All right, meeting adjourned."

He rapped the gavel on the lectern and as was customary during town meetings like this, the residents of the island and town of Massabesic, Maine, stood up and in a ragged but firm chorus, sang "God Bless America."

An hour later he was at the town dock, where his wife Lori grabbed his arm and dragged him behind a pile of lobster traps.

"What the hell do you think you're doing?" she nearly hissed at him.

He gently freed his arm from his wife's grasp. "I'm doing my job."

"Job! You get paid a hundred dollars a year...and get a hundred hours of grief every week. And you and I both know the money's useless now..."

"It's something we've got to do."

"But why you?"

Fred said, "You were there. You saw how folks were wavering. They needed someone to take charge. That was me. If I hadn't taken charge...they'd still be there arguing and they'd get tired, and nothing would happen, and when winter comes soon, we won't have power no more."

Lori stared at him, eyes filled with tears, and she suddenly grabbed him and kissed him hard. She lowered her voice. "You be safe over there on the mainland, got it? You be safe and you come back home to me, Fred Paige. If things...go bad...you leave 'em all behind, you steal a boat back, you swim, by Christ, but you come back."

Fred gently kissed her back. "I'll do my best."

And then he went back out to the town dock.

His wife called out with a hesitant voice. "If...if you find John, let me know, will you?"

He pretended not to hear her.

Massabesic Harbor was shaped like a three-tined fork with the middle tine snapped in half. The town pier—the middle tine—jutted out into the harbor, and the small body of water was flanked by two much longer stone and concrete breakwaters that extended out into the Gulf of Maine, and which allowed for some safe shelter from the waves. About a dozen lobster boats and fishing trawlers, along with a smattering of smaller boats, were at moorings in the harbor.

It was a quiet and nearly windless early afternoon, and Fred thought the scene looked like a damn photo for the Maine Tourism Association, except for a few things.

Like the huge plywood signs posted at the end of each breakwater, painted black and orange, with a skull and crossbones, and large KEEP AWAY painted in white.

Like the M2A1 Browning .50 caliber machine gun at the end of the town pier, secured by concrete blocks and surrounded by sandbags, and where one of the town's police officers stood nearby, on watch. During the chaotic and terrifying days back in May, when "it" happened, Gil Pachter had rolled up in his Jeep Wrangler and with some help, got the machine gun set up. At some point somebody asked Gil where in hell he had gotten the Army machine gun, and the vet had shrugged and said, "Souvenir."

And there was one more thing that didn't belong, that the Maine Tourism Association—if anybody belonging to that was still alive—were the still-bobbing, bullet-ridden hulls and wrecks of five watercraft that had tried to come into the harbor.

Yeah.

A small crowd was gathered at the floating walkway and Fred walked past them, as they patted him on the back and said words of encouragement. He was sweating something fierce, because he was overdressed for the occasion. He had on work boots, two pairs of Carhartt work pants, a leather coat, and leather gloves. Nobody said too much about it, but he was wearing these heavy clothes in case he got close enough to get bit.

Around his waist he had a leather belt, holster, and two spare magazines for his SIG Sauer 9mm. Over his shoulder he carried a Remington Model 870 12-gauge shotgun, with 00 buckshot loads for the shells. Young Jack Tiller and his uncle Brad were waiting dockside as well, both wearing heavy blue jean overalls, thick sweatshirts and gloves. Jack was gaunt, with a scraggly brown beard and long hair tied back in a ponytail. His uncle was a Vietnam War vet, as tall as his nephew, but with a fuller beard and darker eyes. The Tillers lived near Fred and Lori but mostly kept to themselves—which was island life, hell, there were at least three families scattered across Massabesic who hadn't left their homes or property since it began—but the Tillers had a bit of a history. Nothing on the island, but on the mainland, there were stories of OUI's, bar fights, a few burglaries and bad-check charges.

No matter, Fred thought. That was past. They seemed good with firearms and that's all that counted. Young Jake had a pump-action Remington as well, but this one had its barrel illegally shortened (as if the ATF would care nowadays) and his uncle had a civilian AR-15 and was wearing a MOLLE harness with two magazine pouches.

He nodded at them both, and then Janet Wilmot, the town's assistant public works director, showed up, wearing chest-high fishing waders, dungaree jacket and thick leather gloves. She had on a knapsack on her back that looked empty, and had an old-fashioned leather belt with a holster that looked to have a revolver in it.

Janet said, "One good thing, the tide will be high when we get over to Gilbert; the boat'll be at a good height so we can get that generator on-board."

"Okay," Fred said.

From his boat—the *Mona Marie*—Patrick Beecham leaned over and said, "For Christ's sake, can we get going? I'm about ready to crap my pants and I don't wanna do it in public."

Fred started to the boat when a woman's voice said, "Hold on, guys. Hold on."

Doc Molly was there, breathing hard, like she had just run down to the dock. She had a leather pouch over her shoulder, and she reached in, pulled out four heavy thick facemasks with equally heavy elastic bands.

"Put these on," she said. "We don't know much... but before the cable channels and radio stations went off, there was some evidence that it was caused by an airborne virus. These are the best protection I can give you guys. It might not work, but it's better than nothing. Put them on and don't take 'em off until you come back to the island."

From his boat, Patrick called out, "Hey, how about me?"

Doc Molly said, "Patrick, you're at the least risk. Best I can do."

Fred went to the boat, helped Janet aboard, and then the Tillers jumped aboard. Two townspeople undid the fore and aft lines, and then Patrick went to the open wheelhouse, and started the diesel engine. It started right up and then the lines were tossed aboard. Fred looked at the dozens of townsfolk gathered there, staring at them with...hope? Fear? Despair?

He thought he should say something to mark this, the first time in months a boat had left Massabesic to go to the mainland. It was historic, that's for sure.

Fred waved. "Hope you folks remember this next March, when I run for reelection."

He was pleased at their laughter. He said to Patrick, "Let's get going."

The *Mona Marie* burbled its way out of the harbor. The four of them sat on benches in the rear of the boat, which was used for fishing. The stern had removable planks, allowing for a wide, easy opening to let on people and cargo.

Like a desperately needed power generator, Fred thought.

Patrick maneuvered past the moored sailboats and other fishing craft, past the end of the breakwaters with their warning signs, and then out to the Gulf of Maine. Other islands were scattered out there, all the way to the horizon, and Patrick turned and said, "Boy, sure is tempting to keep on going, all the way to England, hunh?"

Brad Tiller, with his AR-15 across his lap, said, "Not enough fuel, Patrick. You know that. Plus I heard that England's a mess, worse than us."

Patrick said, "I was just funnin', that's all."

"Yeah," Brad said.

Patrick turned the boat to starboard, and now they were in Massabesic Channel. The heavily wooded coast of Maine was now before them, with the small buildings and docks of the town of Gilbert. Fred felt his chest grow heavy. When it began, he and other townspeople would sometimes stand on Craig's Bluff, watching what was happening over in Gilbert. With binoculars and a couple of telescopes, they could make out the vehicles moving, the traffic accidents, a couple of buildings burning, and...the people. And the others...

Fred turned and gave a quick glance to his lifelong home. Massabesic Island was shaped like a fat teardrop, with the harbor at the pointy end. The harbor was the only access to the island, for the rest of its coast was jagged rocks, boulders, and underwater ledges that would—and had—ripped open the hulls of any watercraft that came too close.

He turned away.

Young Jake Tiller leaned over the gunwale, seeing the town get closer. "You think there's many zeds over there?"

"Dunno," Brad said. "But you keep your eyes and ears open. One bite from a zed..."

Fred thought of that word, zed. He wasn't sure what they were called in other places, but the word zombie... it just seemed too crazy! All those books, TV shows, movies... and to have it happen? For real? So there was a real hesitation to call them zombies, or a zombie infection, or a zombie apocalypse.

Somebody called them zeds—for the British word for the letter Z—and that word quickly caught on. Fred thought it made sense, because you didn't want to think of what was alive over there being people, people you knew, friends and even a few family members stuck there when the ferry stopped running.

It even made it easier to kill them when the time came.

Fred took the facemask that the doc gave him, and put it on.

So did Jack, Brad, and Janet.

Patrick said, "Crap, I still should have gotten one."

As the *Mona Marie* started getting closer to Gilbert Harbor, Fred stood up and looked over at the familiar town and its docks. A number of boats were still at their moorings, although some were swamped. From what he saw of Gilbert, it was a mess. At least three buildings had burned down; there was an abandoned Gilbert Volunteer Fire Department pumper truck on Harbor Road, along with a dozen cars jammed up in tangled mess. Trash and debris were blowing across the small rectangular park separating the docks and Harbor Road, and the park grass was knee-high. There were lumps of what looked to be clothing scattered here and there. Seagulls flew in and out, some of them strutting around like they owned the place.

Janet was next to him, "Crap. Dina's Diner is burnt out. She used to make a hell of a good Mexican soup."

"What was Mexican soup?" Fred asked, his hands cold, even in the gloves.

Her voice was muffled behind the mask. "Who knows. But it sure tasted fine."

Up in the wheelhouse Patrick throttled back the diesel and said, "All right. The port side of the main dock looks clear. I'm going to switch off the engine, glide in, and you folks can bail out."

Brad said, "Why are you turning off the engine? It might not start up."

Patrick said, "Before the TV went off, I saw something on CNN . . . said the zeds respond to loud noises. I sure as hell don't want 'em running down to the dock, now, do I."

Then he switched off the engine, and it struck Fred just how quiet it was. Other visits to Gilbert before it happened, there were boats going in and out, traffic taking its time going along Harbor Road, music from a couple of the bars, a few honks of horn, and just that little background noise of scores of people enjoying themselves.

Now there was nothing.

Janet reached behind in her knapsack and pulled out a square orange flag. "You see this, Patrick? When we get what we need, I'll be waving this at the end of the dock. And you haul ass to fetch us, got it?"

"Christ, yes, I got it," Patrick said. "You guys . . . here we go."

Patrick might have been full of himself, and told lots of lies like all fishermen and lobstermen, but he knew how to handle his boat, even with the engine off. The *Mona Marie* slid in with less than a foot clearance between the dock and its gunwales, and one by one, they stepped off on the dock. Along the dock were careful piles of lobster traps, fifty-five-gallon drums painted white to be used as trash barrels, and some concrete-and-wood park benches.

Fred turned and watched the *Mona Marie* make a slow, curving turn, and then Patrick restarted the engine and went off at low speed. He leaned out of the wheelhouse, and he waved.

Fred and Janet waved back. The Tillers didn't.

Brad said, "C'mon, let's go."

They all knew where Arjay's was located—about a hundred yards to the south—so at least they weren't bumbling around, tripping over each other, trying to find out where to go. Fred at first found the facemask constricting and made his face sweaty, but now he liked having it on, because it seemed to block off most of the smells of soot, rot, and decay.

There was a strange noise, a low keening, and Brad said to his nephew, "Jack, just don't look. Okay? Don't linger, don't stare. Look at something fine, like that tree or unbroken window. It'll help. Trust me, I know."

Fred swallowed. He knew what was bothering young Jack. The lumps of clothing seen from the water were now visible as torn up and decomposed bodies, with rib cages, leg bones and flesh-covered skulls scattered about. Some of the rib cages were broken, like something strong had broken them apart, desperate to get to the soft organs inside. The struck cars with the bodies inside, barely visible through the cloudy windows, probably having starved or died of thirst, knowing they were trapped in the immovable traffic jam, with the zeds patiently waiting outside. The homes and small businesses with shattered windows, bullet holes in them...

Fred swallowed again. Jack said, "Uncle Brad, suppose we see a zed. What should we do?"

Brad said, "If they're just dragging along and aren't bothering us, leave 'em alone. You only want to shoot them if they're a threat. Thing is, they're hard to kill, they are. Headshots will knock 'em back, but you and Fred, with your shotguns, I'd aim for the legs, the knees. Don't matter how crazed or hungry they are, if they ain't got working knee joints, they ain't going far."

Her voice trembling, Janet said, "Can we talk about something else?"

Brad said, "We can talk all you want about something else, but we were talking important."

Up ahead was the bright red and white sign for Arjay's Hardware, and Fred said, "We're there. Good."

Janet shrugged off her knapsack and said, "Okay. I ain't going in there alone. Who's coming?"

Brad said, "I'll make a quick scan. If it's clear, I'll hang outside with Fred, and Jack, you can go in and help Janet find stuff."

Fred didn't like feeling like Brad was taking charge, but so far, he was making sense in everything he was doing and saying, so that was okay.

The front of Arjay's had broken display windows, and a shattered glass door. Their feet crunched on the glass as they got closer. "Hold on," Brad said, and holding his AR-15 out, he slowly walked in. Luckily the early noon sun was able to light up the interior of the hardware store.

Jack, Fred and Janet stayed together, and Fred realized his shotgun was in his hands. When had he taken it off his shoulder? He couldn't remember.

He kept on looking, up and down, up and down Harbor Road.

Save for the fat seagulls, nothing was moving.

Brad stepped out, nodding.

"It's clear," he said, voice muffled from his facemask. "Jack, go in with Janet. Help her out. You see something moving, shoot it."

"Got ya, Uncle Brad."

Janet and Jack then ducked into the store.

Brad came next to Fred.

"Hell of a thing," Brad said.

"Yeah."

A few minutes passed and then there was something yellow that caught his eye. On the north side of the road, stumbling along. Fred cleared his throat. "Looks like we got a zed over there."

Brad grunted, took out a small pair of binoculars from his coat, and Fred felt a blush of shame. He should have brought along binoculars, too. That had been good planning on Brad's part.

"Yeah, a zed. It's wearing some long type of raincoat. But it's heading away. That's good."

"Sure is," Fred said.

Brad put the binoculars back and said, "It's weird, isn't it. You'd think this place would be crawling with zeds. But where the hell are they?"

"Who knows," Fred said, wiping one sweaty hand and then the other on his pants. "Maybe they eventually died off. Or wandered away. You know, there should be fewer in the spring, after winter comes through. That'd be good."

Brad kept quiet. Fred could hear voices from inside the abandoned hardware story. *Hurry up*, he thought, *hurry the Christ up*.

Brad said, "The Hannaford's Supermarket is only a mile or so from here. On the state road."

"Unh-hunh."

"Thing is," Brad said, "I could run up there while Janet and Jack are still working. Be back in no time."

"With what?" Fred asked, still looking at the faint form of the yellow-clad zed moving away.

"Shit, plenty of vehicles around. Wouldn't take much to get one of 'em started."

"Brad, no," Fred said. "We're here to get spare parts, and a spare generator, and that's it."

"Yeah, but look, it wouldn't take much. Run in there, scoop up a few boxes of canned food, toss it in the back of a truck. I don't know about you, but I'm sick of eating clams, lobster and fish. It's like I'm going to a goddamn seafood restaurant every day. Hell, the stuff at the supermarket will still be good. Canned hash. Beef stew. Even Spam would taste pretty good after all that fish. Plus the canned fruits and vegetables. Help brighten everyone's diet."

"That's not why we're here. We'll stay put."

"Says who?"

Fred paused. There was a tone in Brad's voice that he didn't like. "Says me," Fred said. "I organized this party, got the boat, and I'm the chairman of the Board of Selectmen."

Brad raised his eyebrows. "Yeah, but we're in Gilbert, Maine, ain't we. You're not the chairman of anything here."

Before anything else could happen, Janet stepped out, eyes bright above her facemask. She was followed by Jack, who was carrying two bulging white plastic shopping bags that had ARJAY SAVES YOU TIME AND MONEY in bright blue.

"Pay day," she said, patting the side of her now-full knapsack. "Got more than enough spare parts, picked up some extra tools, and lookee here." She motioned to Jack, who came forward and opened up the bag.

Fred glanced inside, licked his lips. Candy bars, crackers, little containers of peanuts. Janet said, "They had these little grocery shelves by the cash registers. We cleared 'em out, and also got a lot of OTC stuff from the medicine section. Bandages, painkillers, cold remedies. Nothing too powerful but it's better than nothing."

"You and Jack did good," Fred said. "What about the generator?"

Janet wiped at her sweaty brow. "Well, that's when luck comes in. I hope." She gestured to the rear of the store. "Out back there's a fenced-in area where they kept the big-ticket items, like lawnmowers and rototillers, snowblowers in the fall. I came here before...it started, and I know they had at least four generators back there, in a shed."

Brad said, "Hell, let's go."

They walked around the corner down a side street, and Fred kept looking to the rear, thinking about all of those World War II movies he had seen, where the Japs or Nazis would pop out of nowhere and start shooting. But so far, so good. Only one zed sighted and they were halfway through their mission.

The road was narrow, residential, and except for the still cars and the tall grass from the small lawns, nothing looked out of place. To the left was a high chain-linked fence with a two-gate opening, chained, and then Jack said, "Uncle Brad, I need to go to the bathroom."

"Then do it," his uncle replied. "Lots of trees and brush around, go for it. We won't look."

"No ... it's, well, I gotta take a dump."

Brad swore and said, "Then if you're so goddamn shy, then go up there and go around the corner. But keep your eyes open. You don't want a zed chomping on you while you're wiping your ass."

Jack gently dropped the two plastic shopping bags on the ground by the fence, and said, "I won't be long, honest."

He ran up the street, carrying his shotgun at port arms, and then Fred joined Janet at the fence, and she laughed.

"Look," she said. "Isn't this a piece of luck? The gates ain't locked. Just a chain running through."

She dragged the chain through and pushed open the two gates, which swung open without even a creak. Janet walked in, followed by Fred, with Brad bringing up the rear. They walked past rows of lawn mowers, riding mowers, and rototillers. At the far corner was an open shed, and there were wooden pallets on the asphalt floor. Torn boxes, plastic wrapping and Styrofoam was spread around. Janet stepped cautiously forward, pulled away some of the trash, revealing a soggy yet unopened cardboard crate, announcing that it held a twelve-thousand-watt portable gasoline-powered generator.

"Only one left," Janet said, checking all sides of the crate. "One left ... and it hasn't even been opened. Christ, we're full of luck today."

Fred was going to agree when there was a loud noise, and then their luck left them.

He spun at the sound and gaped as a black Ford F-150 pickup truck backed up the short street and into the lot, engine roaring, smoke spewing from the tail pipe, and Jack Tiller stuck his head out of the driver's side window and yelled, "C'mon Uncle Brad, let's go!"

Brad ran to the truck and his nephew leaned over, popped open the door, and before Brad jumped in, he yelled back, "We'll be back as soon as we can! You can thank us later!"

The truck roared out of the lot, striking one of the open gates, and the last thing Fred saw was the truck's Maine license plate and a bumper sticker for last year's Fryeburg Fair.

Janet came up next to him. There was a fresh smell of a gasoline engine. She said, "Mind telling me what the hell that was all about?"

Fred said, "Brad wanted to take a truck or a car, head up to the Hannaford's Supermarket, go in and grab whatever canned goods he could get, and then come back. I told him not to go. He said since I was Selectmen Chairman for Massabesic, and not Gilbert, I had no authority over him."

"Shit," Janet said.

"Yeah."

Using a pallet with wheels and a tall handle to push, he and Janet got the heavy—"And this is what they mean by portable," she groaned—generator down to the town dock, along with her knapsack full of tools and the two shopping bags filled with other goodies. It was hard, sweaty work—especially since they still had on their facemasks and heavy clothing—and it was also nerve wracking. Fred kept on looking around and up and down the street, just in case the zeds burst out of the broken and destroyed stores and homes.

But they only shared their journey with the fat seagulls, and Fred didn't like to ponder over what had made these birds so plump.

When they got to the end of the dock, Janet shaded her eyes and said, "I see Patrick out there, making big circles in the water. I have half a mind to wave the orange flag, have him come in, make the Tiller boys spend the night by themselves in Gilbert. It's obvious they had planned it."

"Yeah," Fred said.

"So why don't we do just that?" she asked. "Leave 'em behind for the night."

Fred looked up the length of the dock, with the heavy park benches, the trash barrels, the piles of lobster trap and other gear still sitting where it belonged. "Guess it wouldn't be right."

From behind her mask, Janet snorted. "What's right anymore? Hunh? The Federal law? Laws of the State of Maine? It's probably just us here on the island that's alive in the whole state of Maine...you know."

Fred said, "Then we'll keep on doing what's right."

"Hunh." She paused and said, "What do you think is going on...out there?"

A splotch of blue that came and went up on the other side of town. Another zed, stumbling along? At least it was moving away from them. "I don't know. I really don't care anymore. I used to care, but now all I care about is the island, the people, and my family."

Janet said, "The diesel and gasoline...it's gonna last us maybe six, eight months more if we're lucky. Then what?"

"Then I guess we go back in time, like Buster said. We'll really be on our own then, won't we."

"But what about those survivors from down Florida way... the Wolf Squadron that Chris Allain heard on his radio. If they found out we was alive, maybe they could help us."

Fred said, "You think so? You're down in Florida and the Bahamas, it's nice and warm, no snow or ice, you want to think about coming all the way up to Maine? With the North Atlantic storms? I don't think so. It don't make sense. We're on our own, and will be for a long, long time to come."

The assistant public works director was going to say something else when the blaring of a horn and the sound of a racing engine reached them, and Janet said, "Oh for Christ's sake, look!"

Fred looked and nearly pissed himself. The black Ford pickup truck was roaring back in town, Jack the driver frantically honking the horn. Fred couldn't quite grasp what he was seeing. It took him a moment to realize the truck was covered with—

"Zeds!" Janet screamed. "They're all over that damn truck!"

It snapped into focus. Two zeds were on the front hood, hammering at the windshield with what was left of their fists. Zeds were also hanging on to both side mirrors, being dragged along, and maybe six or eight were jammed in the open truck bed, trying to get into the rear window, crawling over each other and fighting to be first to break through and get to the two humans inside. Fred had a sudden and terrifying memory as a young boy, watching one of those nature documentaries on educational TV, showing a fast-forward film of a swarm of hungry ants crawling over some animal carcass, stripping it down to its bones.

The horn kept on blaring and blaring, and then the truck rammed right into a concrete planter on the strip of park grass, the truck rearing up like a frightened horse, most of the zeds flying or tumbling free.

The passenger door flew open and Brad ran by the front of the cracked planter and the crumpled front end of the Ford, yelling, "Help us, for Christ's sake, help us!"

Brad spun and, with AR-15 in his hands, fired off two bursts that knocked down three zeds, and then he ducked as one zed nearly grabbed him, and Brad fired another long burst into the zed's back, crumpling him into the tall grass. Brad checked his AR-15, replaced the magazine—and Fred thought *so much for fire discipline*—and Brad screamed, "Come on, help us! There's more coming! And Jack can't get his door open!"

Mouth dry, hands and knees shaking, Fred wanted nothing more to do than to jump in the water and paddle to the nearest boat, but he ran down the length of the dock, lifting up his Remington pump-action 12-gauge, not sure if he was close enough and part of him thinking, *can we really do this,* and two zeds who were in the rear of the truck started running to Brad as he fumbled with his magazine, both of them with teeth bared in their rotting faces, hands with long fingernails extended.

*BLAM!*

*BLAM!*

Both zeds fell to the ground, like they were puppets being controlled by invisible overhead wires that had suddenly been cut, and even the rear side panel of the crashed truck was instantly pockmarked by his rounds.

Brad was at the driver's side door, tugging and tugging, the reloaded AR-15 in one hand, and Janet got off two shots with her .357 Ruger revolver, knocking another zed to the ground.

The uncle yelled to his nephew, "Cover your eyes!" and he smashed the driver's side window with the butt of his semiautomatic rifle, and Jack Tiller managed to crawl out, dragging his shotgun behind him, and he fell to the grass. Janet called out, "Shit, they're coming down the road!"

Fred saw another dozen zeds were coming down the road, most running, others shambling and tripping along, weaving in and out of the stalled or parked cars, and Fred said, "Brad, what the hell did you do?"

"Later, later, come on, let's hole up somewhere," he yelled, and Fred yelled back, "No! We'll fight 'em off at the dock and call in Patrick to pick us up. We can't leave the generator and those parts behind."

Janet fired one more time, in an approved two-hand combat stance. "Fred's right, we hole up, the zeds will chase us in and they won't leave us alone until they kill us. Get down to the dock!"

Janet started running, and Fred was right behind her, and then she reached the piles of lobster traps, and started pushing them over, and Fred instantly knew what she was doing, and he slung his shotgun over his shoulder, went to one of the park benches, started dragging it to the barrier Janet was building. She was breathing hard. "It won't stop them but it'll sure as hell slow 'em down." She turned and said, "Tillers! Haul ass!"

Brad and Jack were running as fast as they could, and surprisingly enough, the older one, Brad, was about two yards in front of his nephew. Three zeds were chasing them, not moving very fast, but pretty damn fast indeed.

Janet shoved more lobster traps, leaving a narrow gap for the Tillers, and Fred held up his shotgun.

"Run!" he yelled.

They kept on running.

And Jack might have made it, except for his ponytail.

One of the zeds—who looked like she might have been a pretty young girl before she changed—snarled and leapt at Jack's back, and managed to grab his ponytail and take him down. His shotgun flew out of his hands and he screamed, "Uncle Brad! Uncle Brad!"

Then he screamed even louder as a larger and male zed shoved aside the zed girl, and bit down hard at the base of the young man's neck and started tearing away at the flesh.

His uncle turned around and fired off a group of shots that killed the two other zeds, just leaving the one on top of his nephew, and Jack screamed again, "Get it off me! Get it off me! Jesus help me!"

Fred had his shotgun in his hands but hesitated, afraid he would hit the boy with the spray of buckshot, and Brad cursed and tried to circle around to get a shot, and then there was a hollow *BOOM!* as Janet fired off a round from her revolver, taking off the top of the zed's skull.

Brad grabbed his nephew at the shoulder and thought enough to also grab the discarded shotgun, and Fred went forward, took another shoulder, as Jack alternately cried and screamed, "It bit me! It bit me hard! Oh Jesus, I don't want to become one of them! I don't want to! Uncle Brad! Oh, Jesus!"

Brad cursed and said, "Jesus isn't going to help you so shut your trap."

The trio pushed through the narrow opening, Jack being dragged along, and Janet was there, pushing a park bench in place, and Fred joined in, putting up more barriers with anything he could drag over. He stepped back just as a growling and hissing zed arrived—an older man who still had a white beard on his shrunken face—and Fred nailed him in his skinny chest with another 12-gauge blast.

Jack was stretched out on his belly on the dock, crying and screaming, and Brad had a knife in his hand, and sliced away the ponytail, tossing it aside. "Fool, you should have listened to your mom, got your damn hair cut."

Janet came up with a bucket and she said, "Salt water. It's gonna hurt but maybe...maybe it'll help."

Brad said, "Pour some of it."

She turned over the white bucket and a stream of harbor salt water hit the open wound at the base of Jack's neck, and he screamed and screamed. His uncle tapped him on the head and said, "Stop with the noise! You're so damn loud we'll have zeds coming up from Portland!"

Brad had a rolled up kerchief in his hand, and he wiped away the blood and salt water, exposing the open wound and torn flesh. Fred looked away, breathed hard.

"More water."

Janet dumped the rest of the water on Jack and he kept it to a low groan, and Brad said in a soothing voice, "I'm gonna bandage you up, best I can, and then we'll get back to the island, and Doc Molly, well, she can work miracles. You'll see."

Jack sobbed again. "I don't wanna change. I'm so scared. I don't wanna change."

Brad patted his shoulder. "You won't. I promise you that. You won't."

"Uncle . . . if I change . . . please shoot me . . . okay? Please shoot me."

He started bandaging up the boy's neck and said, "Where the hell is Patrick?"

Fred said, "Time for him to come. Show 'em the flag, Janet."

Janet ran down to the end of the dock, where the precious generator, knapsack full of tools and other bags of treasures waited. She pulled out the large orange flag—about half her size—and started waving it back and forth, back and forth.

Fred peered around the barrier. Two more zeds were coming up the dock.

*BLAM!*

*BLAM!*

One fell back, and the other, just a kid—he couldn't tell if it had been a boy or girl—fell into the harbor.

But he looked up the road.

More zeds were coming.

Many more.

He stepped back. "Brad . . . what the hell happened? Where are all these zeds coming from?"

Brad shook his head and kept on working on his nephew, like he was too ashamed to raise his head.

"We were gone, maybe a third of a mile, when a zed jumped out from in front of a school bus, full of . . . well, it was full . . . and Jack couldn't stop fast enough, and he ran him down, and the zed screeched some, and that noise must have attracted other zeds, in the houses, and . . . they came out. They just kept on coming out. Like bats coming out of a cave at night."

Fred peered around again. About a half-dozen more were coming straight to the dock, with dozens more coming down the road.

Time.

If Patrick got here in the next couple of minutes, it would be tight going, but they could still safely make it.

Then Janet screamed.

He whirled around, wondering if a zed had gotten her, but no, she was still alone at the dock's end, jumping up and down, waving the orange flag, and she yelled, "You asshole! You son of a bitch! Don't you dare leave us!"

It was like a concrete chunk from one of the park benches was now resting on Fred's chest.

For that's exactly what Patrick was doing.

Turning his boat around and speeding home to the safety of Massabesic Island.

A lobster trap fell and a zed tried to push through, and using Jack's shotgun, Brad blew off its head, and Brad stepped forward, shoved the lobster trap back into place.

"All right," he said, breathing heavy. "What the hell do we do now?"

Janet was crying. "That bastard . . . he left us. He left us behind. That bastard . . ."

Fred thought, well, here you go. Everyone's looking to you as a leader. But this sure as hell ain't approving a town budget or looking at how much it'd cost to transport a new fire truck to the island.

"Three of us stay here, fight 'em off. The other one swims out to one of them boats, find one they can start up, get back here. If we have to, we'll leave the generator here, come back for it later."

Zeds were crawling over the barrier, and he and Janet and Brad blasted them back. These were residents of Gilbert, citizens of the State of Maine, and some were probably acquaintances or folks he knew, but that didn't matter anymore to Fred. They were turned, they were zeds, and they were wearing the remnants of tattered human clothing, but they had to be shot, crippled, killed.

When the gunfire halted for a moment, Fred stepped back and nearly slipped and fell from stepping on an empty shotgun shell. Brad said, "That sounds like a good idea, but I can't swim. And Jack's not up for swimming. Janet?"

Janet had the cylinder of her revolver open, trying to reload it. Both hands were shaking hard. Every other cartridge fell to the dock, and when she was done, she knelt down and frantically scooped up the ones that fell.

She looked up. "Oh, yeah. I can swim. Like a goddamn brick. Fred?"

He licked his dry lips from underneath the facemask. "Yeah, I can swim—"

"Shit, here they come again!" Brad yelled, and stretched on the dock, Jack screamed, "Don't let them bite me again! Don't let them bite me! Uncle Brad!"

Fred wasn't sure if the zeds were learning from what was going on, but instead of going over the jumbled barrier of trash barrels, lobster traps, and park benches, the zeds were forcing themselves against the barrier, like a herd of water buffaloes, pushing against an obstacle. Fred fired, catching the first zed coming through, and one following him was cut down, and then another, and the bodies piled up, and through the hissing, screeching and moans, the sounds of the gunfire just hammered at his ears.

Another pause. Fred was breathing so hard he was tempted to tear away the face mask, but a tiny rational part of him thought, no, don't do that, you might get infected, and he had a harsh laugh, knowing that he was about to get infected in a few minutes anyway. One more zed came over the barrier and tumble of bodies, and he fired again, and his shotgun clicked empty.

With hands shaking as bad as Janet's, he tried to take his time reloading, but time was one thing they didn't have.

"Again!" Brad yelled.

Fred shouldered his shotgun and took out his SIG Sauer, and then three more zeds tumbled over the bodies of their mates.

He backed away. Janet and Brad did the same, Brad hauling his nephew by his coat collar, Jack's eyes just visible above the facemask and scrunched with pain.

Janet said, "Well? You gonna swim or what?"

Brad said, "You better strip then, 'cause those clothes will sink you."

"How much ammo you guys got left?"

Janet said, "Maybe four shots. I'm too scared to look."

Brad said, "I'm using Jack's shotgun. I don't know. Just a few more. My AR-15 is out."

He was going to take a moment to reload the shotgun, and this time, the zeds broke through the barrier.

They stormed up the dock and Fred had another flashback, seeing the clips of the running of the bulls in Spain, but these Maine bulls were ready to tear you open and bite you and eat you and rip you to pieces, and the gunfire started up again, and Lori's voice hammered at him: *"If things go bad, you leave 'em all behind, you steal a boat back, you swim, by Christ, but you come back."*

Bad? They had about three yards of clear space behind them, cluttered with the generator and bags of supplies, and Fred thought, well, he was going to go into the water, one way or another, but Brad was right, he was going to sink like a stone, but better than—

Janet yelled, "I'm out of ammo! I'm out! Oh Jesus!"

As he brought up his SIG Sauer once more, he thought of giving her his shotgun and a handful of shells.

*POW!*

All right, that won't work. Not enough time!

Young Jack was still screaming.

Fred fired again.

*POW!*

A zed who looked to be a nice young woman with open sores and wounds on her ribcage came at him, teeth bared.

*POW!*

Brad yelled, "I'm out, I'm out!"

Fred said, "Behind me!"

He fired again.

*POW!*

And the SIG Sauer's slide snapped back and didn't return.

Empty.

The zeds were a solid mass coming at them now, and for Christ's sake, he could smell them, the smell of death and decay and rot, and he ejected the empty magazine, fumbled in his coat for a spare magazine, knowing he wouldn't make it, wouldn't make it, wouldn't—

The sound of a nearby gunshot nearly tore off his head, and there were yells and he spared a quick glance, and there was another figure there, and he had a wild thought, did a zed just swim around and climb up the dock, but this zed had a military-style cut-down M4 automatic rifle, and he was pushing by them, slowly but firmly walking to the zeds, firing careful three-shot bursts:

*POW! POW! POW!*

Again, and again.

He moved steadily, without fear, shooting off the three-round bursts, and Fred was amazed at how specific and well-aimed the shots were: one to each knee, and then one to the forehead. The zeds collapsed before the man, who had on military BDUs and was carrying a MOLLE vest and small knapsack on his back, black baseball cap on his head. The shooter pressed on, not hesitating, and when a magazine was empty, he changed it out in seconds, hardly interrupting the rhythm. For each three shots fired, a zed fell, either on the dock or into the harbor, and Fred felt his breathing ease.

It was a terrible, horrible, awesome sight to see, a warrior ballet, as the shooter moved towards the broken barrier. At some point the zeds—maybe some of them maintaining some sort of consciousness and recognizing the threat from the shooter—pushed back, falling over into each other, the fire taking them down: the young boy, the housewife with the tattered remnants of an apron dangling from her waist, and the young man, all with rotting flesh, bare teeth, bulging eyes and grasping hands.

All brought down to the now-slippery dock or the unforgiving harbor.

Then it was quiet.

The man gave a quick glance back, started walking backwards, still keeping watch on whatever threat might emerge, and when he got back to Fred and his group, he turned and said, wearing a facemask but eyes shiny with a harsh joy, "Christ, Fred, now I know why you didn't want me to come. You wanted all the fun to yourself!"

It was Gil Pachter, former military man and deputy chief of police.

Fred wanted to say something but the words wouldn't come, and Gil took a quick evaluation of the situation.

"I know you didn't want me out here, Fred, but I felt like doing a little fishing, and I saw Patrick Beecham hauling ass back to the island, with a bone in his teeth, so I figured I'd come over and check things out."

He looked down at Jack and said, "What happened to the kid?"

Brad wiped at his eyes. "He got bit by a zed. Janet washed off the wound with some salt water. We're hoping that might have helped."

"You never know, but Doc Molly will be the one to tell us, once we get back," Gil said. "Janet, it looks like you got your generator and whatever else you need, but none of that will fit in my skiff. You think you can take my skiff, go out in the harbor and find a big enough boat? And get it started and back over here?"

Janet wiped at her eyes as well. "You bet your ass."

The next words were said in a humorous tone, but there was steel in each syllable.

"Make sure you come back for us, all right," Gil said.

Janet went down to where the open flat-bottomed aluminum skiff waited. "Gil, when we get back to the island, I'll give you a night you'll never forget, even though it will piss off my girl something fierce."

Gil said, "Hell of an offer, but just get back here, soon as you can."

He dumped his knapsack on the deck, and pulled out two SIG Sauer pistols and said, "I got four magazines for each. Should be plenty, 'cause I don't expect to be here long. Hey, Fred, can you help me out?"

Fred said, "Gil . . . I mean . . . how can we . . ."

"Stow it for later," Gil said. "Here, take this and bring it down about halfway to the dock. There's a couple of scissor legs. Stand it up. You see the lettering there, where it says FRONT TOWARD ENEMY. Make sure you point it in the right direction, and spool out the wire nice and straight back to me. I'll hold onto the other end."

Fred just nodded, going toward the middle point of the dock, which was still littered with zed bodies and body parts.

Nothing was moving.

Thank God, nothing was moving.

He found a clear spot, positioned the heavy concave piece of plastic—some sort of mine or explosive, he thought—and the metal stands fit well into the gaps between the dock's planking.

There was a shout and when he looked up, a zed was staring down at him.

The zed was big, staring. It was a male with a Yankees tattoo on its arm. The face was nearly covered with a heavy, full beard, and its eyes were wide and bulging and it growled.

Fred grabbed the borrowed SIG Sauer, tried to step back,

tripped on a zed arm and fell, and he yelled, "Go away! Don't come any closer! Go away!"

The zed growled louder and came at him, and Fred fired six shots into it before it collapsed.

He got on his feet and ran back, and Gil slapped him on the back.

"Good shooting," he said.

Fred just nodded. "It . . . it looks like more are coming."

A horn sounded. A fishing boat was coming their way, towing Gil's skiff at the rear, the smaller boat skipping and slapping against the small waves.

Gil said, "Brad, you get your nephew on first. Then come back and help us get everything back on board, including the shotguns."

"You got it."

The boat circled around and although Janet wasn't as good a boat pilot as Patrick, she managed to bump her way up to the dock. She jumped off and secured a line to a cleat, and then Brad got his nephew on board and came back out. It took some heavy lifting and grunts, but the spare generator, the knapsack of spare parts and the two shopping bags from Arjay's were carefully put on board.

Janet undid the lines and Fred looked at the end of the dock, and more zeds were coming, grunting and squealing, even now pushing aside the barriers. Janet, Brad and Jack were on the boat, and Gil put a strong hand on the back of Fred's neck and pushed him flat to the dock.

"Keep your head down, in case there's some ricochets."

"Some what?" Fred asked.

Instead of answering, Gil pressed something in his hand hard twice—*click-click*—and there was a massive *BOOM!* that shook the dock and set up a cloud of smoke and debris, and when Gil grabbed his M4 and battle pack, Fred looked on in awe at the damage the explosive had caused . . . it had shredded scores of zeds and had blown away the rest of the barrier.

Gil tugged at him and brought him to the boat.

"When you care enough to send the very best, seven hundred steel balls will do the trick," Gil said. "God, I love this shit."

Some long minutes later, they were going back to Massabesic Island. Gil took over the helm of the boat—the *Jeannette Y*—and

Brad tended to his nephew, and Janet sat next to Fred. It was crowded in the boat and she rode low, but the water was calm and they were in no danger of being swamped.

Fred tore off his facemask and took a series of deep cleansing breaths. Out here, at least, all he could smell was the diesel. Everybody else on the boat followed his lead.

Janet said, "Ask you a question?"

"Sure."

"Before the mine went off, when you were setting it up ... that big zed was coming at you. The one with a Yankees tattoo."

Fred kept quiet.

Janet said, "Thing is, I remember your brother-in-law John, back when he ran the Gilbert service station, he loved showing off the Yankees tattoos on his bare arms all summer long, he liked to piss off the Red Sox fans around here. Right?"

"Yeah," Fred said.

"And he had a big bushy beard, I remember."

The boat moved along, and Brad was talking softly to his nephew.

"The thing is," Janet said. "That last zed you shot, I could have sworn that was John. Am I right?"

"No," Fred said. "You saw wrong. It wasn't a Yankees tattoo. And it wasn't John."

Janet nodded, peered over the side, looked at Massabesic Island coming closer.

"I guess I was wrong, then," Janet said. "My mistake. I won't mention it again."

"Thanks."

Near sunset and after the short trial, a good chunk of the townspeople were gathered at the town dock, although Fred made sure his son and daughter weren't there. The outcome had been a forgone conclusion, but Fred managed to convince Paul Lucian and Matilda Grant, the other two selectmen, to show some mercy.

Now Patrick Meecham was alone off the dock, in an open rowboat with oars, with as much supplies and clothing that could fit in, ready to face his exile.

His wife Donna, and their kids Roger, Bob and Carolyn, were nowhere to be seen. They had not been sentenced to exile, but they could accompany Patrick if they chose to do so, with another rowboat or two to go along.

Fred thought, well, Donna had made her choice.

Patrick's face was beet red and he called out, "I was scared, that's all! I was scared! I saw all the zeds running down that dock and I thought they was all a goner! And I didn't want a bunch of zeds jumping into my boat."

Nobody said a word. He looked from face to face from his friends and fellow townspeople, and then, clumsily, he took one and then another oar out, and put them in their oarlocks. Just before he started, he called out, "To hell with you all and this damn island. Damn you all to hell!"

A voice came out from the crowd: "Too late, Pat, we're already there."

Some rough laughter at that, and then Patrick started rowing out of the harbor, and most townspeople started drifting away. Fred slipped his hand into his wife's and stayed and watched, fulfilling his duty as selectmen chairman, until Patrick was no longer in view.

Lori leaned into him. "How rough was it over there?"

"Very rough."

She said, "Brad Tiller took Jack back to their house. Doc Molly...she's not optimistic. Brad's watching over Jack. The boy isn't doing good."

"Yeah."

"Franny Jones, she told me that she heard Brad say that if his nephew started turning, that he would do something."

"I believe that."

Paul Lucian came by, slowly pushing Matilda Grant in a wheelchair, and they both nodded to Fred. Matilda reached out a wrinkled and bony hand and touched Fred's arm. "You and the others...you saved us, by God, you saved us."

"For a while, at least," Fred said.

When they had left, Lori said, "I need to ask you something, Fred, and by God, you tell me the truth. Did you see Jack over there? Did you?"

Fred thought of the bearded shape he saw back over in Gilbert, the monster that was no longer human, with a Yankees tattoo.

"I swear to God, Lori, I didn't see him. Not at all."

"All right."

He turned and they walked together, back up the gravel path that would eventually lead to their house, and Lori said, "We've got power for another six to eight months. Thanks to you, Fred."

"Wasn't just me."

"But you pushed it. You made it happen."

"It's my job. We...we need to look out for each other. This island. Our friends, our neighbors."

"Our family," Lori interrupted.

"Yes, always, our family," Fred said, suddenly feeling exhausted by this long and horrific day. "Everyone needs to look out for family."

They soon approached their house, and a couple of candles had been lit by the front door by their children, and they kept walking, hand in hand, until there was a single gunshot, coming from up the road, where the Tiller residence was located.

Lori squeezed Fred's hand, and he squeezed back.

# The Species as Big as the Ritz

## ROBERT BUETTNER

The Himalayan night was so still that when the crusted snow crunched beneath Peter Condon's boots the sound crackled back from the canyon walls like pistol fire. But the sandaled feet of the maroon-robed monk who led Condon glided so silently that the snow seemed unmoved by his passing. One hundred yards above them the monastery hung from the mountainside, more gilded bird house than fortress.

The monk, walking staff in his left hand, sputtering lantern dangling from his upraised right hand, sprang from boulder to boulder with nimble economy born of a lifetime at altitude. Wheezing, backsliding, and stumbling, Condon in that moment realized that Embassy-gym CrossFit was a crap substitute for a lifetime of PT and full-pack forced marches.

*Yeeeooo.*

The wail echoed down the canyon, then was complemented by a second, higher pitched tone.

The monk peered up into the moonless darkness. "They sing to mourn their children."

Condon blinked as the wind revived, and needled snow against his upturned face. He felt with a mittened hand for the .45 holstered beneath his parka. "Are they dangerous?"

The monk cocked an eyebrow at Condon's reflex, then climbed ahead. "Perhaps it is they who are entitled to ask that question."

By the time the monastery doors slammed behind Condon and the monk, the renewed storm screeched outside and rattled the building's window shutters. Smoke from tiers of butter lamps blurred the double rank of lacquered pillars that lined the main hall, and the lamps' flames flickered from the draft Condon's arrival stirred.

In the hall's center Condon's crates lay unopened and unattended, but stacked in precise pyramids. The hired Sherpas had disappeared, as they had the previous afternoon, when they left Condon behind, gasping, to catch up with the monk's help.

As Condon stripped off his parka, and raked crusted ice from his eyebrows and stubble beard, the guide monk took his leave.

Another, older, monk approached and offered, in perfect English, a wide cup of steaming buttered tea. Condon thought it probably the most welcome beverage offer of his life.

He bowed his head. "No, thank you, Venerable Sir. I am quite full."

The monk offered the obligatory second time, which allowed Condon to reply with appropriate restraint. "Well, perhaps just a little."

The ritual lie completed, Condon clutched the cup with both hands, the ceramic's warmth as divine as the scalding bitterness on his tongue.

The host monk stared at Condon's shoulder-holstered .45. "You have not brought fuel for the generator that powers our library lights. Nor have you brought back to us the novice who delivered you our plea."

It was a statement, not a question, but the monk's stare demanded an answer. Lying was Condon's business, but he told the truth, because in this case it served just as well. "The courier who you sent to inquire about the fuel delivery interruption was killed. I assume the Sherpas told you this. But if they have not," he inclined his head again, "I offer both my condolences and my apologies for bringing such unwelcome news."

Condon's host nodded. "Your porters told us that a great and mortal pestilence dominates the land below. And that unfortunately the novice became infected. How long do you estimate before we receive generator fuel again?"

Condon sat on a stone bench and looked down at his boots as he unlaced them.

The truth was that the novice had been savaged short of the embassy by one of the innumerable packs of infected that roamed Kathmandu's ruined and deserted center. He reached the embassy compound's gates bitten through one cheek so deeply that his teeth showed, and he already presented early Level Three symptoms. He would have been put down rather than admitted if the infected hadn't gotten him first.

The truth was also that H7D3 was immeasurably worse than a "great and mortal pestilence." Human civilization had fallen so hard and so fast that no one up here at the Top of the World had heard the thud yet. H7D3 had bypassed, for now, only remote outliers that were geographically isolated or frigid. Or, like this place, both. Condon was a realist, and realists accepted that there would never be fuel deliveries again. Not here. Not anywhere.

But fatigue pressed down on Condon's shoulders as heavily as the burden of telling so many devastating truths. Without meeting the monk's eyes Condon answered his question with a shrugged half-lie. "Certainly not before next winter."

The monk showed Condon to a closet-sized cubicle furnished only with a sleeping mat, left a butter lamp and fresh tea, then turned to leave.

Condon said, "I've come to see Nickelson. He's here?"

The monk said, "He is unavailable to welcome you until the morning."

"Huh?"

The monk bowed as he backed into the corridor, then said as he vanished, "He has gone out for the evening."

Beyond the monastery's walls Condon heard shrieking wind that had swelled into a Himalayan blizzard, and nearby an avalanche rumbled. He had grown up in the Montana Bitterroots, and going out for the evening in a Montana blizzard was to going out for the evening in a Himalayan blizzard as a polite lie about tea was to bullshitting a holy man about the apocalypse.

Apparently, Condon wasn't the only one around here who was having difficulty telling the truth.

∾⊖∾

He slept until awakened, sweat-soaked in the cold darkness, by the too-true and recurrent nightmare of Bria kicking and screaming and reaching out for him as the jarheads closed the tailgate on her and the last convoy of Embassy staff rolled out for the coast. The realist in him had known the destroyer they were to rendezvous with wouldn't be there, even if they ran the twelve-hundred-kilometer gauntlet to the port at Chittagong.

Deluding himself that her chances were better that way, and that his duty still mattered, he had chosen duty over love, and would pay for his choice in nightmares for what remained of his life.

The same monk brought more buttered tea, yogurt, bread, and a fresh-lit butter lamp. Condon breakfasted, shivering cross legged on the stone floor in Gore-Tex long johns, while he reread the note. It was handwritten in indelible marker, and the courier had pushed it through the Embassy compound fence's bars, even as a pack of Alphas had dragged him away, weeping.

To: Condon, Peter, Deputy Cultural Attaché;
U.S. Embassy, Kathmandu, Nepal
From: Nickelson, Walter, Cultural Attaché
Via: Hand delivery, third-party courier
Text: Implement Yellow Hat Rising and you will find me.

The handwriting was unmistakably Nickelson's. So, too, the insistent formality. Nickelson had spent so many postdoctoral and foreign-posted years among the Brits that he wore a board up his ass only when a cricket bat was unavailable.

Uncharacteristically, he had sent the note in the clear. Unless the transparent lie that either his or Condon's real job involved culture counted as encryption. He had also sent the note by unvetted courier. Security breaches, true. But in name only, because the post-H7D3 enemy possessed the decryption skills of velociraptors.

Condon shook his head. It had taken him an hour back-checking files to find it.

Yellow Hat Rising had turned out to be a post-Cold-War contingency plan, still on the books after decades, to provide covert cross-border training and weapons support, in the event the Tibetans home-brewed a credible rebellion against China.

But only if the rebellion happened at a moment when the U.S.

was sufficiently pissed off at China to meddle in Tibet, which was real estate the Chinese believed they had stolen as fair and square as the U.S. had stolen Montana from the Blackfeet and the Crow.

"Yellow Hat" referred to the bon, the enormous, crested, daffodil-hued headgear his current hosts wore when they wanted to really blow it out while chanting and praying.

Condon swore. Despite the diverse workforce required to keep American fingers in all the world's pies, the Agency often made personnel decisions like it was still the Ivy League white boys' club it was born as.

What if the Agency had let employees like Nickelson, a Princeton Ph.D. biochemist, do the jobs they were hired for, which in Nickelson's case had been to defend against biohacker bathtub viruses? Instead of agreeing with Nickelson that a Princeton Man, by definition, possessed the skills and demeanor for third-world field operations? And assigning him to babysit a never-gonna-happen insurrection that some fool expected would be incited by pacifists in funny hats?

Would H7D3 then have never happened? Would Condon have been awakened this morning by Bria's whispered obscenities, in senior NCO housing somewhere warm, safe, and green?

To reinter the ghosts and the what-ifs he forced himself through PT in place until he collapsed, and lay gasping, his cheek wet with his drool as it puddled on the floor's cold stones.

After time passed he stood, dressed, and repocketed Nickelson's note.

The chain of command, at the ass end of which Nickelson and Condon dangled, had been decapitated, like the rest of civilization. But Nickelson remained Kathmandu station chief and Condon his Assistant SC until somebody credible said otherwise. So Condon laced up his boots, zipped his parka, and set out to find the boss he had presumed dead.

Outside the monastery the clear cold after the storm was as breathtaking as the snow that accompanied it was blinding. So Condon blinked when, after just a hundred-meter route march up the canyon, he saw through slitted eyes a shimmering white ghost, advancing toward him and howling.

He blinked again and recognized Nickelson's yowl before he identified the academic's knees-high waddle through a churned

snowfield that marked the previous night's avalanche. The shim-
mers, Condon realized, were the breeze-animated strands of a
half-ass sniper's ghillie suit. Cobbled from white yarn and braided
rags, the suit covered Nickelson from his boots to his egg head.

Nickelson flung his arms around Condon, pounded the taller
man's back with mittened fists. "Peter! My dear boy, I'd given
you up for dead!"

Condon pushed the un-dour, bubbly elf in the ghillie back to
arm's length to be sure it was really Nickelson. He had never
called his ASC anything less formal than Mr. Condon, much
less his dear boy. The religiously hand-scraped face was now
overgrown by white beard, and the joyless blue eyes behind
the wire rims were now afire, and moist with happy tears. Yet
it was Nickelson.

He spun Condon around, took his arm and walked the two
of them downslope toward the monastery. Cross-slung over his
back he wore a rifle, a last-century bolt action Lee-Enfield, its
rear sight filed off and replaced by a receiver-mounted 'scope.

Panting, legs punching knee-deep post holes with each step,
they descended through the lichen-studded chunks and deep
snow the avalanche had plowed down.

"Apologies for the obstacle course." Nickelson patted the leather
cartridge box attached to the sling that diagonaled across his
chest. "I was out hunting last night, but all my booming brought
down was this mélange."

Condon wrinkled his brow. During the two years he had
served under Nickelson, the man had approached annual weapons
qualification like a child forced to eat broccoli. Today he seemed
to have morphed into Santa Claus with a Buffalo Bill fetish.

The monastery's great hall was deserted, and Nickelson stepped
to and ran his hands over the pyramided crates. They had lain
locked away in an embassy subbasement storeroom until Condon, or more accurately the Sherpas Condon had overpaid, had
humped them up this mountain.

Nickelson said, "It's all here?"

Condon nodded. "Smartround long arms, athermal camo,
enough WAASPs to decapitate an infrastructure the size of Rhode
Island. And conventional small arms for the locals. None of it's
state-of-the-art anymore. But then neither are the bad guys." He
paused. "Sir, what the hell is going on?"

"Call me Nick, Peter. What about the team?" He pumped a fleshy fist. "Bright-eyed and bushy-tailed?"

Condon wrinkled his forehead again. "Sir—Nick—Yellow Hat called for a Special Forces A-Detachment sheep-dipped to the Agency to enter Nepal covered as twelve replacements assigned to the Embassy Marine Security Detail. They were to orient themselves, then infiltrate the Tibet Autonomous Region and train the insurgency in the use of the supplied materiel. Obviously, no sheep have been dipped lately, bushy-tailed or otherwise."

Nickelson eyed the equipment pyramids. "Then how did you...?"

"Most of the Embassy Marines escorted the exfiltrating embassy personnel to the coast. Four jarheads volunteered to stay behind and help me degrade the classified material and equipment. When we finished, it made no sense for them to die in place defending bricks and mortar. So, we loaded up the most reliable vehicles we had left and rolled north toward the grid coordinates of the in-country staging area specified in Yellow Hat. Which turns out to be here."

Nickelson smiled. "I was rather proud of the way I did that. Didn't reveal my location. But gave you the key to find it." He extended and joined the fingers of his right hand, palm down, and snapped off a salute. "Semper Fidelis! Yes, Marines should do nicely."

Condon rubbed his forehead. "You're not getting me, Nick. They *did* nicely. They fought like hell for every klick we crossed getting here. But all that made it here is me and these crates. Christ, you must know how hard the trip here was. 'Til I got your note I thought you were dead."

"Yes." Nickelson tapped a forefinger on his lower lip. "Yes, you and I must talk about that."

The monks, who had been on the Buddhist equivalent of mid-morning personal time, trickled from their sleeping chambers, the laundry, and the library, into the central hall. Those who passed close smiled and nodded, but in general the monks treated the pale giants among them as furniture.

Condon narrowed his eyes. "If Buddhists had commandments instead of tenets, the first one would be 'don't kill things.' So why are they letting us turn this place into Fort Apache?"

"Well, the first answer is we aren't. The second answer is they don't know. The third answer is the Agency has been buying their favor for years."

Condon glanced around the sparsely appointed hall. "Buying with what? Yak milk?"

The monks reached critical mass and sat to pray.

Nickelson pointed down the corridor that led to the sleeping chambers. "Shall we continue this discussion over tea in my abode?" He swayed side-to-side as he rolled his eyes. "Once the chanting starts you can't hear yourself think."

Judging by Nickelson's abode, whatever currency the Agency had been buying favor with, its exchange rate was crap. His chamber was the size of two closets, compared to Condon's one. The furniture consisted of a five-gallon oil tin converted into a charcoal burner, that vented some, but not all, its smoke through an unglazed wall slot that passed for a window.

Nickelson poured two teas from the dented kettle atop the burner, handed one across, then sat on the stone floor and motioned Condon to join him.

"Peter, Buddhist monks are mendicants. Their vow of poverty permits them to solicit and accept four requisites of life: food, clothing, shelter, and medicines. That last one is the hardest to come by from, or for the benefit of, lay Buddhists." Nickelson sipped. "Therefore, the Canadian Physicians Buddhist Foundation, a Canadian not-for-profit which the Chinese tolerated, because they didn't realize it was us, has been sending volunteer physicians each summer, and also donating funds, materials, and volunteer labor for the construction in this valley of a free clinic to serve the local population while researching the effects of altitude on their physiology. Been going on since before I took over in Kathmandu."

"The 'clinic' has *actually* been what?"

"A clinic. Sometimes the best way to make useful friends is to make friends. And we have. We even wired the monastery library with electric lights that run off the clinic generator. Therefore, this was my obvious option once I had my epiphany."

Condon shifted from his left butt cheek to his right. Getting to the point had never been Nickelson's forte, and that, at least, had not changed.

The station chief said, "You were in charge in Kat while I was running our human source trap lines in western Nepal when the H7D3 virus sacked South Asia."

"And last I heard you ran into a bad pack of infected out west. I made the only realistic assumption. Obviously, I was wrong."

Nickelson unbuttoned the cuff of his right sleeve, rolled it up to the elbow, and displayed the scars of opposed half-moon puncture wounds.

Reflexively, Condon gasped as he crabbed backward.

Nickelson shook his head. "In fact, you were largely right. As you see, I was bitten by a particularly nasty zed. I made the same assumption you did. I was a dead man walking. But the local source I had been cultivating, a second-generation Tibetan refugee whose lineage traced back to this valley, didn't know what you and I knew at that time. He dragged me, unconscious, back to the home he shared with his grandmother. Let her nurse me with home remedies, unaware that within ten days I would die. Or worse, I would turn, then murder them and devour their flesh, like the brain-dead beast I had become."

"But..."

"But neither happened. I recovered completely, as you can see."

Condon saw nothing of the kind.

About five percent of the population survived H7D3 infection, but with various permanent effects. Nickelson 2.0 may have inhabited the same body but H7D3 most viciously attacked the brain, and Nickelson's brain was so thoroughly rewired that he didn't even realize that Nickelson 1.0 had been a total prick.

Condon's own brain remained wired by a lifetime of duty. And duty didn't include telling the boss he was insane.

Instead, Condon said, "You're the one in twenty who survives, Nick. That's all."

"Applying Occam's razor, that's the simplest answer. Nickelson chose his ancestors wisely. Full stop. But why didn't my recruit and his grandmother contract the virus during days of close contact with me?" He shook his head. "No Princeton Man worth his education settles for an answer so pregnant with imperfections." He stood, reached for his coat, and tossed Condon his parka. "Peter, it appears it's just you and me. But I believe that, at this defining moment, we possess the means to rebuild civilization. Free of imperfections, this go-round."

Condon narrowed his eyes. "Nick, we're sitting in an unheated closet drinking tea with yak butter. Exactly what means do you think we possess?"

"My dear boy, we have the species as big as the Ritz."

A half mile up the canyon from the previous day's avalanche the clinic was so completely dug in to the mountain that Condon barely spotted it.

Nickelson keyed in the front door combination, smiling. "Blended with the pristine landscape as seamlessly as any environmentally rabid Canadian physician might want." He winked. "Also, as bombproof a headquarters bunker as any revolution might need."

Nickelson stepped inside, the lights came up, the heat kicked on, and somewhere a generator hummed to life.

"I thought they were out of fuel."

Nickelson shook his head. "They're merely disconnected. The Buddha didn't teach electrical engineering. It was the simplest way to get them to send a courier to you."

Across the clinic's unfurnished vestibule, a door stood open. In the center of the room beyond, Nickelson raised his arms and turned slowly. "Welcome to my la-*bore*-atory. Bwa-ha-ha."

Counters along the far walls were set with a microscope, a sleek box that Condon recognized as an in-clinic bench-top centrifuge, and additional sleek boxes he recognized as boxes about which he had no earthly clue.

Condon shook his head. "Nick, since things went to hell we've heard frag reports about vaccine research back in the first world. But I don't think a little old lady in Western Nepal got her hands on any. And vaccine keeps you from *getting* a virus. It doesn't cure it. Nothing cures H7D3. Full stop!"

Nickelson waved his hand as he nodded. "I should think there were been massive efforts to develop a vaccine. Or would have been while the requisite infrastructure survived. Another requisite would be neural tissue of infected organisms, in which to culture the virus. Which would be high-order primates. Specifically, humans because we appear to be the only hosts within which the virus was targeted to propagate."

"Grow this stuff in live people's brains?"

"Spines could do, I think. But your question highlights the difficulty in infecting healthy people, or in rounding up and vivisecting the living infected. The yield would be inadequate in any case. And the course of treatment, especially for early stage already-infected individuals, would require a series of injections similar to rabies treatment. But more painful and less effective."

Condon turned his palms up. "Back in the monastery you said something about us being special. A big species?"

Nickelson threw back his head and laughed. "I spoke metaphorically. You're from Montana. You're familiar with the classic novella *The Diamond as Big as the Ritz*?"

"I'm from Montana. I'm familiar with guns and sugar beets."

"Oh." Nickelson frowned. "Of course. Well, to begin with..."

Condon pointed to empty space along the wall behind himself. "I should sit down for this?"

"We both should." Nickelson stepped to the counters, opened a drawer beneath one, held up a pint of Canadian whisky and grinned. "A cover legend without detail is just bad fiction." He swigged from the bottle, then shrugged out of his jacket, laid it on the cold stone alongside Condon and sat on it.

"During the first half of the last century F. Scott Fitzgerald wrote fiction. As a fellow Princeton Man, I would argue it was *far* from bad fiction. In Fitzgerald's short novel *The Diamond as Big as the Ritz* a Montana resident discovers that a mountain on his presumed valueless property is in fact a single, gigantic diamond. *Bigger* than the Ritz, actually." He passed the bottle, tugged his impractical but correct fountain pen from his breast pocket and unscrewed its cap. "Have you something I can write on?"

Condon dug Nickelson's note from his pocket, handed it across, blank-side up, and Nickelson smoothed it on the stone floor between them. "These two diagrams—" He drew hexagons, and connected strings, of the letters C, O, and H, then straightened and said, "represent proteins manufactured by a body's immune system. Antibodies. Antibodies bind to foreign substances in the body, such as bacteria and viruses, and cause them to be destroyed." Nickelson pointed with his pen's nib, "*This* represents a well-known and typical antibody that's been effective in treating cardiovascular disease. *This* is an antibody I isolated here in this lab. It turned up in material with which I was treated for my H7D3 infection."

"They're different."

Nickelson nodded. "And *vive la différence*. Obviously, this peculiar rascal here not only vigorously attaches to and destroys the H7D3 virus; it acts as a template that the human body readily copies. It's naturally sourced, easily refined, can be administered orally and absorbed through the digestive system, and once introduced, self-propagates within the host organism. Absorbed through my intestines, it rapidly yielded an army of virus fighters."

"You're not exactly a double-blind FDA study."

"H7D3 isn't exactly the flu. Mankind must take the risk and deploy this gift *now*. Or perish."

A lifetime of service had taught Condon that it was not his place to second-guess his boss. And Nickelson, a biochemist, was right about the need to play a longshot when a winning ticket could save mankind.

Condon said, "So, exactly what is this stuff?"

Nickelson stood, walked to the whisky drawer, and returned, cradling in both hands a grapefruit-sized stoppered brown earthenware jar. "I was given a literal pinch of the powder in this jar in warm tea immediately and twice daily for two days thereafter. As my host's family had been given for various ailments for years."

"That jar's a sample," Condon pointed at the antibody diagram, "of this. And those letters you drew are carbon and oxygen and hydrogen. You can draw it. So, you can make more. Right, Nick?"

Nickelson shrugged. "Given facilities, trained personnel, and time. Of which mankind is presently fresh out. And my diagram is part conjecture. A mass-produced synthetic knockoff of the real thing could prove as dysfunctional as a street vendor's Rolex."

"So, this little jar is all there is? And you still haven't told me *what* it is."

"It is hand-ground desiccated epidermal tissue. Dried skin. Presumably well-vascularized skin, because dried blood is disproportionately included. A scalp, for example."

Condon nodded. "Head wounds bleed like a bitch. So what kind of scalp?"

"The very old kind, according to the woman who saved my life. And who I therefore vastly overpaid for this jar. Similarly represented relics have on closer examination turned out to be the scalps of Asiatic black bears and snow leopards. But this antibody's uniqueness, its effectiveness in combatting a virus that attacks only high-order primates, caused me to suspect this powder is just what the old woman claimed it is."

"And?"

"Peter, this jar contains the ground-up scalp of a Yeti."

Condon shook his head to clear it. At altitude a little Canadian whisky went a long way fast.

But actually, things were coming clear enough. Nickelson was one of the tiny minority who survived H7D3. But Nickelson's mind hadn't survived. Or perhaps his mind was suppressing guilt that if he had done his biochemical cop duty, instead of pursuing James Bond fantasies, the world wouldn't be screwed. Or both. Nickelson was insane. But what kind of insane?

He was a different person. In a good, if slightly goofy, way. But it was time to reel him back in to reality and determine whether Nickelson 2.0 was also a *sane* person. Or whether Nickelson's violent encounter with the infected had accelerated dementia, like altitude accelerated the kick in whisky.

"Look, Nick, last night, my imagination, and a monk who wanted to prank a round eye, made me mistake *wind* for howling boogey men. Let's apply Occam's razor again, and go with the simpler explanation. One, Abominable Snowpersons are third-world myths. Two, a long time ago a medicine man scalped a bear. Three, it turns out that bear had great genes. The realistic question is how do we test your, um, hypothesis that this stuff cures H7D3?"

Nickelson smiled. "How indeed." He crooked a finger, and led Condon to a set of double doors deeper inside the clinic, alongside which a wall plaque read SURGERY.

When Nickelson pressed the wall plate beneath the surgery sign, the doors swung inward, and frigid, stinking air spilled out.

Nickelson stepped into the room, triggered its motion-sensitive lights, and Condon realized why the cold stank. It was a meat locker.

On a wheeled gurney at the room's center, spot-lit from above, a cadaver lay, face up and frozen. It was far from the first cold body Condon had identified.

But this cadaver's calves and feet overhung the gurney's end by nearly a yard, and its arms, biceps as massive as a nose tackle's thighs, hung off the gurney's sides so far that the massive hands lay flat and palms-up, bent at the wrists. Coarse white-gray hair four inches long covered the body, except for the feet's soles, hands' palms, and face.

Condon inched forward, jaw agape, less from stupefaction than to avoid nose breathing, and the stench that would come with it. The face was too long to be simian, too different to be, well, anything else. The dead, pink eyes stared. The lips had frozen in a teeth-bared rictus that could have been a snarl as easily as a postmortem muscle contraction.

"This helps." Nickelson handed Condon a surgical mask, twin to the one he had put on. "Myth, Peter?"

Condon whispered through the mask, "They're even bigger than the stories say."

"Actually, these two are juveniles."

"Two?" As Condon turned to Nickelson his boot brushed something solid. He looked down, then sprang backward, eyes wide, from the second body on the floor. "Jesus!"

"I've sampled tissue from both specimens. They are beyond doubt the antibody source."

"How did you...?"

"Improvised toboggan. If it hadn't been downhill all the way I couldn't have. Even the small one weighs eight hundred pounds."

Condon inched away from the body on the floor, then held his breath, leaned over and peered, without touching the fur, at a red brown stain on the brighter-lit cadaver's left breast. "I don't mean how did you get them back to the lab." He paused, afraid to ask because he was afraid he knew the answer. "I mean, how did you get this 'specimen'?"

"Lucky shot. His companion limped for a half mile."

Condon shuffled backward out of the room, sat on the lab's floor again, and ran his hands through his hair. "Jesus."

Nickelson came and again sat alongside him. "It's a great deal to absorb, I know."

"The monk wasn't pranking me."

"Hardly. Buddhists are wretched comedians."

"So, are the survivors hunting *you*?"

"Now there's a terrifying thought. You saw those incisors. The tips alone are larger than Brazil nuts. Hypothetically, if you were a betting man, Peter, would you choose one of these in a match versus a Kodiak bear? Assuming competitors of equivalent weight and maturity?"

He turned and took Nickelson by the shoulders. "Nick, are they... intelligent?"

Nickelson cocked his head. "Fair question. That *would* change the odds."

"I don't care about the *odds*. I care about whether this was murder."

Nickelson retrieved his bottle, stared at the opposite wall as he drank. "Well, with the survival of the human race at stake I don't think it could be, regardless. But no. Don't let that concern you. They're clever, to be sure. Since I bagged these two the entire population has gone to ground. I've barely spotted a footprint. But a communal flight reflex isn't intelligence. Deer learn to avoid hunting preserves by the second day of deer season. White sharks, which are even more mindless eating machines than deer, vacate vast expanses of ocean when a killer whale pod takes even one of their number."

"What *is* their number?"

"They're limited by the sparse food supply in a harsh environment. And so dominant in, and well-adapted to, their niche that they hardly need to produce extra heirs to serve as spares. I estimate their number stable at around seven hundred individuals. All within the surrounding valleys within a one-hundred-kilometer radius of this one."

"If you just wanted to be sure they were the source of the antibody, why did you kill *two*?"

"The possibility of sexual dimorphism. It's unlikely, but if only the males or the females had been chock full of the antibody, the contributing population drops by half. I shot two that were walking *ensemble*, expecting a mated pair, not two males."

"Contributing? Contributing how?"

Nickelson wagged his index finger and shook his head. "Data first. Conclusion after. Which is where you come in. I need a female. And you're just the man to procure me one. Not in the pimp sense of the expression, of course."

It took until noon of the following day, with the monks' help, to transfer all the crates to the clinic vestibule. "Medical supplies," Nickelson had told them.

All the sophisticated systems that the Yellow Hat cadre would deploy to support the locals, as opposed to the weapons the cadre would teach the locals to use, were packed in a single hard-shell crate.

Condon knelt beside the crate, removed its lid, and lifted out the vacuum-bagged athermal camo ghillie suit.

Nickelson, whose wet operations experience had been limited to having human sources in bars spill drinks in his lap, peered over Condon's shoulder. "Is that better than the suit I've been using?"

"It's lighter, temperature controlled to deliver comfort between minus twenty and plus one hundred twenty Fahrenheit. The hood has a built-in earpiece, mic, and water nipple, and the wearer can inflate and deflate built-in knee, elbow, and butt pads to enhance comfort during extended surveillance, when bone-to-support-surface contact is noncritical. So yeah." Condon spoke about the suit like a man who had lived in one, because he had.

His last Army years, before he had followed a common career jump from special ops to Agency ops, had been as an Eighteen Bravo, a twelve-person Special Forces Operational Detachment-A's Sergeant specialized in weapons foreign and domestic. And sometimes, as in Condon's case, trained as a sniper.

He slit the Vacpac open with a trench knife and the ghillie swelled like a shaggy white balloon.

Tapping a thumb wheel that overlay the wearer's collarbone he said, "For this job, this makes the difference. It switches on a thermal sensor net built in to the suit. It monitors ambient surrounding temperature, air or surface, and tells that part of the suit to match, second-to-second. The wearer's boots are the same temperature as the ground he stands on. The wearer's head is the same temperature as the air he's breathing. In thermal imaging a normal GI, or you in that ghillie of yours, shows warmer than the surroundings. He, and you, glow in the dark. The same GI in this ghillie disappears off the thermal. When the shooter is controlling his breathing, even his exhalations barely show."

Nickelson pursed his lips. "You're sure?"

"Bet my life on it twice. You say our nocturnal pink-eyed friends see infrared waves, a longer wavelength than what humans call visible light. So, they've seen us coming, warmer than our surroundings, for centuries. If you're right, this should change the game."

Underneath the ghillie's bag, the WAASPs were packed in gross lots, one hundred forty-four of the little bastards fitted into a hard-shell box the size and shape of a cigarette carton. Condon clipped the seal on one box and shook out five into his palm. Three for overwatch surveillance plus two spares.

No bigger than the first joint of Bria's pinky finger, the

Weaponizable Airmobile Autonomous Surveillance/Penetrator was a shiny black pill of a nanodrone. Standardly configured with a long-life battery, a WAASP could spread its tiny, membranous wings and loiter, as unobtrusive and mobile as the insect it was named for, monitoring a battle area for days, infiltrating a head-quarters, casing a prime minister's residence, or hiding beneath a fallen leaf. It could be remotely piloted like its bigger cousins, or preprogrammed to autonomously and unjammably seek an optically, or auditorially, or thermally, acquirable target and look, listen, and report. That was the nifty part.

The nasty part was that with purpose-built tools included in each carton, basically tweezers and a jeweler's loupe, each WAASP could be reconfigured with a payload packet that swapped some battery mass and range for a high explosive warhead tip, plus face-recognition optics and software. The warhead was a pip-squeak, but once the WAASP wriggled itself into an ear canal, up a nostril, or into a snoring mouth, it was plenty to blow the target's brains out.

A WAASP could feature-match and assassinate a particular individual, or could be programmed to seek and attack within a designated area by facial descriptors, uniform, even height or weight. If a field operator chose to wipe out every bearded midget *gendarme* in the Sixteenth Arrondissement of Paris, all it took was the included electronic Field Manual and a couple boxes of bugs that would fit into a backpack.

Condon lifted out and set aside eight cartons of WAASPs, which would have been plenty to decapitate, literally, Tibet's Chi-nese security infrastructure overnight. From "reeducation" torture squads to militia commanders to Prefecture police chiefs to the Regional Secretary of the Communist Party of China. If Condon was honest, WAASPs had put snipers like him out of business.

However, Condon would conduct this immediate business the old-fashioned way. More or less. He leaned in to the case and lifted out the tool of his trade, a .50 caliber sniper rifle, its dis-assembled components packed into a meter-plus long, flat, case. Neither rifle nor case had changed all that much since before the millennium turned.

What had changed was the rifle's ammunition, and the target-ing 'scope with which the ammunition interfaced. Once the scope was trained and locked on the target by line-of-sight, each fired

round adjusted its flight and struck center-mass on target virtu-
ally regardless of the rifleman's skill or the target's movement.

Condon embraced smartrounds when shooting bad guys that
endangered fellow soldiers who his marksmanship protected. But
the idea of killing *game* so unsportingly, as he was about to do,
he despised.

He opened the case, ran his fingers over the flat white finished
scope and muzzle-braked barrel, then frowned as a shadow obscured
them. "Nick, that sailboat on your head is blocking my light."

"Sorry." Nickelson stepped around, bent, and peered down as
Condon plucked out, and fumbled to fit together, components that
in his prime he had literally put together, blindfolded, in seconds.

As Nickelson bent, the crest of his bon hat hung above Condon's
hands like a construction crane. Nearly as massive and every bit
as Caterpillar yellow. Nickelson supported the weight of his torso,
which was draped in maroon and gold off-the-shoulder robes, by
resting his palms on berobed knees. Today he wore the uniform
of the Gelug, or Yellow Hat, school of Tibetan Buddhism. Which
Nickelson had, apparently and improbably, joined, and trained
in, decades previously.

As Condon worked he said, "I thought the monk thing was
like the Army. You can't just walk away from your duty because
you feel like it. And if you do you can't just come back and say
'Here I am! Give me back my big hat.'"

"Actually, it's more a matter of living by Buddhism's tenets.
Once you have learned the Buddhist way, you're a Buddhist as
long as you live the Buddhist life. There really is no in or out.
Not really so different from what you're doing here and now.
Picking up where you left off. Just as long as you do the right
thing, nothing else matters."

"Are we, Nick? Doing the right thing?"

"Can saving millions of lives be wrong?" Nickelson straightened,
then resumed pacing back and forth, squinting at a minitablet
in one hand that he thumbed as he paced. In his other hand
he held a monk's walking staff topped with maroon and gold
braids, with brass bells that tinkled with each step as he tapped
the staff on the floor.

"Nick, if it's so simple, what are you working on?"

"Supply chain management. The fellow in the story with the
big diamond realized that as long as he didn't chip off and sell too

many diamonds, they would remain precious. His wealth could be whatever he chose it to be. With absolute control of near unlimited resources, he would be able to structure the world as he chose. Similarly, control of this cure will allow us to restructure a better world."

"Better according to who? Because I'm not interested in playing god and deciding who gets the precious cure and who dies."

Nickelson stopped tapping and pointed his staff at Condon and the nearly assembled rifle. "That's why the right thing for you to do is to get on with it and bag a female. That will allow us to maximize production. Simple matter of making the diamond as big as possible. Do your duty and we can change mankind's nightmare into a dream come true."

Condon woke from the recurrent nightmare again, shivering in his own sweat inside the heated ghillie, and concealed in the shelter he had burrowed in the mountainside's snow.

In the dark he bit down on the radio's talk switch and whispered, "Base, you copy?"

"Copy. How long 'til you summit?"

Condon dug out of his shelter, shrugged into his pack and climbed, already sucking wind. "Moving. One hour, tops."

The summit toward which he had been climbing for two days was at the center point of, and commanded, the valleys Nickelson had identified as the Yeti population's home range. The WAASPs' thermal imaging had proven able to pinpoint and track individuals as they emerged from dens and burrows each night and ranged actively during the hours of darkness. It also confirmed Nickelson's estimate that there were perhaps seven hundred out there, altogether.

But on this clear, moonless night Condon was only interested in one. He attained the summit, ate and drank, then radioed Nickelson again. It took time before the old man came back, and when he did he sounded even more breathless than Condon himself was.

"Base, transmit the grid reference for her den and I'll set up where I have line-of-sight eyes on."

"Done. Out."

"You'll have ample time to recover the body, Peter. They ignored, indeed avoided, both my kills. Though cannibalism would be a natural enough behavior, given the scarcity of protein in this environment."

"Not that hungry yet." As Condon scanned the terrain with the rifle's massive, separate spotting binoculars, he punched up the magnification and I.R. sensitivity, but he didn't really need to.

A single bipedal track line in the new snow led away from the dark, low opening beneath the ledge that overhung the valley floor. The tracks topped a distant ridge and disappeared down the reverse slope. Sets of smaller tracks looped out from, then returned to, the den. No meander ranged farther out than fifty meters.

Nickelson continued in his ear. "Their abstention from eating their own dead may be a learned response to a long-past species-wide viral pandemic similar to H7D3. 'Dead cousin's meat make us sick.' That would explain why this surviving population is so small, and why it carries this antibody. The fittest few survived because their bloodline carried the right protein."

Condon had chosen the broad rock ledge on which he had anchored the rifle's bipod legs because it was eighty meters below the mountain's absolute summit, on the terrain's military crest. He wouldn't be silhouetted against the sky, as he would have been on the topographic crest. His firing position was twenty-nine hundred meters from the den. Once upon a time, a conventional shot from one point eight miles would have been the longest kill in history. But with a smartround this kill would be less challenging than hitting an ox with a shotgun from ten paces. However, that wasn't Condon's greatest sporting reservation.

"I confirm it's a female. I do not have eyes on, but I think she's left a cub to hang around the den while she's out foraging."

"Agree with your assessment. WAASP Three has eyes on her as we speak and will continue tracking. Her return ETA is three hours. Recommend you nap and I will wake you in plenty of time."

"What about the cub?"

"It's unnecessary to kill it."

"Exactly. Orphaned it will die."

"Peter, our first duty is to mankind. Not to hand-wring about minimal, justifiable collateral damage. Take your nap and dream about making a brighter future for our species, rather than about accepting a future in which we are reduced to a handful of snowbound cave dwellers. Out."

Condon lay there staring down at the small tracks in the snow until sleep overtook him.

"I survived." Bria, her cheeks chevroned with makeshift charcoal camo, a Marine-issue carbine in her right hand with its muzzle pointed at the sky, winked. "Bad girls are good at that."

He had found her barricaded on the bright, sunbaked rooftop of a burned-out warehouse overlooking the green sea at the Chittagong docks.

He said, "Were you afraid?"

She shook her head. "You never understood that I can be nastier than your worst nightmare and slipperier than your wettest dream. I was never afraid whether you would find me. But I was terrified your sense of duty wouldn't let you come looking."

"Now what?"

She extended her free hand to him. "Now we quit pretending there's anything left to be duty-bound to. Screw your duty. Screw me instead. We'll make babies. Teach them to read. Teach them to laugh. And we'll laugh with them. Again. Peter..."

"Peter! Dammit! Do you copy?"

It was dark. It was cold. It was reality. Again.

"Copy."

"WAASP Three's battery quit. I'm blind here. Do you see her?"

He fumbled for the binoculars, swept the landscape until he located the female, two hundred meters left of the den and inbound. The sight reticle measured her at nearly three meters from broad feet to skull crown.

Her gray back bore a distinct chevron pattern of darker streaks, and Condon wondered whether they distinguished her as an individual, or were what Nickelson would call sexual dimorphism, or didn't matter. She moved fluidly, confidently, but with her head on a swivel, like she was walking point and presumed something was out there but couldn't spot it.

Condon whispered, "Got her."

He laid down the binoculars, extended his fingers through the slits in his mittens' palms, then rolled alongside the rifle and switched on its 'scope. He kept his fingers against the 'scope, felt its silent clicks as it powered up, ran its diagnostics, and shook hands electronically with each round in the magazine.

By the time the weapon beeped the last of its ready tones in his earpiece the female was already just fifty meters from the den. The cub popped out, one third her height, ran to her, and she scooped it in massive arms as she loped forward.

"Shit." What had he been thinking? If she disappeared into the den...

Three heartbeats later he relaxed.

She carried the cub to a low, wind-cleared ledge five meters left of the den, sat, pulled the cub's face to her breast and began nursing.

"Shot?"

"Obstructed."

"Obstructed how?"

The least he could do was let the infant suckle a final meal, give itself a fighting chance. Adoption of orphans wasn't unheard of among mammals in the wild.

He would wait until the cub and mother separated. Not because he was afraid of hitting the cub. A clean head shot was guaranteed as long as he had the crosshairs laid on that target when he fired. But if a half ton body fell on top of the cub it could be trapped, or suffocate.

"Condon! Damn you, talk to me!"

"Base? Base? Say again last transmission."

Nickelson had given up shouting into Condon's ear by the time the cub stopped nursing, or at least Condon assumed he had because he had switched off his receiver. But after she released the cub and the round struck, all would be forgiven and forgotten.

Except she didn't release the cub. She cradled it in one arm, knelt alongside the ledge, and began drawing her forefinger through the snow, moving her hand left to right. Then she lowered the cub down to the snow, took its hand, and manipulated it to mimic her previous movements.

She nuzzled the cub, returned to the bench, raised a thin slab of slate that lay there, and held it in front of the cub's face. Then she traced a finger across the slab, as her lips moved alongside the cub's ear.

Condon rolled away from the rifle, stared up at the sky, eyes wide, his jaw open.

The mother was teaching her baby to write and read.

It only took a moment to decide.

He rolled back to the rifle, sighted on the pair, relocated the point of aim fifty meters up and right, then fired. By the time the slowing round struck harmlessly in the snow high right, the shot's sound rolled in close behind.

Alerted, the mother whirled, eyes searching the darkness, and as he peered through the 'scope it seemed that she stared directly at him. He may have been invisible, cold as his surroundings. But in the moments after the shot the rifle's barrel wasn't.

A heartbeat later, she had scooped the cub and sprinted away, more two-legged cheetah than lumbering grizzly. She disappeared over the ridge seconds later.

Condon sat still, rocking, with his arms wrapped round his flexed knees. Finally, he switched back on. "Base?"

"Base copies. What the hell happened?"

"I missed high and right."

"I thought with that equipment that was impossible."

"That equipment hasn't been calibrated in years. Neither have I. Nick, the pooch screw's a hundred percent on me."

"No matter."

"Oh." Condon frowned. "Really?" He gathered the binoculars, policed up the single round's ejected brass. "I'm coming down."

"No. Hold in place."

"Why? She's halfway to Kathmandu by now."

"I'm coming up."

"Yo-da-lay-hee-hoo!"

Condon woke on the ledge from which he had taken the shot, and sat bolt upright. After days of exertion at altitude, followed by a tension release, he had slept, dream and nightmare free, until dusk of the following day.

He squinted toward the summit and spotted Nickelson, silhouetted against the sky in his homemade ghillie, peering out over the summit's snow lip, grinning. He flapped a mittened hand, poked with an ice ax at the snow as he tested for a path across the overhanging lip. "Don't come up! I'll be right down."

"Jesus! Don't! And quit yodeling! You'll bring the damn summit down." He pointed left. "There's an easy clear-blown rock path down to this ledge fifty meters that way."

∞ ⊖ ∞

Nickelson arrived on the broad ledge a half hour later, bent beneath a pack as large as Condon's, with the Lee-Enfield strapped along its side. Condon greeted his boss with tea he had boiled on a pocket stove. Because of the altitude, it was barely warm.

"Nick, how the hell did you get here so fast? It took me two *days* to get here. You only left the clinic twelve hours ago."

"*Au contraire.* I left the clinic six hours after you did. And I don't mind admitting it's been a bugger keeping up, even with the aid of your trail breaking."

Condon narrowed his eyes. "You didn't give a shit about testing a female for antibodies."

Nickelson shrugged out of his pack and plopped down in the snow. "Oh, I did, at first. It all seemed too good to be true. So, I assumed every untied knot was a noose. But the probability of that sort of sexual dimorphism is too small to worry about."

"*I* never worried about it."

"But you immediately and demonstratively worried about the morality of advantaging our species to the disadvantage of another."

"I suppose you know they're intelligent."

Nickelson snorted. "You needn't be righteous about it. If intellect guaranteed virtue, mankind wouldn't be in the crapper today." Nickelson unstrapped the Lee-Enfield, laid it on the ledge beside himself. Then he unzipped his pack and withdrew a full carton of WAASPs.

"Really, Nick? If you plan to expand this monitoring and tracking program so you can round them up for forced catch-and-release blood donations and breast milk pump-offs that's not 'disadvantage.' It's not game management. It's slavery."

Nickelson slid open the carton. Each of the little WAASPs' nose cones were now olive, circumscribed with a yellow ring the width of sewing thread. Markings denoting live explosive ordnance.

Condon's jaw dropped. He spun away, clapped his hands to the side of his head. "Christ. *That's* what you were programming on your tablet. And what you did for six hours after I left. You got a twofer. A trail broken to this summit and also your squeamish subordinate out of your way while you reconfigured WAASPs with weapons payload packets. So they could hunt and kill anything that looked like your two dead Yetis. You're not planning to catch and release. You're planning to stock the freezer. Then grind 'em up for your magic powder."

He spun back, pointing at Nickelson.

And found himself staring down the Lee-Enfield's barrel.

"Of course I am! As you've suggested, an intelligent species couldn't be counted on to submit like sheep to forced shearing. Even if these ungovernable peaks were as patrollable as a Montana prairie. Peter, was I supposed to wait until society was irretrievably down the tubes? Don't you agree that I—we, if you come to your senses—can more competently manage this resource than the boobs and charlatans who visited this apocalypse on us?"

"Buddhists like you harm no living thing. What would the Buddha say?"

"Had the Buddha ever met a virus he would have acknowledged that a virus and a human being are not equivalently valuable living things. Once the fallacy that all living things are equal is exposed it's just haggling over the appropriate exchange rate. If Yellow Hat had indeed been implemented you would have done your duty and assassinated a thousand Chinese cadre overnight. With a salute and a 'boo-yah' fist bump."

"Because my country decided they were oppressors. And if I did, there'd still be a billion Chinese left."

Nickelson rolled his eyes. "Rationalization proves *my* point, not yours."

Nickelson 2.0 turned out to be not merely a little goofy but delusional and murderous. Inside Condon's parka the .45 hung over his heart, potent but hopelessly buried. The .50 was disassembled luggage.

Condon raised his hands, palms out. If you can't kick the shit out of your adversary, negotiate. "Okay. Let's talk resource management. How much powdered Yeti can the market absorb? One carcass a month?"

Nickelson kept his rifle trained on his assistant while he rummaged through his pack until six open cartons of weaponized WAASPS lay on the ledge, the tiny assassins gleaming in shiny black rows.

"Peter, picking them off to order, whether one a month or one a week opens up too many variable outcomes. They may learn to hide better. Or fight back. Less enlightened humans may intrude. It's a bad plan."

Condon nodded at the open cartons. "Seven hundred Yeti.

Eight hundred sixty-four WAASPs. That's overkill by a margin of one hundred sixty-four. I call overnight genocide a worse plan."

Nickelson shook his head. "Hardly genocide. Yellow Hat's infrastructure decapitation plan projected two percent survival among Chinese cadre. If anything, tonight's survival percentage will be higher. Among a *minimum* fourteen surviving Yeti there will surely be several breedable pairs after the plan's executed."

"Nick, Clausewitz said plans don't survive contact with the enemy. Put down the antique and let's talk."

Nickelson smiled. "Peter, engaging me in conversation is sound negotiating. Your Special Warfare instructors would be proud. But you can't change this outcome now. The hay, as you say in Montana, is in the barn. When we pass from End of Evening Nautical Twilight to full dark each WAASP's photo sensors will awaken it. The swarm will perform its assignment as programmed no matter what either of us does now."

As he spoke, one of the tiny drones twitched, wings buzzing, and Nickelson said. "See?"

"Nick, there is no cure for H7D3. The best that what's left of mankind can do is survive and rebuild our species the best we can. And exterminating another species that's been through the same wringer, to chase a fantasy, is no way to begin." Condon inched forward.

Nickelson gripped his rifle tighter, shook his head. "Peter, stop. Do your duty or I *will* shoot you."

Nickelson wasn't the first commander who had given him an order he thought was stupid. But Condon hadn't disobeyed one yet. So, he kept talking. "I wouldn't, Nick. You boomed down one avalanche since I've been here." Condon kept his hands high but waggled one toward the summit and the snow overhang. "If that comes down, we—you, me, the bugs—go down with it. And wind up dead and buried under a snow mountain on the valley floor." He pointed. "Especially *that* drone. It looks like you screwed up and programmed it to home in on your own face."

Nickelson flicked his eyes down.

Condon seized the instant of distraction and dove forward.

Nickelson fired.

Condon, breath hammered from his body, chest burning, lay gasping on his side in the snow, as the shot's echoes rebounded from the distant peaks.

Beyond Nickelson's shoulder the snow bank still hung, stable and gray in the deepening twilight.

He stared down at Condon, eyes glistening, head shaking. "Oh, Peter. Why?"

Condon hissed through clenched teeth, "Because even if we could cure ourselves, we wouldn't deserve to survive this way."

"You're wrong. The species that fights hardest for its life at the last is the one that deserves to survive."

Behind Nickelson, silhouetted against the twilight's last flare, something crept along the overhang. Condon recognized the Yeti's gait, saw when she turned the chevrons that marked her back. She had circled back to the place from which the shot that had threatened her family had come.

She dashed back and forth along the overhang, then howled. The combination of the disturbance at the snow bank's hinge point and the pitch of her cry provoked a deep groan within the snow. Nickelson turned and faced the vast bank as it cracked loose from the summit, slid down, rumbling, and swallowed him, Condon, and the nanodrones. Then it carried them all over the ledge and plunged down.

Condon realized, as he clawed to float atop the surging tide, alternately tumbling and suffocating, that without even so much as a Neanderthal's sharpened flint the Yeti had weaponized her environment, and defeated an existential threat. The species that had fought hardest for its life at the last was the one that was going to survive after all.

White light surrounded Condon and silence rang in his ears like an eternal bell. But his chest hurt, which a dead man's chest shouldn't. He was alive but buried in the avalanche's debris. His legs were pinned, as was his left arm, but his right he could move. The light seemed strong above, and he was breathing, although with effort. He wriggled his right arm, punched a hole that let blue sky in, then dug with his right arm until his left was free and he could see and breathe unobstructed. Then he rested and wept.

Finally, he sat atop the avalanche debris, dangling his feet in the hole that had been his grave. A blaze erupted in his chest with each breath, no matter how shallow. The round Nickelson fired had struck Condon's .45, driven it back against his body, and broken a rib.

It took him ten minutes to stand, then he picked his way to the dark shape atop the snow twenty meters from him.

Nickelson lay spread eagled and face up, wire rimmed glasses lost forever beneath tons of snow, as were the WAASPs and the fifty cal and the Lee-Enfield. His dead blue eyes wide open to a sky equally blue, his neck was broken, so his head was cocked as though he had posed a hypothetical to God.

Condon felt in his own pocket for Nickelson's note, which had separated him from Bria and ordered him to this place, chasing a duty that no longer existed. Meltwater had soaked the sheet, so Nickelson's inked magic diagrams on the page's reverse side had blurred into illegible blue tears. He tucked it into Nickelson's pocket, gathered blocks of crusted snow, and erected a cairn over the body.

To stabilize his rib, Condon held his left arm pinned against his body with his right, then gritted his teeth and crabbed and slid down the avalanche mound's fore slope. Then he limped south along the valley floor, beginning a fourteen-hundred-kilometer march to the sea.

Whether he found Bria alive, or dead, or he died trying, he would finally be chasing the only dreams a man had the right to grab for. His own.

Behind him he left a man who had grabbed for dreams too big, to make his peace at the top of the world with the species as big as the Ritz.

# The Cat Hunters

## DAVE FREER

*"This is Auckland Islands Science Base. Is anyone receiving us?"*

When the world was busy falling apart and the H7D3 virus was spreading like wildfire across it, Eric Anderson, "Weasel" Jepsen and "Devil" Moroi were somewhere to the south of Mount D'Urville, just off Tagua Bay setting cat-traps, baits and freezing their buns off sitting in the hides.

Auckland Island, about two hundred and fifty miles south of New Zealand, was one of the most remote places on Earth. It was also the place that New Zealand government's conservation arm was spending a shed-load of money, to try and keep-up-with-the-Joneses—or rather, with Australia and South Africa. Both of those countries had successfully eliminated the animals that the sealers and whalers of the 1800s had introduced to their chilly Subantarctic islands, to protect the birds and vegetation. On Auckland Island, New Zealand had got rid of the goats, the cows and rabbits...but the pigs, mice and cats were still there. At a mountainous hundred and seventy square miles, with large tangled Rata-tree forests as well as a jagged coastline of drowned valleys, Eric thought there was more chance of him falling pregnant, than of success.

225

But they were prepared to pay professional vermin hunters very well for a six-month stint—which was why he wasn't arguing, and just taking their money and doing the job.

Comms to the temporary main science base in Port Ross meant walking three or four miles through wet megaherbs and tussocks and snow patches. When Eric last bothered all the outside world had for him was a demand from his ex-wife about her alimony. Fuck her. Mind you, that had been his mistake in the first place. It was why he'd taken a job on the ass end of nowhere, in the rain. It never seemed to bloody stop, with more than three hundred days a year on which it rained. And after three hours of waiting in the hide in the rain, the only cat he'd seen spooked before he could get a bead on it. His own fault, he admitted. He was too used to only taking head shots. He was a wallaby shooter and the value lay in the meat and hides.

So when he walked back to the camp to find Weasel and Dev there, and they hadn't got the billy boiling or picked up the traps, he was ready to rip someone a new one. Even in those two, and you didn't want to do that. "Who does all the sodding work in this place and why do I?" he said, dropping his butt in the camp-chair that was close to their only luxury. "Where are the bloody traps, you useless drongos?"

"Got orders to leave 'em. And the rest of the kit, and hotfoot back to the base. Weasel took the radio up to the D'Urville ridge," said Dev, shoving his spare parka into a bag.

The Weasel looked up from where he was squatting and oiling his pet rifle, its padded waterproof case open and waiting. Most of the shooters had gone along with the recommended .223, even if they brought their own, because it made ammo supply easier. Eric had a bolt action Sauer as well as his .223 Rock River Arms Mountain rifle. The .223 was adequate for outright kills on small targets. Not for the Weasel, however. He'd even brought his own brass and did his reloading every time they went back to main camp. He was a fanatic who had spent a few years working out his loads to the grain, only using new brass—and getting fantastic groupings at five hundred yards with his beloved Nosler 30-06. If they had had one hundred yards visibility it would have been deadly. Mostly they didn't, and the Weasel spent his life cleaning it. "Got the satellite phone working. That bit of sun yesterday charged the battery up. I thought I'd give my missus a thrill."

"I reckon that's enough reason to recall us," said Eric, reaching out and snagging the Inox from the Weasel, giving his RRA's action a spray.

"And when she didn't answer, I tried me brother. And then me dad and Uncle Ted..."

This could go on a long time. The Weasel's clan covered half of South Island, and most of Invercargill. "And they all said she'd won the Lotto and run off with the milkman."

"No, no one was answering. So I got worried about an earthquake."

Eric stopped himself from a smartarse comment. New Zealand. Coming, as he did, from Oz, you tended to forget that New Zealand's problem wasn't just shagging sheep. They had earthquakes. Big ones and plenty of them. "Yeah?"

"So I walked up the hill, and they said they've been trying to raise us for two weeks. Was going to send a search party down. We're to get ready to evac."

"Why?"

"Pākehā's have all gone mad and started killing people. My mob's gone bush," said Dev, laconically. "I used the 'phone to try call my sis. Couldn't raise her so I tried the old man. He tells me they're ripping their clothes off and eating people. And then I lost him because the battery is flat again."

"Some kind of disease," said the Weasel. "That's all they told me. Anyway. Apparently they're goin' to chopper us out."

"Yeah. Well, I reckon they won't go without us, and knowing that lot they'll probably change their minds, or charge us for the gear. We pack up proper, at least try and keep the mice out. We're never going to do Base before dark, and I'm not going to sea at night. No ways."

"You got a point," admitted Dev.

"Yeah. And I got no tea," he said, putting the rifle down on his sleeping bag and getting the burner going.

They had the Zodiac down in the water by just after first light. By helicopter it would have been around twenty-four miles. If they followed standing instructions and stayed within 250 yards of the coast... it would be close on a hundred, dipping in and out of the fiords. Even the jackasses setting the rules expected them to bend the rules, because they didn't have enough fuel to do that. It was still thirty-six miles in an eighteen-foot boat in the Southern ocean, full treacherous waves and unmarked rocks. Their lifejackets had neoprene liners. That improved your time in the water from about a minute to...maybe three.

Everything in the boat was in watertight containers, and tied down. It was relatively still here in Carnley Harbour, at least today. It wasn't going to be, once they got out onto the east coast. Still, you wouldn't even try on the West, where the wave-splash would sometimes get up the two-hundred-foot black basalt cliffs. To make a change from the last three weeks—at least it wasn't raining. That, when they hit the big swells on open coast, was a plus. You could at least see the foam of a breaking rock well in advance instead of having to rely on guesswork, your ears, and fast reactions.

None of them were saying much. It wasn't a great place for conversations, and, anyway it wasn't the time for normal biting either a bit of shit. There was too much in their heads for giving the Weasel a hard time.

They slid into Port Ross just after mid-morning, and skimmed past a pod of Southern Right Whales, and into Erebus Cove. No one came down to meet them, but the other Zodiacs were tied up and floating, so it looked like everyone was home.

"No point in taking the kit out," said the Weasel, who didn't like carrying more than he had to. "We'd probably just have to put it in again. And that stupid cow will want us sign the rifles in and lock them up." The chief scientist had issues about guns.

"Yeah. Let's go find out what's going on."

They walked up the track to the base, where the first person Eric saw was the other Australian shooter. He was first, because he wasn't inside the base, but sitting outside on a rock, looking glum. That was about normal for Strife Thomas. He was a 'roo shooter from Queensland who normally said at least a word a week if he wasn't drunk, and then he only said as many as it took to start a fight. Except now: "Big Eric, yer Bastard. I was beginning to think I was last Ozzie left in the world, but." And there was a tear running down his face.

Eric wouldn't have thought Strife even had tear ducts, let alone could use them. "What's going on, Strife?" he asked.

"Half the fucking world is dead, Eric. We're fucked. We're stuck here. They keep pretending someone is coming to fetch us. My kid is out there in that shit, and there is nothing I can do about it."

"What the hell?"

The details came spilling out of Strife. His group had got back to camp about two weeks back, seen some of it on satellite TV, tried to contact families and friends. "So what are they doing?" asked Dev. "I mean, in there." He waved a hand at the base building.

"Nothing. Bickering. And crying," said a tired female voice behind them.

Eric recognized her—half the scientists hadn't bothered to introduce themselves—but this woman was also the camp doctor. She looked like she needed herself. She had a black eye. He managed not to say: "What's up, Doc" but got it out as: "Are they really coming to evacuate us?"

"No," she said with grim finality. "It's just wishful thinking. We've had no transmissions from New Zealand for weeks. The satellite TV broadcasts went from horrific to giving emergency information, to silent. Creek has convinced herself she's important, and we're going to be saved."

"Didn't need a lot of convincing," said Dev, managing a sketchy smile. The chief scientist had delusions of grandeur—and some political clout. It was because of her they had shooting teams and traps, not dogs, which was just plain stupid.

"So, Doc, what's actually happening?" asked Eric. "What's being done? I mean we may be here a long time..."

The slight woman took a deep breath. "Absolutely nothing. Absolutely fucking nothing! They're all too scared of that woman. So they're just sitting here, eating, drinking and falling apart. What can be done?"

Eric tugged his beard. And then said: "Well. I reckon I can go back to the Zodiac and collect a few cans of fuel and go back to our camp."

"Why? You're just like that stupid bitch trying to pretend everything is normal..."

"Nope. Going down to collect the tent, the rest of the food, stove, solar panel, fuel. We'll need them. We might be here a while."

"Oh." She took a deep breath. "Yes. Sorry. I just flipped out because Creek has gone to her sea-lion colonies on the North Coast. It's pointless..."

"She was feelin' sex-starved. She's a hot date for a sea-lion

bull," said Dev. It was true enough—the domineering chief scientist looked rather like one of her research subjects.

"She's a Lizzie. She just wants to steal some of their cows,"
said the Weasel.

It took a few seconds for the comments to sink in to the doctor. A few seconds of incredulous open-mouth staring at them.
Then she started laughing. Laughing so hard that she had to sit
down on the rock next to Strife. Eventually she stopped, wiped
her eyes. "Sorry. I...Everyone tiptoes around her."

"We aren't much on tiptoes," said Eric. "Especially not me.
My feet are too big. I'm heading out. I want to get back before
dark and start carrying down the gear."

"We ought to ask," said Dev.

Eric shrugged. "Sounds like some jackass might tell me not to.
Besides what they gonna do to us? Send us home? Dock our pay?"

"You got a point," said Dev, nodding. "Okay, let's go. You
coming, Weasel?"

"All I want to do is kill something, but I might as well," said
the Weasel. "I just got off that bloody boat. Why now, Eric?"

"Because I might have someone try and stop me later. And I
need to think, and I need to do something." Out of...well, pity,
not because he really wanted the morose man along—he wasn't
sure he wanted anyone along, just to deal with the sea as a nice
immediate problem, and to think—he asked, "You want to ride
along, Strife?"

Strife shook his head. "No. I get sick. I'm going to clean me
guns."

"Don't go shooting yourself. That kid of yours might need you."

"I can't get there."

"I'm gonna work on that. We'll do it somehow, I reckon."

That got a long slow nod. "I was going to off myself." He stood
up. "But now I'm going to clean me guns. Anyone's hurt her, I'll
have them. Yer a good man, Big Eric. You'll do it."

The doc got up. "One less on the suicide watch. Look, do you
mind if I come along? I...I just have to get out here. They...
they can just look after themselves for a bit."

"Yeah sure. You don't weigh much. Just get a lifejacket and
sleeping bag."

"Sleeping bag?"

"We got nine hours of daylight, and it's half over. We're not running back in the dark. It's bring your own, or share the Weasel's. There's no room in mine and Dev's stinks." They all did of course. They'd been nearly four weeks out there. He wouldn't mind her in his sleeping bag... "And the Weasel's missus gets touchy."

"They're all dead. How can you make jokes?" The thin edge of hysteria was back in her voice.

He shrugged. "Laugh or cry. And I don't cry well. Anyway, I reckon the military will sort it out, if the government can't. It won't be as bad you make out. It never is."

She shook her head. "You don't understand. It's worse than you could understand. But I meant I didn't know you needed to stay overnight."

"It's about four hours run. You want to do it in daylight. See you down at the boat."

He doubted she'd come along, but she was there, less than five minutes later, when they were changing over fuel tanks, getting a few bits of gear off the boat. Two minutes later they were heading out of Erebus cove again.

On the run down they learned far more than they really wanted to about the H7D3 virus and the horrors of the stage two effects. Of the wave of destruction and death that had swept out of the USA and across the world. Of the "zombie" hordes tearing people apart and eating them. Of the scenes that had come to the helpless science team through their satellite TV... until that stopped. Doc Lyn seemed to need to tell them, to get it out. She was going to be hoarse, talking above the wind, outboard noise, and then repeating herself so others heard too. But she wanted to talk about it.

That was more than she wanted to do about the black eye.

They got into their landing rocks, tied the boat up and headed back up the hill to the camp, and started packing things until dusk, ate freeze-dried crud and talked over the lousy coffee, sitting around the fire they weren't supposed to light, using up the last of their dried wood. "So, look, I have this right: whatever this thing is, it spreads like flu," said Eric.

"In the first stage. Then it needs blood or body-fluids," she explained.

"Yeah well, what I'm saying is flu—it spreads because there are lots of people. And if it's killing people, sending them mad, well, pretty soon it's got to stop spreading."

"The infected..." she shuddered. "Well, it seems they live while

they can get food and water. And they can infect with a bite...
or their body fluids."

"You'd avoid sex without protection," said Dev.

"Yeah, well, my point is you're gonna run out of tucker pretty
soon. Even eating each other. And New Zealand...well, South
Island they're in for a rough winter without clothes and heating.
It can't last. Make one hell of mess. But it can't last."

"Yeah. I reckon that's what the first guy to catch flu said too,"
said Dev. "But it keeps comin' back."

"You've both got a point. But isolation and quarantine could
work," said the doctor. "Could have worked, for all we know.
And we probably never will," she sounded despairing again. "We
can't survive here."

"Speak for yourself," said Eric. "I'm not dead...until I'm dead.
There's plenty of firewood. There's food...pigs. Seals. Birds. Fish.
I know, all protected, but who is gonna stop us? We've got shelter,
we've water, we got food. We've even got a doctor and medicine.
Anyway, I don't plan to stay here."

"How do you plan to leave?" asked Dev. "We can't do it in
a Zodiac. The sea out there will kill us. This is the Southern
Ocean, not the Bass Strait. And these twisty Rata trees and tree
daisies won't do for a boat."

"I'm thinking about it, but now I'm going to hit the sack."

Eric would have been ready to sleep the sleep of the dead tired,
but it seemed he was wrong about how much room there was in his
sleeping bag. It'd been a long time since he'd been with a woman,
and his need was pretty urgent...but it seemed hers was too. And
she clung very tightly to him in the darkness. It seemed like being
in the middle of zombie outbreak made smelling like a fox's den
acceptable to a woman. But before she left at the first birdsong, she
told him what it was that made him attractive. "I need hope. Everyone else...just doesn't know what to do. Or has given up," she said.

"I don't do give up well. I don't know about succeed, but I
don't give up," said Eric.

"The black eye," she said, suddenly. "We've got less medical
supplies than you think. I...I caught my partner...my ex-
partner, in the act."

"Banging the sea lion?" he asked, putting his arm around her.

"No. Taking my keys and stealing the morphine. He...he said
it didn't matter anymore. It was escape."

"Fucking dickhead."

"So we've got almost no major analgesics. Someone...sometime will need them. I don't know how to deal with some things without them."

"As and when the time comes, we'll deal." And privately, he planned to make sure he got her to some. So maybe it was rebound. Or fear. Whatever...what was 250 miles of ocean to him? He knew women made him stupid. That didn't stop him. And the ex might be needing painkillers soon. "What happened to him? The ex, I mean."

"He ran off to Creek. She was just getting set for the sea-lion trip. He told her he wanted to join them, and I was upset about the idea...then when I showed up, the bitch didn't listen to a word I said. She wouldn't believe me. Even said I hit myself in the face."

"I think we're gonna need a bit of reorganization..." He put his finger to his lips. Dev was stirring. He opened his eyes as she scooted back to her own sleeping bag.

"You're not fooling anyone, you know," Dev said cheerfully.

"What?" said the Weasel, waking up.

"Shows how much you know, Dev." Eric knew the world was in trouble, and they were stuck on a Subantarctic island, were probably screwed. But...this morning he was ready to take on the world, and make it right again. For a miracle it was an almost clear morning, with fairly little wind, a high between fronts in the September change of seasons.

They loaded the rest of the gear and the fuel and were out on the gray swells before the sun, chasing a white-capped albatross skimming the waves.

It was interesting—on the way down they'd been listening to Lyn tell them how the plague had destroyed cities and countries. Now...now they were talking about how to feed themselves, how to build boats. What they each knew about. After weeks sitting in the bush together, Eric had thought he knew his two mates. But you tended to talk about what you had in common: which was shooting, chasing skirts and the problems that had caused all of them.

He knew that Dev had worked on a farm for a while, before moving into deer-shooting. He had too, but it was a sore point: having had to sell the family farm to pay out his ex-wife, so she could continue to keep up her lifestyle and horses. The Weasel was a diesel mac—at least he'd finished his apprenticeship, because they wouldn't have him in the Army. Thinking back on his own time in the Australian Navy, the New Zealand Army and the Weasel had both dodged a bullet. The five foot two, hundred pound nothing squirt was one of best shots of any fanatical gun-nut Eric had ever met, and he'd met a fair number. He just didn't do taking orders from anyone, especially if they were bigger than him.

They knew each other, knew the base tech officer, knew the other nine shooters—professional vermin hunting was not a big world. Back at the base and on the ship, that was who they'd socialized with. The sixteen scientists and the doc, they'd had little to do with. Ten of the scientists were women, and after a few weeks in the bush, you didn't mind trying—but it didn't cut both ways. However, Lyn did know the scientists, and knew what their fields of expertise were.

If they needed botanists, entomologists, zoologists, marine biologists, ornithologists, limnologists and even a microbiologist who had changed her mind and ended up specializing in pollens...they'd be right. "And the archeologist and historian," she added, with a wry smile.

"What the hell for?" asked the Weasel. "Not much history here."

"Well, partly because she was the doctor, and married to the limnologist. And partly to do some research on the shipwrecks and their survivors, Charles Enderby's colony, and the Ngāti Mutunga Chief Matioro's colony and to look for other East Polynesian sites."

"Ah. Yeah, those colonies come to grief, didn't they?" asked Eric.

"Yes. And they had a lot more people. Enderby brought a hundred fifty people, carefully choosing them for suitable skills, and Chief Matioro had thirty Māori and thirty Moriori slaves from the Chatham Islands. And they both failed. It's a hard place," she said, looking at the forested coastline behind the bleak rocks.

"Yeah. I guess we'll have to be harder and smarter," said Eric, putting an arm around her. "But I reckon Weasel was wrong about the history part. I could get interested in it myself. I'm not keen on repeating their mistakes."

"Anyway," said the Weasel. "We've got less people to feed. That's better isn't it?"

She pulled a face. "So long as this isn't the whole human race.

Not so good on the gene pool. The colonists came at the tail end of the sealing and whaling...and those populations have recovered a lot. But...you've got some biologists who're going to resist any killing. Of anything."

"Then they can resist bloody eating," said Dev, voicing all their thoughts.

"Well...um. I don't want to say this, but well, they have got control of all the supplies. And Creek wouldn't hear of it. And most of the scientists...well, she had final say in the selection. She picked them young, and a lot of women. She claimed it was to give them career opportunities and help correct the female imbalance in the sciences...but I think she was working on building her power-base. She's got a lot of political influence."

"And no common sense. The stupid bint is why we're down here in winter, and without dogs."

Just then the stupid bint's voice crackled over the radio. They all started. It had been silent since they left Port Ross the day before—so even if it hadn't been Dr. Creek speaking or she'd said anything less earth-shattering it would have a surprise. "A ship! A ship! They've sent a ship for us! A ship. A ship!"

Eric looked at the coastline, and the sea. They were about a mile short of Ewing Island and the entry to Port Ross—if you were in anything bigger than a Zodiac. Wherever the vessel was, he couldn't see it. "Relax. We'll easily beat them in." He picked up the microphone and called: "Zodiac Three calling in. What's the position and size of the vessel? We're near the mouth of Ross and can't see it. Over."

There was silence. Then another voice, a male one, answered. "Dr. Creek is trying to signal to it. Um. It's uh, heading toward the north coast. A few miles from us...we're just west of Matheson bay...above the rookery at North Point now. Uh. It looks like...a container ship. It may not be coming for us at all. It, it could be going to just hit. What do we do? Um. Over."

"Go Channel sixteen and see if you can get a response. Base. Base, if you're hearing this, send on sixteen. You've got a more powerful radio. Over."

"This is Auckland Islands Science Base, receiving you. Going sixteen."

Eric and the others on the Zodiac could hear the attempts at contacting the ship...and no reply. And then, suddenly a slightly high pitched voice, saying something in a foreign language. Might have been "Santa something-or-other."

"This is Auckland Island Science Base. Say again. Over."

"Is Third Mate Miguel Ferrego of Container ship BELLA FOR-TUNA. I am need assistance. God, help me!" came the voice in heavily accented English.

"This is Auckland Science Base. Will do what we can to assist. What is your position? What is the problem? Over."

"What is the problem! What is the fucking problem?" screamed the man, his voice on the wrong edge of hysteria. "Everybody she is dead or they go mad! The captain she is dead, they *eat* him. I don't know what to do! Help me! Over."

"You're going to wreck your ship," squalled Dr. Creek. "Steer away from the rocks! We need you to rescue us."

"Which way I go?" demanded the third mate. "Which way I fucking go? Over."

Dr. Bint got in first. "Right ... I mean starboard. You've got go around to Enderby. Over."

"Starboard! I see entrance. I make it starboard. Over."

It took Eric a few seconds to work it out, picturing the map in his head. The stupid bint was using *her* left and right. He yelled into the mic. "Not fucking starboard! *Port! Port!*" and realized he hadn't pressed the send button. So he did. But whoever was manning Auckland Base was already yelling the same thing.

The accented voice came back. "Say again. Say ..."

Then there was just Dr. Bint squalling. "He's going to wreck—unless he gets into North Harbour."

North Harbour was the only one of the long, narrow inlets typical of the East of the Auckland Islands, which graced the North coast. It was about three miles long by a third of a mile wide—with a tricky cape at each side and a river at the head of it. Neville, Strife and Fat Boy had been based there. It had some of the densest Rata forest on the island. Good for cats, good for the shooters to whinge about. Reachable by Zodiac on a good day.

And today was about as good as it was going to get in these parts, thought Eric, looking at the sea and reaching decisions. It was as flat as his first girlfriend in the lee of the land on the east. It could be a bit exciting in the open water around North Cape. "What do you say we run the Rose Island gap? We're pretty close on dead low by the looks of it." The tidal rip through the shallow rocky gap made it risky at anything but slack tide, and best at high water.

"So long as you don't want to do the Enderby Island one," said the Weasel. "Maybe we should drop the doc off inside the point."

"It sounds like they may need me," she said.

The radio brought them the voice of Dr. Bint. "We'll make our way down as fast as possible. We need all available people for the rescue."

"This is Zodiac Three just inside Tucker point. We're going via the Rose gap. Over."

"Roger Zodiac Three. I'll get the others teed up. Two of the hunters are walking back to their base. I'll see if I can contact them too. They know the terrain there. Over and out," replied the male voice.

"Reckon we should change tanks here, where it's quiet, before we run out of fuel out there," said Dev.

"Good point." The water inside Port Ross was limpid. It wouldn't be off the north shore.

So they did. It didn't take long...but seconds count.

Soon they were nosing into the channel between the islands, with the sound of breaking surf along the teeth of the reef, and the treacherous still water that betrayed the racing current under it. Then they were bucking their way through the churn of foam and racing the peaking swell...and out, running on a rolling sea. The open water and bigger sea made this a much harder task, and all Eric did for the next while was concentrate on that. Once they got around North Cape, things might ease off a little. Lyn made her way back to him. She was trying to say something, but it had to wait....

And it did. As soon as they were inside the lee of the point he eased the throttle and said "What?"

"I realized," she said. "The people on that ship. They could be infectious. No, they must be."

"What the hell do we do about that?" asked Dev.

"Um. Don't know," she answered. "Stay away from them... the virus has about a ten-day incubation. If we can quarantine for...say six weeks?"

"Huh. That third mate didn't sound good for six hours. But we don't know if they made it into North Harbour. Not seeing any signs of a ship so far."

"We just need to be careful," she said.

"It's not exactly my strong point, but I'll keep it mind." He opened the throttle again, and they headed inshore toward the mouth of North Harbour—it was about a third of a mile wide, three mile long gash into the high bluffs of the north coast. There, at the head of it, was a container ship, its bow deep in the wash of the small waves foaming on the gray and black volcanic pebble beach.

Stark against that beach...

"Those are people!" yelled the Weasel.

Eric dug into the box strapped onto the top of the safety barrel. Pulled out the binoculars. Took a look...and shook his head and handed them to Dev, as they closed on the vessel. It was quite still in here, and he started to cut the throttle.

"They're all fucking naked!" said Dev. He scanned around the bay, looking at them. "What the hell! Hey. Weasel. Get that rifle of yours out. You'll be able to see better though that demon scope of yours. It looks like..."

Eric cut the throttle more. They were just outside the small break zone, not fifty yards off the stern of the vessel. He could see, clearly, without the binocs, people climbing down the lines hanging from the lifeboat-davits and dropping into the shallows and scrambling up the black cobbles. Some were staring at them...others—others were on hands and knees...eating something. The air was full—not of yells for help or waving, but a terrible inhuman yowling chorus.

There was the sudden crack of a shot...loud and echoing in the narrow valley.

"What the hell are you shooting at, Weasel? Stop it," yelled Eric, as the small man worked the bolt, his eye still to the scope.

"Trying to get him off her," said the Weasel. "Next shot I'll blow his fucking head off."

"Look," said Dev, shoving the binocs at him. "Over there." He pointed. "I'm getting my rifle."

Eric looked. Screwed up his eyes. Looked again. There was a knot of the naked people, more running towards the scene on the rocks, some 150 yards before the rocks gave way to the black beach. On the second last piece of basalt before the kelp fringe, one of the naked men was busy raping someone. Someone with a very recognizable head of hair. Dr. Creek was very fond of that shade of hair dye. Eric handed the binocs to Lyn and swung the Zodiac across. "Dammit. I am trying to aim," said the Weasel. "Hold her still."

"We'll be able to get there," he said as he pointed the Zodiac towards the rocks.

"Eric! Eric. No! They're infected! Oh, oh no! That's Paul!" screamed Lyn.

Paul was the ex. Dev was quicker off the mark than Eric, and grabbed her arm before she jumped over the side.

"Going in. Fifty yards should be safe, Doc? We can deal with it from there." He'd reverted to "Doc" without thinking about it. Half a minute later he had the Zodiac nudging the edge of kelp, and flicked the outboard out of gear. Took the shocked woman's arm. "You drive. You can handle a Zodiac?"

"Yes...of course. What are you going to do?" she asked.

The Weasel answered that with a crack of a shot. The rapist's head jerked back, and then a second shot from Dev, hitting the man's temple, sent a spray of blood, brains and bone fragments out of the Weasel's entry wound. Eric had his Mountain Rifle out and chambered the first round. The shots and sudden death hadn't put the naked infected off—instead there were more loping towards the scene. He put his eye to the 'scope. The first thing he saw, close up, was one of the infected picking pieces of the skull off herself...and licking them. He managed not to reflexively shoot, but to sweep across the mob with the scope—there. Under that lot was a glimpse of clothing—typical expedition orange parka. And that one there...was eating an arm. Chased by two others who wanted it. So he started shooting at the scrabbling pile-on. Might be someone alive under that.

It was like spotlighting 'roo, but in daylight—and they didn't run after the first shot. The other two both had bolt-action rifles, unlike his semiautomatic—more accurate, they said, more what they were used to from deer shooting here in New Zealand—where you got one shot, at range. Eric's Australian 'roo shooting experience was different. If you were fast at acquiring and nailing the target, you could make a living at it, but that took shooting fifty to one hundred a session. If you weren't fast...well, you were out of business. And it was head-shots only in his trade. Ten shots and nine down—one moved at the last moment, and he'd clean missed it, which had kept it alive for about two seconds.

Dev and Weasel were shooting too. But it wasn't making infected run...except towards the bodies. "Drop them farther back. On the beach," he said, digging out a brick of ammo and the spare mags from the waterproof box. "Lyn. Can you put rounds in the spare mags?" he asked as he refilled his. There was still a scrum over the place where he'd seen the parka. And one of the infected had simply replaced the rapist—while another was pulling the fragments of the first's skull apart to stick its face into the bloody brain-feast.

Eric started shooting again. Both of the other shooters, especially the Weasel, were probably better at range than he was, and were dropping infected on the beach—where other infected were rushing in join the cannibal feast. Eric kept his bullets for the scrum on the rocks, taking out the brain eater, and the rapist, and, one-by-one, the pile-on.

He nearly shot the expedition member in the orange parka, as the man, streaming blood, somehow got to his knees.

"Can we get to them?" asked Lyn in what was bordering on a shriek.

"Clear a few more," said Eric, taking another mag from her hand. "Load the next."

"It's just him," said Dev, tersely. "Dr. Creek's dead. Look at her throat through your scope."

Eric did—once he'd taken down two more infected attacking the bloody masked man in the parka trying to get to his feet. If Dr. Creek wasn't dead, she wasn't bleeding much out of that ripped hole in her neck anymore.

The parka-clad man managed to stand. And headed, staggering, toward the tangled forest margin. They all yelled at him, as Eric pushed his rifle into Lyn's hands and grabbed the tiller, and pushed them another twenty yards inward—but the kelp was a solid mass.

The yelling might have been a mistake. Heads lifted from the cannibal feast Dev and the Weasel had organized on the beach. It also made the bloody, bitten-faced man turn toward them. He'd been fleeing blindly...because he was blind. His eyes had been gouged out. One still hung from the socket. His cheek was ripped open to the bone.

"Keep them off. I'll see if I can push us in. This kelp's a problem. Don't want to foul the prop." He lifted the motor and grabbed the paddle, as the parka-clad man staggered blindly towards the water...and then fell. A female infected—eyes empty, mouth wide to bite, had snagged him by the legs. And she was on top of the victim, grabbing him by the hair, pounding his head against the rock with brutal, killing force, howling with delight.

The first bullet—Dev's—hit her in the chest. The hollowpoint .223 round didn't have enough impact to stop her—even though Eric was sure she was dead. What was left of her brain hadn't told her that yet. The Weasel's shot must have hit her spine because she flipped backwards, with the nerves giving their last message.

She lay still. But so did her victim. Eric continued to push the Zodiac in. "It's too late for him," said Dev. "And they're coming thick and fast. Must be fifty, sixty of them. Let's get out of here, Eric! We can't hold them!"

"We'll make sure he's dead," said Eric. "We can't just leave the poor bastard..."

"He'll be infected," said Lyn, quietly. "Even if I can save his life, now..."

"Big Eric! What the hell is going on!?" The yell came from farther into the inlet, probably forty yards from the black cobbles. Closer to the infected...who had also heard it.

It was two of the other cat hunters—Neville Matthews and Strife.

"Hell's teeth! Strife! Nev! Get away from that lot on the beach! They'll kill you."

Both men were down to shirts—they'd plainly run the track to their camp back from base. Eric shoved the Zodiac back as hard as he could with the paddle. Dev grabbed the other paddle and was pushing too. "Get that motor ready to drop as soon as we're out of the kelp!" he yelled at Lyn and the Weasel.

"Do it," said the Weasel to her. "I'm going to see if I can slow them on the beach." He took as careful an aim as he could manage in a moving boat. It wasn't a kill, but one of the infected went down—and three of the others attacked it, as Lyn was frantically trying to pull-start the outboard. "Kill switch key," yelled Eric, dropping the paddle into the boat and snatching his rifle before it slid off the waterproof box and onto the wet deck.

That was the issue, and the outboard roared to life. "Take her in. 'Ware rocks!"

She nodded and pushed the boat in toward the two hunters, both of whom were running towards them. Neville was ahead—Strife was older, and probably a little less fit—besides having just taken a run across the mountain. The kelp fringe was thinner here. Eric started shooting into the pursuing mass, with the Weasel.

Neville dived in. Strife, just ten yards behind, stumbled and fell, as the surviving leader of the infected pack reached him.

Eric didn't shoot for fear of hitting him, as the infected, with a triumphal yowl, grabbed Strife. There was a cracking crunch they could hear even above the outboard, as Strife head-butted his captor's nose—before shoving him off and kicking him in the belly so hard the attacker went down on the rocks. Dev was hauling Neville into the boat.

"Strife—get into the water!"

The hunter kicked his attacker once more and scrambled into the kelp and pushed his way out. "I can't swim!" he called.

"Bloody hell. Here. Rifle. I'll get him." And Eric dived in. The water was limb-numbing, painfully cold. It was hard to move, let alone swim, but he did. He was aware of rifle fire ... sort of, as he hauled in on the kelp.

Strife plunged towards him, and disappeared under the water.

Eric managed to grab him as he came up. "Hold the life-jacket," he said and started kicking out. It was hard to move in among the kelp, dragging someone. And the infected were trying to walk onto the kelp to get to them.

"Rope, Eric," shouted Dev, and flung a coil at them. The Weasel was still shooting, as Dev hauled them in.

Half a minute later he was shivering in the boat. He heard Lyn say, "Did you get bitten?"

"No," he answered. And then realized it was Strife she was speaking to.

"The bastard tried, before I give him one." The brawler sounded incredulous about it.

Neville was already wrapped in one of the survival blankets. The Weasel hauled a second blanket out—Dev had taken the tiller and was balancing three rifles—the butts might get wet, but the actions and barrels were well away from the sloshing deck. "You bastards will have to share," said the Weasel. "Watch my scope, Dev. You're gonna scratch it on Big Eric's piece of crap."

"You were shooting them," said Neville, shivering, his eyes wide. "You were shooting people! That's murder!"

"Yep," said Eric, pushing the blanket onto Strife, and pulled himself up onto the pontoon. "And we just saved your fucking sheep-shagging New Zealander hide by doing it. Now, we need to go and let me murder someone else."

"Can't we just leave them? They don't seem to want to get into the water," said Dev.

"I just need to make sure that poor bastard that was with Doc Creek is dead. That's all we can do for him."

"Too true," said Dev. "Mind if we stick off shore a little further? The Weasel can use his wondergun."

Eric shook his head. "I'll do it myself. Neville here is going to accuse me of murder, I might as well wear it properly."

"If he's gonna accuse anyone, he can accuse me too," said the Weasel. "You prick, Nev. Look. Look hard. There are the binocs. They're eating each other. They're not even worried because we shot the shit out of them five minutes back. Watch. They're following us. When we get to where they were raping Doc Creek and they killed the others...you goddamn watch. Or I'll shove these binocs down your throat." Which, as the Weasel weighed maybe a hundred and ten pounds, and Neville Matthews two hundred and twenty, would have been funny under other circumstances...not right then. The Weasel looked like he might even do it. Neville took the binoculars. You didn't need them at this range, and his hands were shaking a lot.

They got level with the body-pile on the point where Dr. Creek's body lay, as the loping gaunt naked infected started climbing the rocks to it. Eric reached for his rifle. Dev pulled it away. "You're wet. I'll do it."

"Got him in my 'scope already," said the Weasel. "If you just hold as still as possible. But he's dead, I reckon."

Eric put his hand on Lyn's arm. "I'm sorry. Was that your husband?"

She shook her head. "No. That was Dr. Jansen. I...I saw Paul with one of them after him, running. Please...Walter. Just to be sure. Shoot him. I couldn't bear..."

Hearing her ask was almost as much of a shock as having the Weasel called "Walter." But he did as he asked. The shot didn't even worry the infected who had got there, and had started to pick at the bodies and eat them.

"Holy...! Shoot them! Shoot them all," said Neville. "I think I'm going to throw up."

"Change of heart, mate," said Dev. "Hey look. There's another Zodiac."

"There should be two of them. They've kept three at base," said Strife. As he said it, the second boat came into sight.

"Let's get out there. Tell them what is going on," said Eric.

"Are we just going to leave them to eat...?" asked Neville.

"There's more of them than we have rounds with us."

"We could at least recover the bodies..."

"They might be infectious. You want to end up like that?" asked Dev.

They headed towards the other two Zodiacs. Eric noted that the infected were trying to keep up. That was a whole new worry.

The two boats had brought four people each—and ropes, emergency blankets, spare clothes, and extra life jackets. Someone had been thinking. The crews were a mix of shooters and scientists. Eric was ready to bet that whatever they had been thinking about, it hadn't included guns and ammunition—which was a pity. The infected would spread out.

"What's going on?" shouted the skipper of the nearer boat. "Any people to be rescued? What have you got guns out for? Are those people on the shore?"

"I think you'd better come and see. Don't go too close. They're infected. They killed three of ours, including Dr. Creek. And it looks like there are thousands of them. Follow us. And you can give us some dry kit and life jackets—or better still, take Nev and Strife on your boats. Ours is a bit more loaded."

So, after transferring the two shooters, the three boats set off inward. The howling infected on the shore... mostly turned to follow them. Soon they were level with the bloody cannibal feast. There were enough scraps of expedition parka to tell the story. The newcomers stared in horror. Other than looking hungrily at them, the infected paid no attention, and went on feasting and squabbling with each other over choice morsels. Several people in the Zodiacs threw up, and hid their faces.

"You gonna shoot the bloody things or just look at them?" said one of the cat shooters from the other boat.

"Was holding onto our ammo."

"You can't shoot them. That'd be murder. They're human. Just sick," said one of the scientists in his boat.

Everyone else looked at her like she'd maybe caught the disease too, in a sort of stunned silence.

There was always one, thought Eric, trying to choose his words carefully. "Yeah. And if they bite you, you'll be sick too. Now, we really don't need them to follow us back to the base. I suggest we go—making as much noise as possible, across the inlet, and see if we can draw them along the western side instead. Then we run out to sea, and turn east and go home. We give the base a call on the radio as soon as we're out from under the bluff. Tell them to start packing. We need to move across to Enderby Island."

"Why?" asked the same woman who had insisted the infected were just human.

The woman must be simple, despite having a Ph.D., decided Eric. "Because we want water between our base and them," he answered as patiently as possible. "Otherwise they'll try and kill us."

"But ... can't we help them? I know ... but they're not in their right minds."

"No," said Lyn tersely. "All the governments, medical facilities and effort in the world have failed, Rae. We're not suddenly going to succeed. The kindest thing is to kill them."

The argument was broken up by one of the hunters pointing to the half-beached ship, and saying: "Someone is flashing something at us from the bridge."

"Try Channel sixteen."

As someone said this, the foreigner spoke from the radio. "Please don't shoot me. I am not sick. Over."

"Copy that. We are only shooting at those who attacked our expedition members. You are quite safe. Over."

"Shoot the mad ones. They kill the crew. They kill each other. I am trapped here on the bridge. Over."

"Are you able to keep them out? Over."

"They are not trying to break the door anymore. They are going off the ship. Over. Can you rescue me? Over."

Eric looked at the others. Shook his head. "Not immediately. We need to get more firearms. Have you sufficient food and water? Over."

"Have water. Little food. Over."

"Can he drop a rope?" asked someone. So Eric asked. The answer was a no. The best they could do was promise to return.

"For planning: we need to know how many of the infected you have on your vessel? How come you have all of these infected on a container ship? Over."

"We bring general cargo, heavy machinery from China. We come to Wellington. We take on bunkers from the barge, come to unload. Is no cranes working on docks. Instead Army orders us to take five hundred refugees to Chatham Islands. Take ten containers off deck, put some with supplies, and some empty for shelter. Only come more than two thousand. Would be more but we cut cable. One day out of Wellington ... some people go mad. Chatham will not let them land. More going mad. More fight. Me, I am sick, and captain tell me to stay in my cabin with food. The mad ones break in to the bridge. Kill crew. Three weeks now. You come back, please. They getting off ship. Is no more food for them. Over.

"Will do. Over and out."

"So ... if we want to try and draw them away from our base, we should run across past the stern and then make lots of noise—and see if we can draw them to follow us along the Western shore," said Eric. "If they stick on that shoreline—where the walking is easiest and there is some food for the infected, that's about a hundred and seventy miles to us. If they go east along the coast, it's only about eleven miles. Ten to one they'd show up after nightfall. I don't want to deal with them in the dark. It's bad enough when you can see them."

"Too true. And those rotting cliffs on the West coast might get a few. They nearly got me," said one of the shooters. The terrain was all pretty rugged, but the West coast had spectacular cliffs, with even more spectacular waves driven by the prevailing wind.

So the three Zodiacs moved around the stern and towards the western corner. They had some followers but the cannibal feast was still drawing stragglers, sending them questing eastward, where they'd reach the Base Camp far too soon. They tried shouting. That got some attention. Dev started giving them a Haka. That really got attention.

"Let's sing to them," suggested the Weasel.

"That should send them running," said one of the crew.

It didn't. It brought them running. More and more. Howling.

"It's hard to make yourself heard over that noise," complained someone.

Dev grinned. "Weasel. Get that bloody beat box of yours out."

The Weasel's luxury was his music—which he normally had to listen to with headphones. They all had some sort of iPod, with earphones—sitting in a hide got very long—but the Weasel had speakers ... and volume, once he powered it off the boat's battery. And that really got the infected interested, swarming. "They got your shit taste in music," commented Dev, complaining about the Weasel's Pearl Jam.

"So gimme some of yours."

Dev did. The infected liked Eagles of Death Metal just as much.

And . . . seeing as there was food there—each other, and the possibility of sex, the infected added a bit of cannibalism and rape to the party. "I think we need to start to lead them away," said one of the scientists, looking as if she was about to throw up again. So they did—rather like Zodiacs full of pied pipers.

The music was overwhelmed by a sudden yell of absolute rage. A couple of the crew of her boat had to hold onto Rae. Shaking, red faced and yelling at two of the infected on the shore bickering . . . over a bird. A penguin. The first intelligible thing she managed to say was: "Kill them! Shoot them! *Now!*"

"I thought they were human, and it would be murder," said Dev, who never could resist stirring.

"They're eating a yellow-eye! They're endangered!"

Eric had one of his rare moments of tact and didn't point out that there was no government to protect anything. They'd be eating "protected animals" taken from a protected area themselves, soon enough. Instead he said: "They're going to kill anything and everything they find. Birds. Seals. Sea lions. They don't care how rare it is or how protected."

"You've got to do something!" she demanded.

Eric shrugged. "Come over to this boat and I'll let you use my rifle. You can 'do something' instead of making it my problem."

"I will!"

The shooter driving that boat was about to say something. Eric caught his eye and shook his head, slightly. So the ornithologist climbed over into their boat. Eric calmly put a round in the chamber, showed her the safety, and gave her a good rest. At thirty yards with a good scope she probably still couldn't hit a barn door from inside . . .

She proved him wrong. Wasn't trying head shots, but she hit one. Tried again. He took the rifle away before she had a third try. He'd made his point, and there was no sense in wasting ammo. And what she'd done dawned on her.

"Look at the shore," Dev said to her. "Humans would be running away looking for cover. They're packing the one you shot, to eat him."

"It's a bit like a rabid dog," said Eric. "You have a dog, and it loves you. But if it gets rabies—it'll attack you. A rabid dog doesn't know or care if you used to be its beloved master. It's not same dog anymore. They aren't humans anymore. Now let's get on. We want to catch the high tide for the Rose Island gap."

Sea conditions had flattened a bit more and they led the pack of infected around the end of the Cape before heading out to sea. The swells were big but regular, and it was tempting to think of doing the run to New Zealand in the Zodiacs...except, it usually flattened out before a big blow. And when that happened... well, this was the Southern Ocean.

Anyway: what waited for them in New Zealand?

Instead, they made contact with the Base. Somehow, Eric found he'd become the spokesman, and he had to work at persuading them to start loading the remaining Zodiacs and heading for Enderby Island. There was a lot more than they could ferry in one trip: the ship that landed them had provided labor, cranes and several more boats for landing all the expedition's gear, all those months back. There were three old buildings at Landing Beach on Enderby Island, and at least that would provide some shelter.

They had an easy passage through the reefs in the Rose Island gap, and through into the sheltered waters of Port Ross. In this weather that was several square miles of water that was quiet and still—which was more than you could say about the Base. They hadn't managed to load a single boat let alone do the less than four miles to Landing Beach.

"What the hell is wrong with these bloody people? They've got a ravening pack of infected heading for them, and they can't even organize to move to safety," grumbled Eric.

"They couldn't organize a fuck in a brothel," said Dev. "They need someone to give orders."

"They're used to Dr. Creek telling them what they can do, or not. She chose them for that," Lyn said quietly. "You'll have to tell them what needs doing."

"Hell's teeth." They tied up the boat, and Eric noted that everyone from the expedition was there milling around, asking questions. "All right—shut up for a minute, everyone."

Silence fell. "Dr. Creek is dead, so are Dr. Jansen and Dr. Smith. We need to evacuate to Enderby Island or they'll kill us too. You've all got five minutes to gather sleeping bags and one bag of warm personal gear, and be back down here with it. Hunters. I want you armed. Get your rifles first. Dev. Weasel.

You take up observation positions. Shoot first and ask questions later. I'll load your kit. Get to it."

"Who put you in charge?" said one of scientists, as most of them turned to leave.

"Oh shut up, Maria," said, of all people, the ornithologist, Rae. "Someone has to do it, and he at least knows what to do. You don't."

"You can argue about it once we're safe," said one of the others, who had been on the "rescue," pushing her. "Now get on."

It took, inevitably, a bit more than five minutes, but the kit got piled into three boats. It had only taken Eric a few minutes to get his, Dev's, and the Weasel's bags off the landing rocks and back into the boat, so he'd had a few minutes to write lists. "Right. You're in teams. You, you, you, you." He picked them out, trying to put at least one shooter with each team, and one of those who had been on the rescue, in each team. "And you six will take three of the loaded Zodiacs across, offload above high tide, and scoot back, and take the next three. Fat Boy, join Dev and Weasel on lookout. Other teams, here are your lists. Carry gear down, be ready to drop and run for the boats if you hear any shooting. Fat Boy—tell the other two I expect them to drop any infected at range, and then beat anyone who can't run back here."

"Can't we fight them off?" said Fat Boy—a skinny beanpole of a man.

"No. We're not fucking soldiers. We're hunters. We'll stick to what we're good at."

"A private word, sir," said Lyn.

He nodded. "The rest of you jump to it. The doc will catch up with her team."

She waited until everyone had moved to their tasks, and the Zodiacs were already heading out. "You need any more medical stuff carried down?" he asked. "I was making this up on the fly."

"No...I've got the essentials, as best as possible—on one of the boats going across. I...I wanted to ask about Paul."

"I'm assuming he'll get back before we evacuate. I can't send anyone out to look for him." He was afraid she was going tell him that she was going, because, kicking and screaming if need be, he was going to see she ended up on Enderby Island. Even if she never did speak to him, let alone sleep with him again. They needed a doctor.

"No." She bit her lip. "I...understand. I suppose I've spent years looking after him. He...he had a drug problem when we met. I...I felt I'd rescued him from it. I spent a lot of time making sure he didn't get tempted or miserable or vulnerable, to keep him like that. It didn't always work. That's partly why I took this job. But...what I wanted to say..." she closed her eyes. "If he's been bitten...can you order the others to shoot him? Please."

Eric felt that you could have knocked him down with a feather. "Ouch. I don't know if I can ask someone to do that."

She took a deep breath. "Then...can you put me on guard and lend me a gun?"

He put an arm around her. "No. But I'll go up and talk to the boys. They have binocs and telescopic sights. The Weasel's 'scope will let you see a flea at two hundred yards. They can look him over. Fire a warning shot if they can see he's bitten. And let him approach to fifty yards for close examination if they can't. We'll offer him a Zodiac, a tent, and half a gallon of fuel and some food. That won't get him to Enderby, but will get him to Shoe Island. We'll come and fetch him in...what's the incubation again?"

"Around ten days. So two weeks would be safe." She smiled up at him, her eyes wet with tears. "You're a wonderful man, you know. I've been tearing myself apart. I still feel I have to look after him even if don't love him anymore. I don't think I have for some time, but when he told Creek I had been using the morphine..."

"I should bloody shoot him for that. But I won't." He wanted to kiss her.

"I suppose caring for him was a habit. Hard to let go. But I will. And now I will go and carry loads. Sir."

"What's this 'Sir'?"

"I told them you were a Navy officer. They'll be happy taking orders from that, under the circumstances."

"Bloody liar," he said with a grin.

"Well, I couldn't tell them you were great in the sack and made me go weak at the knees," she said with the sort of smile that made him go weak at the knees.

"I'm just a big, ugly vermin shooter," he said, feeling even if the world was going to hell, it wasn't such a bad place.

"That might be the new Alpha male in this situation."

It was near dusk and they'd ferried a lot of loads across to Enderby Island, when the unwelcome sound of a shot rang out. They pulled back to the boats, with the shooters arriving moments later.

"Just one," said the Weasel. "And he won't be telling his friends."

"I reckon we may as well go across to Enderby anyway. Food and sleep. We can decide what the hell to do in the morning."

So they did just that. Eric wondered what had happened to Doc Lyn's ex. But...in a way he was just relieved that it hadn't turned into the issue he'd feared. He was also pleased he wasn't sleeping alone that night. He was also somewhat taken aback by Lyn saying quietly. "I'm letting you know that I want you to father my babies."

"Uh. That's not an invitation a guy gets every day. It's kind of why I got divorced."

"You don't want children? I...understand. Paul didn't either. But we're going to need them. And we need all the genes we can get. A couple of the women and I were talking about that already yesterday. They're biologists. They understand that."

"Oh, I want kids. I always thought we'd have them. I even went for infertility checks. I thought it was me. Only...she was on the pill. I found her stock of them and I completely lost it. We had one hell of a fight, and ended up divorced. I lost my farm in the process." Even saying it now still hurt. It had been Anderson land for a hundred and fifty years. He'd always thought he'd hand it on.

"We're going to need farmers," she said.

"And mothers," he said, pulling her closer.

The morning brought howling wind, flurries of rain and sleet, fresh council, and, Eric noted, some people plainly emerging from each other's sleeping spots. It looked like the rigid cat hunter–scientist divide had gone to hell, in face of everything falling apart. Breakfast was a relatively silent meal. Afterwards, Eric decided it was time to bite the bullet. "Time for a meeting, folks. We need to decide what to do next."

They all looked at him and waited for him to say something. So he did. "Yesterday some of us got to see the effects of this disease, firsthand. It's...bloody horrific. I reckon you all shared stories, no need for me to say it again. But civilization as we know it is shot to hell. The New Zealand government is not coming to fetch us. Nobody is."

"But surely...surely there will be some survivors?" said someone.

"I reckon. But for a while, they're just going to be trying to survive. We might end up helping them, not them us."

"So...is that what you think we should do? I mean, we'll run out of food."

"No. There's food to be had here, from the land and the sea. We've got a safe—or safe-ish base," said Eric.

"People have lived here. Some of them for years. We have knowledge and equipment they didn't have," said Lyn. "What we don't have a lot of is the skills we need."

"We could last a while. We've got some skills, some tools. I'm a cat hunter, but I've been a farmer, and I was in Navy before that. Most of us know more than just one trade."

"Not this entomologist," said the bug hunter—the one who had been giving him lip about who had put him in charge, only yesterday, with a wry smile. "But go on. I can learn, I suppose."

Eric nodded. "Most of us are going to have to learn. Well, here is what I propose. I've been talking to the third mate on the container ship this morning. We've got much better radio communications here, a better aerial, and no mountain in the way. Now he knows there is help and a chance at relief, he's had some rest, and he's quite a sensible bloke. He was pretty near cracked when he got out of his cabin and up onto the bridge. He hadn't slept for about three days when he brought the ship in. About a third of her bow is aground in the shallows. North Harbour is very gently shelving. We're of the opinion that if we lighten her, and get a high tide it may be possible to refloat her."

"How are you going to deal with the infected on the ship?" asked one of scientists. "Because, yes, I think we need to try—but I just don't see how. I couldn't believe what we saw on the beach, yesterday. The ferocity, the swarming—I don't know. Can you shoot all of them?"

"Well, I was talking to the third mate, as I said. He hasn't got a rope—but he's cutting up the carpets to make a cord. Then he can pull a rope up from one of the Zodiacs. We can get him food, and we reckon get someone up to him. I know we've got a rock-climber among you, and there's a method to climbing ropes...If we can't, we'll get a rifle up to him. He's got a nice clear line of sight to the davit ropes they climbed down. He says he's only seen one climbing back. I think there's not much food left on the vessel. We reckon of the original couple of thousand, less than half made it this far. We don't know how many of those are on Auckland Island—but it's a lot." He shrugged. "We'll bait them onto the beach, and shoot any that try to climb back. You scientists don't know much about us hunters. We're just people you got in to do an unpleasant job you wanted done, but didn't want to, or have ability to do yourselves. Well, we can do it. And it has to be done. We do it quick and as clean as possible, because that's how we earn a living. We're not soldiers, not as good at what they're good at—not war, or close combat, sure as hell not at taking orders. But shooting efficiently is our job."

"I think I have had a bit of an attitude change with what we saw yesterday," said the scientist with a wry smile. "I'm enormously grateful you're here, sir. Before yesterday...well, I thought you were just a big, dumb guy who liked shooting things, and that I did something worthwhile. I'm not sure how much value a marine biologist is anymore. Or ever will be again. I'd rather be able to shoot well. And I'd like us to have that ship."

"Before this is over you probably will have to shoot well. All of us have spares for the trip. When we build up again...one day they're going to want marine biologists again. Anyway—the ship. She's near full of fuel, and has a lot of containers full of what could be useful stuff, including some earth-moving equipment. If we get her floating and running—we can use Port Ross as a base, and try to contact other survivors. Maybe fetch them here, if they need rescuing. Maybe leave and try for a place that's not so bleak. If we get the ship going...we have resources and choices. But it's going to be hard. Going to be dangerous. Or we can just sit here and wait to die. I know what I'm going to do. But what do you lot want to do?"

"I'm with yer," said Strife, making about his longest public speech ever.

He was only the first. They were actually cheering! Eager... excited and willing.

Beside him, Lyn said quietly. "Told you."

"Lots of babies," he promised. He'd make a future for them.

# Alpha Gamers

## GRIFFIN BARBER

"Careful...once you have the crosshairs on him, squeeze the trigger like I told you."

The rifle's report rent the morning quiet.

James watched as, two hundred yards away, the target folded around the shot and started screaming. Its companions quickly converged on it and started the feeding frenzy. Within moments the twisted steel and broken asphalt of what remained of the Bay Bridge was dripping blood into the Bay again.

"Got him in one. Good job."

His son lifted the custom molded-plastic mask every one of the Island's residents were issued once they were assigned guard duty and smiled over the butt of his gun.

"Ready for another?"

"I want to try for the head, Dad."

James shook his head. "Waste of ammo, trying for that kind of shot."

"Mao taught me to use the reload bench, remember?"

"Until the primers run out."

Jalen looked away. "I don't want him to scream. Used to be human."

"But it ain't anymore. Once they turn, whatever made 'em human is gone."

"All right."

"And put the mask back on. Best get used to sweating under it, the zombies like cheek meat."

Jalen sniffed but did as he was told.

"Again, take your time, pick your target, aim, keep your breathing as even as you can..." James kept up the steady stream of calm instruction and watched the kill zone, mind elsewhere.

Better part of a year since the Fall, and the zombies were still thick as shit on what remained of both spans of the Bay Bridge. Temps just didn't get cold enough, long enough, to give the naked fuckers a good killing-off. Mild temperatures combined with good rainfall made for easy living for zombies, too.

His son's sudden shot made James flinch. The head of a zombie splashed across the front of a Buick.

"Jalen."

"What, Dad? I was aiming for his chest, honest."

"Little man just rolled a crit, James," Mao said.

James's head snapped around to see his oldest friend standing just outside the watch post.

They bumped fists. "Mao, you one sneaky motherfucker."

A bright smile. "Did I scare yo black ass?"

"Shit, yes," James said. "Trust a brother with a Chinese name to creep like a ninja."

"Ninjas are Japanese, Dad."

James shot his son a look, testing him. "And how would you know?"

"Shayu told me."

He glanced at Mao, who was hiding a smile behind a hand. "She did, did she?"

A serious nod from the twelve-year-old. "And the Magus backed her up."

"Well then, it must be so." It was pointless to ask Jalen to use Sam's actual name: the younger generation had all grown up hearing the nicknames their elders earned sitting round a table, gaming.

"Speaking of the Magus: James, she wants to see us. Looks like we got a job."

"All right. You got this, Jalen?"

"Sure do, Dad."

∽ ⊖ ∾

They found Sam with Drake and Shayu in what they'd come to call the war-room. They joined the ladies at the big circular table that always reminded James of *Doctor Strangelove.*

"Marc and Tanya are running a bit late. Some maintenance issue with the boats," Sam said, hiking up her robes to sit down. Her nickname was a better match for her than the monikers of the rest of the gamers who made up the core of the fighting arm of Treasure Island's survivors. It wasn't just the robes, either. Had it not been for her, none of them would have survived. She was the wizard who made sure they all got the vaccine in those first weeks, smuggling it out of her lab in the last days before the Fall really got going. She'd come a little unglued back then, taken to wearing one of her cosplay wizard robes all the time and failing to answer to anything but Magus, but she'd come through—and kept coming through—for all of them.

Marc bumped his leg as he took the next seat over, drawing James from his thoughts.

Once everyone was settled, Sam opened the meeting: "So I wanted to discuss going in after the ammo Louis told us about before—" she stopped abruptly, swallowed.

"Before he ate his gun," James finished silently. He didn't blame Louis for killing himself, not really. James figured Louis had done a lot more than most: his skills at the helm of the little Coast Guard boat brought most of the survivors out of their initial, failed attempt to hold out in the Port of Oakland. He'd survived the death and destruction of his entire command, and the sinking of the local cutter...yeah, he'd done a lot. Couldn't blame him for giving up when it became clear just how unrelentingly cruel the new world was.

"Which armory?" Mao asked, his deep voice filling the room.

"Coast Guard range. Should have a couple thousand rounds of nine mil, an equal number of twelve gauge and five five six. Should be a number of guns in the safes, too."

"Think it's still there?"

Sam answered that, "Louis said not a lot of people knew about it, so yes."

"Do we really need it?" Mao asked, pointedly putting his machete on the table.

"If we're ever going to get off the islands like we all agreed we need to in order to start over again, we have to secure a landing somewhere. To do that, we need guns and ammo sufficient to shoot everything that slobbers and howls, not to mention a shit-ton of other supplies. That in mind, if this proves as easy as we hope, then we'll start planning a mission to the air rescue facility opposite it. They should have medical supplies as well, and the chopper is still sitting on the tarmac."

"All right, but won't everything be locked up?" Mao had mad skills with a blowtorch, come to that, but it was time-consuming work and the equipment was heavy as shit.

"Yes, two big gun safes. Louis gave us the combinations."

"Combinations?" Shayu groused. The Shark thought herself a real-life rogue, practicing to pick every lock she'd found on the islands once they'd been cleared. Even with all the practice, she was still slow as fuck at it. The same could not be said for her skills with a sword, at least no one who had seen her in action against the Lord of the West back before everything went to shit or against any number of zombies in the time since...

James shook his head. Swords. They had a new lease on life these days. Not rapiers and shit, but Conan the Barbarian–type: straight, heavy-bladed weapons that cleaved bone and chopped limbs. Had to in order to stop zombies.

"As to the layout, Marc has some pictures."

Marc stood up, powered up the laptop and the projector. "As you can see, concrete rubble shore to a height of eight feet at low tide. The backing-stop berms for the range rise to a height of twenty-five feet on the water side and ten feet on the sides. Other than that, there's lots of flat terrain, which will make us easier to spot. The safes are in this doublewide Louis identified as the office. The whole facility has chain link around it on all sides topped with razor wire. The land side has that thin aluminum privacy crap, so viz in and out of the range is minimal. Only problem is that the gate to the parking area is open and might be broken; I couldn't get a good look. That said, most of the fences between the airport, warehouses, and hangars are still up and capped with razor-wire, making it a bit of a maze beyond the range.

"Can't count on that to slow any zombies, at least not for the first few," James said. They had a lot of experience, by now, but Marc was a mariner, and had less experience on the ground with the howlers than the rangers and fighters. James also believed in reminding everyone of the simple shit they should already know. Simple shit got you killed when it was overlooked.

Marc stopped.

James explained: "Any that get attracted from a distance will likely be slowed, but the first ones to respond... got to think they're like any predator, and familiar with their territory by now."

"Right... well, aside from that, the zombies should be fairly thin on the ground relative to the numbers we've seen in the more populous areas of the Bay: no big source of water, nothing to eat, and not a lot of resident population on the water side of the freeway to begin with. Then there's the lack of wildlife. Each time I took a look, I saw zero activity, but I kept at least two hundred yards from shore to avoid drawing any in."

"So, we go in on the RIB and creep?"

"That's the plan. Old-fashioned unless things get out of hand, then we go hot. Rangers in first to scout and try to get the gate closed, fighters to follow. Marc and Tonya's Mariners to provide covering fire from the boats if it hots up. Because of the shape of the coast there, they should be able to get a good crossfire for everything between the berms and the offices."

They couldn't have done this sort of thing just a few months ago. The zombies were too thick on the ground, even where the population had been relatively thin before the apocalypse. Now, though, they'd proven their tactics worked. It wasn't easy, and required some balls, but it could be done.

"Just make sure they shoot the right targets," Mao rumbled.

As soon as Marc and Tonya signaled they were in position at the other side of the point, Drake nosed the RIB up against the rubble.

James and Mao slipped over the side and put in rat lines to hold the boat close. That done, they swarmed up the rocks as quickly as their postapocalyptic war-gear would allow.

At the top Mao pulled his bolt cutters and set to work.

On overwatch with the compound bow, James felt sweat start to pool under the motorcycle gear and distracted himself by keeping to his job: they were in between and behind the backing berms, which limited their field of view, but James could see the target of their little raid about fifty yards away.

The place was not the pictures, but it was close enough: the doublewide range office sat like a fat brown log on the expanse of gray concrete, a couple blue shitboxes and series of converted shipping containers with a porch running their combined length.

The gate, though, was a wreck: all bent to shit down at the ground—there was no way they could get it closed.

No movement or noise other than the water lapping the rocks and the repeated sharp clicks of Mao's progress through the fence.

If there was one thing about the postapocalyptic world that took the most getting used to, especially for a city kid, it was the total lack of mechanical noise, music, or even the periodic shouting—or shooting—matches between neighbors.

Mao rolled the fence back to the posts and wired it in place, leaving a huge triangular opening. Always better to have space you didn't need than need space you didn't have.

He signaled Drake and Shayu, who came ashore clanking and took up positions at the fence.

The door to the office was open—a bad sign. Adjusting his mask and pulling his hatchet, James nodded at Mao.

Mao quietly pushed the door wide.

Taking a deep breath, James entered as quickly and quietly as he could, nearly bouncing off the far wall of the tiny room he found himself in. A single, closed clerk's window was right in front of him, doorway on his right, battered door lying on the floor beyond.

The smell hit: shit, rotting flesh, and the large-mammal unwashed stink of zombies. Problem was, he couldn't tell if the smell was fresh or not.

Mao's bulky shadow crept in behind on silent size 18s.

Clicking the LED headlamp mounted in his mask, James led the way through the next doorway.

Larger room, counter on the left, beyond it: wrecked space full of human remains...quite a few people, and from the lack of meat on 'em, an old kill. A doorway at the far end, dark.

Something pushed James's button, made him pause.

Mao edged up behind him, his very nearness asking a question.

James looked around, trying to find the source of his unease... he saw it after a moment: a well-worn trail through the wreckage—human and otherwise—leading to the doorway.

He hefted his hatchet and nodded that way.

A tap on his shoulder to acknowledge the signal. Mao didn't normally use the headlamp mounted in his mask, preferring to avoid notice until things got ugly. It had worked in their favor in the past, with the zombies rushing toward the light, never seeing Mao till the bigger man cut 'em down.

Picking his footing with care, a sweating James slowly closed on the doorway. Despite his precautions, and in standard horror-movie fashion, James stepped on something—perhaps some finger bones—that crunched loudly underfoot.

Snort, then snarling, and a tall, rather big zombie appeared in the beam of James's headlamp. It rushed him with the reckless abandon they all showed.

James timed its approach and brought his hatchet down in a fast overhand blow that intersected the zombie's forehead with a crisp thwack and a spurt of blood. A practiced turn of the wrist broke the weapon free.

A second zombie stumbled over the corpse of the first.

Cursing under his breath, James backpedaled.

Mao stepped from the darkness, machete edge a glittering arc that swept across the zombie's neck. Blood shot into the darkness as the zombie fell at their feet.

James ignored the female's gurgling death-throes, making sure there wasn't another one. He cleared the back office, finding a nestlike setup he hadn't seen before.

"No threat," he announced before exiting the back office. Mao had almost got him once, back in the early days, when James had come out of a room unannounced.

"No threat, got it."

James came out, found Mao already cleaning his machete on the heavy drapes someone had installed in an effort to hide from the zombies.

Mao nodded at the safes: "Looks like Luis was right."

One safe was open, ammo boxes spilling from the shelves to the floor. The other two were closed and, presumably, locked.

"Hope the combos work," James said. Suddenly overheated, he took his mask off and whipped it around, cast-off sweat pattering amongst the pooled blood already soaking the floor. He put it on the counter with his gloves and pulled the edge of his chain coif up to unzip the synthetic biker jacket.

He kicked aside some bones—a pelvis or something—to get in front of the first closed safe. A quiet moment spent recalling the combinations, he began spinning the tumbler through its paces, came up empty. He moved to the other safe and tried the same combination. This time it worked.

The safe opened with a satisfying clunk. It opened to reveal a rack of ARs and two shelves filled to the top with ammunition.

"Nice."

Mao moved to the door, summoning the others.

Drake and Shayu entered as quietly as they could. Plate and mail wasn't exactly quiet, even if it wasn't quite as loud as the role playing games they'd all played would have it.

James started the third combo on the other locked safe.

"Need me?" Shayu asked, hopeful.

"Nah, I got this," James said, hoping it was true as he rolled the tumbler to the last number and tried the lever. Thankfully, it swung under his hand.

James winked at her as he pulled the heavy door open.

He immediately regretted the wink as the air horn rigged to blow once the safe was open went off with a thunderous blast that went on and on.

James leapt nearly out of his skin.

Shayu was saying something as the horn finally ran flat with a noise not unlike the tightest asshole farting a dirge.

"What?" he shouted, ears ringing and heart racing.

"You didn't check for traps, did you?"

"What? Traps? Fuck, no! Why the fuck would I check—"

Shayu pointed at the horn. "That's why. First rule of opening treasure chests: check for traps!"

Mao's bulk darkened the door. "What. The. Shit. James?"

"What?" James shouted, reaching for his gloves. "Fuck, man, I can't hear shit."

The first few howls were a ways off, but loud enough for James to hear.

The rest of the party certainly made sure he knew why the zombies were coming as they all scrambled to pack as much as they could into the duffel bags Drake and Shayu had brought.

"Jesus, James!" Drake said.

"It was fuckin' inside the damn safe, how was I to know? Who the fuck does that, anyway?"

"Hell, could simply be some vindictive dick making sure any looters attract the zeds," Drake said.

"First one in the perimeter," Mao rumbled from the outer door, statement quickly followed by the hum-slap of a bowstring and a grating shriek.

"One down."

"Ammo only."

"Right," James answered, slamming boxes into the duffel.

"Group coming about...ten, but they are looking for a way through the fences..."

"No time," Shayu said, heading for the door.

"Fuck," James agreed, looking helplessly at the guns and ammo still remaining in the safes.

A sweating Drake nodded. "Let's go."

"They've almost found the gate. Flare up," Shayu called over the hiss-pop of the flare launching.

The mariners opened up a moment later. The chatter of Chinese-made AKs always reminded James of the worst night of his life prior to the apocalypse. Now, though, he was happy to hear the sound.

Gunfire naturally led to more howls. But the zombies would be more likely to rush to the guns than go after the quieter shore party. Zombies might be hell on wheels for sprinting, but they were shitty swimmers. As in, they didn't.

James and Drake each carried a heavy duffel to the door, where Drake handed his off to Mao.

Despite the murderous fire from the boat and his slowly recovering eardrums, James could still hear howling from behind as he and Mao ran past Shayu and Drake on their way toward the boat. The fighters would take on any leakers that made it past the fences and the mariner's guns.

Leaving Drake and Shayu to cover their retreat was standard. Rangers were always the first in and usually first out because, as the less heavily armored team, they could carry more of any recovered loot. Mao quickly outpaced James, even carrying the heavier duffel. Sometimes he couldn't help resenting Mao's many gifts.

The guns went silent as the mariners reloaded.

James swore.

They weren't supposed to go empty at the same time, but shit happened. Several zombies howled as they charged toward the shore party.

Behind James, Drake muttered something.

A meaty *thunk* and wet *plop* as a heavy blade dropped a zombie.

Shayu's high-pitched giggle followed. "You see that?"

Drake grunted something that could have been an affirmative. "Watch your six."

"I got it." Again the wet hammer sound of a blade cleaving flesh.

The clatter resumed as both fighters started jogging after the rangers.

"Did you see that?" Shayu asked.

"Yes," Drake grunted. Fifteen years older than Shayu, he was breathing hard. Drake's plate and chain might be custom fitted; that didn't make it light.

Another giggle. "I mean, not every day you see a zombie trip on his own guts trying to get at you."

The AKs started chattering again. Zombies started squealing.

Mao was between the berms, James a few steps behind. The boats always seemed farthest away when you were being chased by a horde of slavering zombies.

Mao went through the fence and reached the water's edge. He started down the rubbled shore as James reached the top.

James turned to check on the fighters, found the pair in a clattering jog between the berms. A lone shadow moved behind them, eventually resolving into a zombie that had escaped the fire from the boats and was pursuing the shore party on silent feet.

Shouting a warning in such circumstances almost always summoned more problems than it solved, so James dropped his duffel and started pulling his bow out. He was nocking an arrow when Shayu spun on one heel and her sword flicked out.

Shayu had already resumed her jog when the zombie hit the ground, half its neck severed.

"Show-off," he muttered as they ran up.

Another giggle was her only reply.

The mission debrief seemed to take forever, what with everyone giving James a ration of shit over failing to check for traps. He was past ready for a distraction when Marc walked in.

"What's up?" Sam asked.

"We got a radio message."

"From someone new?" It had been a while since there had been any new contacts. The last year had seen a declining number of holdouts on the radio as the zombies overran sanctuaries, or people ran out of power, components, or simply the will to live.

Marc started to shrug, then nodded. "You could say that."

Sam went full Magus, drawing herself up in her seat. "Could? What does that mean?"

"They claim to be the good ole U. S. of A."

"No shit?" three or four people said, all at once.

"No. Shit."

"And they want us to do what, exactly?" Sam asked.

James was pretty sure he knew what she was thinking: Been getting along just fine despite the failures of government—local, state, and national—over the last year. His own thoughts were less abstract, and more angry.

"For now: keep the flame alive."

"The flame?" she snorted. "It actually says that?"

Marc shrugged and handed her the transcript.

She read incredibly fast: "They say the President—er, that would be the former Vice President, now President—has been restored to power . . . that they want survivors to rejoin the union as and when they are able."

James got up, chair grating against the floor as he pushed away from the table. Dimly, he saw Mao getting to his feet.

"James?" Sam asked.

He barely heard her, blood rushing in his ears as he set the knuckles of his fists on the table.

"No." James did not realize how loud he'd been until he saw all the looks on everyone's faces.

"No, what?" Sam asked.

"What if we don't want to 'rejoin the union'? It never did anything for me but put me behind bars."

"That was the State of Californ . . ." Sam trailed off.

James looked down at the table.

Mao answered for him: "Doesn't matter."

"Look, I'm no fan of the way things were run around here before the Fall, but we can do better, make things better . . ." she trailed off again, this time with a helpless shrug.

"I didn't fight to restore anything. I didn't bleed to bring us back under some distant government that doesn't give a fuck about me or my kid." He spread his hands. "I fought to keep us alive—killed all those zeds—to build something out of the ashes and shit the old world order left us in."

Mao was nodding. The rest looked...uncomfortable in a way they hadn't in a long, long time. It gave James pause. He spent a moment examining his anger. It was burning more brightly than at any time since before the Fall. Carefully, he put the leash on it. The men and women at this table weren't the people he was angry with. Most of *those* were long dead.

He snorted, shook his head. "Been a long time since I had to worry about my supposed 'place' in things. My anger hasn't forgotten, though. Not one bit. Right back to being mad as fuck."

Mao was nodding again.

Sam gave an uneasy smile. "I'd like to see some changes in government, myself." He remembered Sam used to call her politics "anarchist with a strong social conscience," whatever that meant. She gestured at the transcript: "May be a while before they get this far, anyway. So far they've only been active around San Diego."

"Still, though, we ought to get our questions answered before we agree to anything," Marc said.

James shrugged. "It doesn't sound like they're asking, more like they are assuming we're gonna want to go straight back to the way things were. I ain't down with that."

"Me neither." She thought a moment before going on, "I'm no scholar, but it seems to me there might be some room under the old U.S. Constitution for some alternative forms of democracy. Something that more equally represents us all. We might be able to work from that, get the folks we've managed to keep in touch with to agree to a Congress—"

"No way the Delta Free State Militia will agree to that."

"Or the Alameda Axis," Marc added.

"Not right away, but they may see reason once we are up and running with a plan..."

James shook his head. "We had a plan, one we told each new arrival: Stay alive. Rely on one another. Never let them do this again."

"James, I'm not saying we don't have problems to work through, but shit-canning the whole idea without—"

He interrupted with her own words, said to each newcomer that survived quarantine on the Island: "Them being some distant government or faceless organization that spread the fucking plague in the first place, us being: everyone contributes, everyone gets a share. Know who you work with. Know them. If they can't hold their end, help, but don't go under with them if they can't—or won't—learn. This ain't no suicide pact."

Sam hung her head. "I know my own spiel, James. Ghu knows I've said it enough myself."

A bitter retort slamming against clenched teeth, James took a deep breath and tried to find an answer that wouldn't do more harm than good.

Sam surprised him when she looked up. Silent tears were rolling down her cheeks. "I . . ." she started, voice shrill. She stopped, held up a hand, swallowed once and then continued more steadily: "I don't know if I can go on making these decisions for us, James. I'm not built for it. I feel them, like fucking spears in my side: Vic, Rachel, the families that turned in quarantine, all of them. I want to hang up this responsibility. I want someone else to run the game . . . I need a break, otherwise I'll break, and I . . . I'm afraid I'll take us all down with me. This—this news from the old government—is the first bit of good news we've had since Luis blew the bridges and we got set up here. I . . . I think we owe it to ourselves to consider how we'll contribute to the greater good and the saving of fucking humanity! If that means working with the remnants of the good ole U.S. of A, then that's what we'll do. It's at least a start."

James and Mao shared a long look. After a moment Mao gave a spare nod.

"Shit," James said it slow, savoring the word while he considered things. After a moment, he went on, "I'll go see if the library's law books cover any odd shit like how far we can get from the old system and still be protected by the Constitution." Prison hadn't just made a gamer of him, it had made him interested in the law, and given him the time to make a study of it. His interest wouldn't have meant shit without the law library left behind by some lawyer who'd lived on the Island before the Fall, but some days God smiled on a brother.

He even smiled a bit as he left the room. Gamers were creatives of a different stripe: give them a world to play in and some rules to govern it, and they'd have the system suiting them in no time. James figured all he had to do was learn the basic rules and how they applied, and the group would pull together to make it happen.

Like they always had.

"Alpha Gamers," the local game store owner had called the group.

He'd no idea how apt the name was.

# True Faith and Allegiance

## MICHAEL GANTS

"Fucking nukes."

Machinist Mate Second Class William Berner stuck his head out from around the $CO_2$ scrubber he was working on.

"Can the attitude. I take it that you did not get the check-out?"

Fireman's Apprentice Machinist Mate Moody shook his head side to side.

"No. I just don't get why they are making it so hard. It's not like anyone needs to care. The world is gone."

"Gone or not, we are still part of the military...U.S. Navy according to our uniforms. Part of the submarine force," Berner said.

He put down the socket wrench he was using inside the scrubber. Turning a bit so he could face Moody he spoke very carefully.

"Whether you think that the Message means everything is gone...does not matter. Not one bit. You swore an oath. Protect and defend and all of the other stuff.

"We still have a job to do. That job, that very hard job, is keeping the *West* running. If for no other reason than she is our lifeline right now. To do that very hard job, Seaman, requires that each person is able to properly perform certain tasks on board."

He paused. "Those tasks are maintenance, watchstanding, and

most important, damage control. So the reason that the nukes are so hard on checkouts is that they have the most equipment and systems that need to be known. Once you get your dolphins, then you can bitch about the nukes being a bunch of stuck-up over-brained pains in the ass. Until you achieve the honor of fish, get it through your tiny dense skull that while submariners make up some of the best and the brightest that the Navy has, nukes are the cream of that crop."

Berner tapped his socket wrench. "Now, to finish fixing this piece of junk I need a nine-sixteenths. Since you obviously are not in the mood to study for a checkout, go find me one. Should be in the toolbox next to the R-12 refrigeration plant."

The petty officer rotated back into the internals of the machine and returned to his work.

Edward Land ducked his head slightly as he calmly ambled into the Machinery Room. At six foot one, he was a bit above expected height for a submariner. His unruly straw blond hair and the way his shirt sleeves hung from too thin arms had garnered him the nickname "Scarecrow" when he was younger. The enforced weight loss from the post-Message diet had increased the resemblance. He glanced around for the watchstander then knocked on the side of the diesel control booth. The metal boomed hollowly.

"Machinery Room?"

"Behind the scrubber," came the muffled reply.

"How are things going?" asked Land.

He stood looking over the shoulder of the petty officer. The NCO was bent over and rummaging in the internals of the number one scrubber.

"Not as bad as it could be, sir. I think that I can have number one up by the end of the watch. Moody! Where's that frigging nine-sixteenths I sent you for?"

"Busy. That's good. I'll let you be then."

The XO clapped the petty officer on the shoulder and walked out of the room.

"That is one tough man," Berner stated firmly when the XO was out of hearing.

Moody handed the requested socket to the petty officer.

"What do ya mean?"

"Do you not bother to keep up with things, NUB?"

The look of confusion on Moody's face was amusing to Berner. He took pity on the junior sailor.

"His wife was one of the first cases. Thankfully she died from it rather than turning. She lives, well lived, back in the states. California if I remember right. Their daughter was in high school and XO didn't want to make her change schools to Guam. So he knows that his wife is dead. Has no idea if his kid is still alive. Yet still takes time to check on all of us during midwatch. With a good attitude I might note. As I said, one tough man. A man that understands family."

Moody pointed to the interior of the broken scrubber.

"So you think it can really be fixed?"

Berner sighed.

"I've seen worse. Hell, last deployment the nukes managed to fix the high-pressure brine pump that failed. While, by the way, we were on station near somewhere we shouldn't have been. First they tore the thing down at sea. Normally a job that requires a shipyard team. Then they used a sledgehammer to straighten the bent drive shaft until they could stick it in the freezer to prep it for putting bearings on.

"While, I'll add, another group of them was using the oven in the galley to heat the set of bearings they had somehow managed to MacGyver into working. Finally those crazy idiots put the whole thing back together so that we could stay on station doing whatever it was we were doing there. So this is nothing."

A loud bang from below the deckplates caught the two men off-guard. Berner pushed himself out from behind the scrubber and headed for the noise. Cold water sprayed from below a deck-plate just aft of the huge diesel engine. He tore open the hinged plate and stuck his head down into the hole.

"We are so screwed," whined Moody as he gazed at the water spewing. "We're going to sink, or have to surface and all of us are going to get the plague and turn zombie. Or get eaten by someone else who turned zombie."

"Shut your pie hole, NUB," Berner half-shouted.

Berner had joined the Navy during his last year at high school. He knew that he could not get away from high school or central New York City fast enough. Now, four years later, he was stuck listening to some non-useful body whine about things instead of buckling down and getting them done. Just like high school.

He studied the cracked valve and harrumphed to himself.

"Call the conn. I don't think I can fix this alone."

He pointed to a sound-powered phone.

Moody lifted the 4MC damage control phone and spun the charging handle.

"Flooding! Flooding in Machinery..."

"No dammit...controlled leak from potable water!" Berner screamed as he rolled to his knees to get to Moody before things got worse.

It was too late.

"...Flooding in Machinery Room!" crackled over the 4MC repeater.

The United States military trains constantly for emergencies, believing strongly in the axiom the more you sweat, the less you bleed. The U.S. Navy trained on steam line ruptures, crashed aircraft, fires, and for submarines especially, flooding.

This training lays out the methodology to survive flooding in a series of carefully orchestrated steps. The steps are designed to inform the crew of the situation and ensure the submarine is placed in the safest condition possible. They include announcements and alarms, increasing the submarine's speed and angle, performing the emergency blow, and checking for other vessels in the path visually with the periscope and audibly with sonar. Drills ensure that the crew reacts in an efficient and orderly manner during an actual emergency.

Instead everything happened at once in barely controlled chaos.

The *Key West*'s commanding officer ran into the Control Room yelling, "I have the conn!"

"CO has the conn," replied Commander Land calmly. "XO retains the deck."

The expected chorus of "CO has the conn, XO retains the deck aye" only arrived from the Radio Room over an amplifier. Everyone else ignored the words and focused on their actions.

Upon hearing the words flooding, the chief of the watch sprang to action. He turned in his chair and slapped the yellow handled general alarm. His motion continued, ending with his hands grasping the emergency main ballast tank actuators. He slammed the actuators down and shifted his attention to the valve board. As soon as he verified all of the seawater valves in the forward compartment indicated closed he shouted "Commencing emergency blow!"

The diving officer gave his seat belt an unconscious tug to tighten it. Glancing down at the Engine Order Telegraph he noted that the helmsman had already dialed AHEAD FULL without order. The planesman pulled back on the dive plane controls.

"Twenty degrees. Slack them up some, you're at twenty-seven already."

Rushing for the periscope, the CO knocked the junior officer of the watch out of the way. Land grabbed JOOW and steadied him. "You need to watch out. CO can be a bit rough when his ship is in trouble."

The young officer gave Land a sickly grin and nodded.

Land held onto the stanchion bar and leaned forward as the USS *Key West* surged surfaceward.

"Dive, ahead full. Full rise on the planes. Chief of the Watch, sound collision and blow the tanks," the CO barked unnecessarily.

He then reached up and twisted the orange ring bar at the number two periscope to the RISE direction. As soon as the eyepiece cleared the edge of the periscope well, the CO slapped the periscope handles down and began walking the scope in circles.

"Damn its dark out there. Cannot see anything." He continued to walk the scope around and asked "Sonar, any transients prior to the blow?"

The freighter should not have been there. Originally it had been scheduled to dock in Port Adelaide in southern Australia. Now she was a derelict silently drifting in the Indian Ocean. Since being abandoned by its crew, the high winds of the storm continued pushing it steadily southward out of the main shipping lanes. No noise emanated from the abandoned vessel and the slap of waves on her hull were inexorably mixed with the wave sound generated by the rapidly worsening storm.

The *Key West*'s sonar dome passed just under the keel of the freighter, missing even the barnacles that had begun colonizing the sharp edge of the vessel. The sail and fairwater planes, however, slammed into the side of the ship at a speed in excess of twenty knots. Steel plates buckled and tore as the mass and speed of the rising submarine pushed hard into the hull of the stricken freighter.

The commanding officer flew backwards with the force of the impact. There was no time to flail his arms before the metal of the secondary quartermaster plot table crushed the back of his skull. Land and the JOOW managed to stay on their feet only because they were holding the metal rail around the conn. Books, logs, and coffee mugs tumbled out of stowage spots and became dangerous missiles flying through the compartment.

Belts kept the diving crew and chief of the watch in their seats. The on-watch quartermaster tumbled out of the control room and screamed as he slid down the ladder towards Operations Middle Level. The screech of tearing metal, thumps, and bangs from both inside and outside the compartment filled the air with a cacophony of sound.

Land had heard the impact of the commanding officer's head and noted the sudden severance of his gasp. Pulling himself around to face the diving officer he called out over the thundering noise.

"All stop . . . back full! Sound collision!"

Without first acknowledging the command, the diving officer reached between the helmsman and planesman and twisted the Engine Order Telegraph to ALL STOP, hit the ringer once, then immediately turned the knob to BACK FULL.

"All stop."

Three rings broke in on the chief's report.

"Maneuvering acknowledges back full."

The general alarm cut out as the *bawoop bawoop bawoop* of the collision alarm rang over the 1MC.

The click of the alarm circuit was enough to wake MM2 Nicholas Jordan from a surprisingly sound sleep. He rolled out of his rack and was slinging a pair of submarine coveralls on before he was fully awake. Just over five years of time in submarines had taught his subconscious to listen for the important sounds. The bawling of the general alarm brought him to full wakefulness.

Jordan grabbed the edge of a wall to keep balance as the ship suddenly pitched upward. The roar of the emergency blow air surprised him nearly as much as the change in angle. He dodged other sailors as they hurled themselves out of their racks and everyone raced to put on clothing. The mass of bodies was collectively thrown off their feet as the deck of the submarine shuddered under them.

The collision alarm overrode the general alarm.

"What the—!" Jordan exclaimed as he regained his balance and ran aft to his duty station.

Many others he passed were carrying clothing and running in only underwear. Living just wearing your skivvies beat dying full clothed any day.

Commander Land felt the change in ship's motion through his sneakers. He called to the chief of the watch.

"Damage report?"

"Don't have all the reports in yet, sir. So far, Torpedo Room reports they have a torpedo that has bounced partially off the starboard rack. Machinery Room reports that it has a controlled leak from the main potable line, not flooding. Maneuvering has not reported yet for the Engineering Spaces."

The chief of the watch pressed a hand to the sound-powered phone headset he had tossed on. "Crew's Mess has four injuries, including the quartermaster. Broken leg, compound fracture."

There was a shuddering and grinding, but the dive angle indicator and log repeater both showed that the submarine was not moving.

"Dammit...all stop." Land ground out the words. "We're stuck on something."

Looking over his shoulder, Land noted the blood pooling under the CO's head.

"Captain's down. I have the conn."

The shuddering stopped as the strain from the cavitating propeller reduced. Pops and groans continued as the submarine settled in the water, listing to starboard at sixteen degrees with a slight downward angle. Murmurs and orders drifted up from the decks below. Extra personnel now poured into the command space as the crew was finally able to set the damage control watches.

The JOOW pulled the 1MC microphone out of its holder. "Corpsman to the conn," he ordered into the microphone.

Land glanced over his shoulder as the weapons officer hurried into Control, a pair of sneakers hanging loosely from his hands as he attempted to zip up his coveralls.

"Weps, you have the conn. I will be in the Wardroom. No, best use my stateroom, the Wardroom will be where the doc is working on the injured. Have the COB, EDMC, A Gang chief and the engineer meet me there."

The short dark-skinned officer nodded, now attempting to slip on his left shoe.

"I have the conn aye. Have the COB, EDMC, engineer, and A Gang chief meet in your stateroom, aye."

Four minutes later the group had assembled in the XO's stateroom, standing uncomfortably crowded in the small compartment.

Land began without preamble.

"We hit something. And it appears we are now stuck. COB, put a working party together and go topside. Let's see what we are stuck on. Chief Hearns, I need to see how bad the periscope systems are damaged. Number two was up when we hit..."

Land paused a moment. The four men stared in open horror at him.

"Sir, if we open that hatch, we expose the entire crew to the plague," Chief Hearns, the A Gang chief, blurted.

"Now wait," the COB said and held up a hand.

The COB was a short and wrinkled sailor sporting an impressive and just barely in regulation white mustache. The spitting image of the 1950s movie portrayal of the storied Chief Bosun Mate of World War Two. He seemed to have developed the personality to match the image. He tugged on the end of his mustache.

Behind the engineer the stateroom door was pushed open, squeezing the A Gang chief against the bulkhead.

"How about I send one of the guys up in a set of firefighting smocks and an SCBA," the COB continued.

"That way he is breathing our air rather than outside. We can flood the trunk when he is ready to come back in."

"Use the anti-c's. They're designed to minimize radioactive contamination," the EDMC said.

"They are, in no means, biologically secure but we could put one of the disposable Tyvek painting suits over that and tape everything. Have him remove everything in the escape trunk and seal it in a bag. Then we could get him back and destroy the bag...launch it out of the trash disposal unit."

"And wash the SCBA down with bleach, betadine, and hydrogen peroxide. That should kill everything else," piped the corpsman as he finally entered the compartment.

Submarines, unlike most ships in the USN, only have a single senior enlisted medical complement in place of a fully fledged doctor. Gunny Doc was a broad shouldered corpsman whose last assignment prior to the *West* had been patching up Marines in the sandbox. He came to attention in the tiny space and handed Commander Land a printout with short bit of text.

"Sir, I regret to inform you that Commander Manuel is dead. You are now in command."

Gunny Doc nodded slightly to the other four men, turned and shut the door behind him.

Land looked at the paper in his hand, the quick notice of death of his captain. He shook himself. He scanned the room.

"Good ideas all. Let's try and keep everyone as safe as we can. Back to what I was originally saying."

He focused on the A Gang chief.

"The attack scope was up when we collided with whatever it is we hit, so I suspect it is screwed up pretty good. Not sure about number one scope or if there was any damage to the seals. I need your guys to get on that as well as fix the potable leak that led to all of this."

The heavily tattooed A Gang chief nodded in silent agreement.

Land turned towards the engineer. "I didn't catch anything wrong from your end of the boat. Anything I need to know about right now?"

The lieutenant commander in charge of Engineering had never been the most decisive of men, and the current stress of a damaged boat and dead CO on top of a zombie plague had reduced him to nothing more than a figurehead for his department. As the engineer mumbled a few incoherent words, the EDMC spoke up.

"The Engine Room is overall in good shape. Some bumps and bruises, but nothing is broken or leaking beyond what it normally does. I've got the guys doing a full sweep just to make sure that everything is getting back to where it needs to be," the EDMC finished confidently.

"Good." Commander Land, new CO of the USS *Key West*, nodded once firmly. "Let's get things moving. Dismissed."

Lukewarm water cascaded down on Electricians Mate First Class Galecio as he shoved open the forward escape trunk upper hatch. Wind blew gusts of rain into his faceplate as he strained with his legs to lock the hatch into the upright position. The sun had set some hours before and the storm blocked any light from the moon. Galecio could barely see the sail, though he could see enough to tell it was damaged. Crumples had formed in the metal at the base, and the entire multistory black structure was canted over about twenty degrees.

He reached down and fished the large black Maglite up on the coil of shotline it was hanging from. Galecio turned it on, and a beam of white light speared the darkness to the port side of the submarine. Careful in the hot and cumbersome combination of anticontamination clothing, disposable white Tyvek paint suit, and forced air SCBA, he made sure he was securely positioned in the open hatch. Satisfied that he was not going to find himself sinking into the Indian Ocean he played the light over the damaged sail.

A large portion of the starboard side fairwater plane disappeared into the mangled remains of a blue wall of metal. A large wave splashed over the side of the submarine, momentarily blinding the petty officer. He scrubbed the saltwater away from his SCBA masks with his left arm. Streaks of salt remained though he could once again see fairly clearly. He played the light upward, catching sight of a yellow crane arm swinging about above the deck of the ship the *Key West* was now coupled to. A continuous groaning acted as a soundtrack to the damage.

Galecio swept the light as far right and left as he could, then keyed his headset.

"Looks like we hit a freighter of some kind. I can see at least four cranes. No people," Galecio shouted into the sound-powered headset. "Name is *Nord Hakata*...Hotel Alpha Kilo..."

The COB replied in a tight voice.

"I don't give a damn about the name, what's the damage look like?"

"Sail's broke. Worse than the USS *Hartford*'s after her collision I would say. Looks like the starboard fairwater is jammed clean into the side of the freighter. She, the freighter I mean, is kind of sitting on our bow, which is probably why we have a down angle."

Galecio paused and aimed the light towards the point where the freighter's hull and the water met.

"There's a crack in the freighter's plating nearly to the water line, but it doesn't look like much water is getting into the hole. At least not yet."

"Right," said the COB. "Come on down. Don't forget what we talked about. Remove all the gear and bag it except the SCBA. Flashlight and phones too."

"Aye."

Galecio nodded to himself and dropped the flashlight so that it hung from his wrist and slowly climbed back down the metal ladder in the escape trunk.

The CO's compartment, one of the largest personal spaces on board, was filled with reminders of its last owner. The COB, Land, and a harried looking Gunny Doc avoided looking directly at any of the pictures on the desk.

Commander Land opened the Jane's Merchant Ships 2011/2012. He read from the entry.

"She's seventeen thousand tons. Four cranes. Cargo consisting of mainly dry goods. Crew size of fifteen to eighteen. Galecio didn't see anybody moving around, correct?"

"No one. Still, could be infected personnel on-board," the COB replied, grimacing.

Gunny Doc shook his head. "Doubtful. You might not have seen the message, but according to Fleet, the infecteds are drawn to light and sound. We made plenty of both. However, I think that sending at least one sailor, if not two, armed with rifles is a good idea."

Land nodded as he looked up from the book. He looked at the two men and grimaced.

"As I see it, we don't have a choice. We open the ship, risking the crew's possible exposure to the plague. Then we, hopefully, get the *West* out of this predicament. If not, we may have to abandon her with everybody in survival gear."

He paused and looked at the frown on the COB's face.

"Or," he said with emphasis, "we can wait and die as the freighter fills with water and sends us to the bottom."

He held up a hand as the COB opened his mouth to speak.

"I'll grant you that there is a small, very small, chance that we could back out during the sinking. As far as I am concerned that chance is too small. Tons of water and broken ship headed deep at a high rate of speed."

The new CO turned to Doc. "What are our chances for infection?"

Gunny Doc, his midwestern accent a bit out of place with the Norse blond hair, began, "Well, last set of reports that AMRIID and the CDC managed to put out suggested that the virus was weak."

"Weak?!? It killed the entire god-damned planet," shouted the COB.

"Medically weak," Doc continued.

"It is suspected to be a manufactured virus. Flus tend to burn out fast anyway. Since this is an airborne flu, it means that you need a decent number of people around to keep it virulent. Not going to happen here in the British Indian Ocean Territories. Not enough people in the BIOT. If we were still near Diego Garcia, might be a problem. As far south and west as we are now, probably not. It's been four months since the message. Flus don't usually stay active more than three to five weeks.

"So at this point, as far out to sea as we are and with the suspicion that there are no living infected sailors on the freighter, I would say that the chance of infection is minimal. And better odds than trying to save the boat as it begins sinking with a huge freighter on top of it."

Shaking his head in frustration, the COB threw up his hands. Then the short man pointed a knife hand at the CO.

"Fine. I'll support you on this, sir. But I'm not telling the crew. You get to do that."

He paused for a moment, stroked his mustache and then held up two fingers.

"Two things though. First, the shotguns will be better close-in weapons against infected so I would suggest that we send at least one shotgun up. Maybe in place of one rifle to cut down on how many crew we have topside."

He paused and stared into the distance.

"And the second?" Land asked after a moment.

"I lead the first team up."


"Careful up there, COB. With the waves and storm, I think we are all going to need to wear harnesses."

"Hence why I am decked out in my fancy duds," the COB said playfully as he held up the deck rail connector from his safety harness and slipped past the young petty officer. The COB began ascending the ladder. He glanced over his shoulder.

"Tell the rest of the topside crew to get ready. And send Galecio up as soon as I clear the hatch."

"Will do, COB."

The petty officer ducked out of the black vinyl bathtub that was now in place to direct the water coming in through the open hatch into the bilge in the machinery room.

"Galce, COB needs you topside."

EM1 Galecio grabbed the cord to his sound-powered headset and looped it over his right arm. He barely had gotten safely situated when the COB began rattling off his report in rapid patter.

"Tell the XO . . . er . . . CO I'm going to have to figure out a way to cut some of the metal away from the fairwater. I'd say that when we did that back full the fairwater jammed into the hull just below where it came in. See how the area's kind of bulged out there?" he asked.

The COB pointed his flashlight's beam at the affected plating. Galecio nodded.

"I think that our best bet is going to be grinders with cutting wheels, but have the guys send up anything that might work. Pull snips out of the damage control bags, that should be good to clear some of the thin stuff. Crowbars too. Oh, and have them send all of the sledgehammers up too."

Fifteen minutes later Machinist Mate Chief John Dorsett followed three Engineering Department sailors up the forward escape trunk ladder. He stopped at the top of the ladder and ensured that the air hose the sailors were dragging was unkinked. Dorsett was young for his rank at only eight years of service. Everyone that had worked with him understood why he had made rank so quickly. He had the three qualities that made an excellent sailor. He was extremely knowledgeable, good at his job, and was graced with the unusual talent of actually being a chief who listened to and understood his sailors. His guys would walk through fire for him.

Inwardly he thanked his stars that he oversaw the craziest groups of sailors available. Because crazy was what it was going to take to solve the problem, he mused as he cleared the top of the escape trunk and saw the situation. Deck spot lights had been attached at various locations along the long hull of the *Key West*. They all pointed at the towering face of blue metal, the hull of the freighter the sub had slammed into. Salt spray and rainwater sparkled in the beams of light. The combined spots illuminated the area enough for work but cast deep shadows where they did not reach.

Chief Dorsett carefully walked to where the squat COB continued directing sailor's efforts. "COB, we brought the grinders and the air hoses. I went ahead and hooked a three-way splitter onto the end of the main hose so we can run multiples off of it. Jordan's got the crowbars and Daly brought up the sledges from the damage control bags."

"Good. I've got a couple of guys trying to rig up something to get the guys higher. We need to cut that portion away," the COB said as he shone the bright beam of his flashlight near the rent in the *Nord Hakata*'s hull where the fairwater plane was driven through.

"I think we can have a group cutting and banging away near the base of the impact area and the higher group cutting below the plane. Just got word from A Gang that the sail's hatch is warped so bad that they can't get it open. Chief thinks that it might be able to be cut away with torches..." the COB trailed off.

"Except we only have welding gear on board, not cutting torches. They keep those on the tender." Dorsett glanced up again at the dimly lit freighter. He rubbed his chin, nodding slightly. "Interesting," he half whispered to himself.

"Shit, we're screwed," said Jordan to Electronic Technician First Class Doug Lewis.

"You think?" Lewis snorted.

Jordan eyed the ET1. He really had never taken to the man, finding him a pain in the rear.

"No, now I know," Nicholas stated strongly. He pointed at the M Division chief with his chin. "The only times I ever see that man rub his chin and say 'Interesting' is when things are hitting the fan. Firm believer in Chinese curses that one is."

"What?"

"You know, 'May you live in interesting times' and all that."

"That makes no sense." The ET1 turned and began hauling one of the grinders and hose towards the hull of the freighter.

"Sure it does you maroon," said Machinist Mate First Class Ian Daly as he came up behind Jordan. "I agree we're in it pretty deep this time though. I mean, it's a dark and stormy night, our boat is stuck in the side of some...what kind of name is *Nord Hakata* anyway? Swedish or something? Anyway, dark and stormy night, busted boat, no comms, and in the middle of a zombie apocalypse."

"Well, to quote the third Indiana Jones movie, at least there aren't snakes," Jordan said as he helped another sailor pass up a box of cutting wheels.

MM1 Daly turned his flashlight towards the water on the lee side of the submarine. Two long white and black striped shapes undulated just below the surface. "We're in the middle of the Indian Ocean. More sea snakes than anywhere else. Most venomous in the world too."

Jordan feigned astonishment and dropped into a fake Harrison Ford accent. "Snakes, why'd it have to be snakes?"

The rain petered off, though the sailors working in the dark hardly noticed. They continued rigging a set of ropes over the damaged sail to attach to one of the orange Jacob's ladders the submarine owned. The plastic and rope emergency ladder normally was used to allow someone in the water a way to climb the rounded hull. Now it was going to be used as a jury-rigged lift to get a couple of the sailors near the hole where the *Key West* had punched through the *Hakata*.

"How close?" asked Dorsett as he continued to pull the dull red air hose up through the hatch.

MM2 Jordan shouted from where he was now swinging against the hull of the damaged freighter. "Looks like about another ten, twelve feet. I guess we could start cutting here, but I'd rather get us higher."

"Roger. Galecio, tell them we need another fifteen feet of hose."

The dark-haired petty officer nodded and bent over to speak into his headset.

"Crew's Mess, topside. Send additional fifteen feet of hose." He paused and listened. "One five ... shit. Send everything you can then."

Galecio turned back toward Chief Dorsett.

"They say they only have about eight feet left. They're scrounging for more."

"We'll use anything they can send us." Dorsett turned and hollered to Jordan and Lewis.

"That's it. Start cutting. And for God's sake Lewis, watch how you're swinging that cutting wheel around. Focus on just cutting the hull, not the ropes or Jordan."

"Yeah whatever you say Chief," the surly Lewis replied.

"Hey, the man is trying to keep us safe," Jordan protested.

"Not like there is anyone else out in the ocean doing that for us. All we have is each other."

He shook them aside and shifted the cutting wheel to come into stronger contact with the hull. Sparks flew molten orange bright through the storm-dark night.

The chief of the watch reported as he shifted to let a petty officer third class retrieve a set of fire control logs that had become lodged in between the Ballast Control Panel and the locker.

"Sir, we're gone down about half a degree forward since they started cutting,"

Land looked up from where he was conferring with the quartermaster of the watch at the plot.

"Commence a low-pressure blow. That's about all we can do to overcome the enormous weight of the damned freighter sitting on us."

He wiped a hand over his eyes.

"Sorry about that Chief, uncalled for. Commence a low-pressure blow."

"Low pressure blow aye," replied the chief of the watch.

He passed the order to the roving watch. The chief of the watch then turned and leaned over to the diving officer, whispering "He's really stressed. Usually doesn't snap at us like that."

The diving officer replied in a low mid Texas drawl. "What can you expect? Man just inherited the *West* from a dead captain. Bad luck that. Bad luck. Like we needed more bad luck."

Both chiefs nodded and the chief of the watch patted the flat portion of the panel.

"She'll keep us alive. Has so far."

As soon as the Aux Forward watch informed him the lineup was complete, he started the blower and called topside.

"Commencing a low-pressure blow," Galecio shouted over the squeal of cutting wheels.

Dorsett felt the rumble of the low-pressure blow through the soles of his shoes before he heard the suction valve pop open. He opened his mouth to shout to Lewis and Jordan.

The low-pressure blow not only pushed water that had slowly entered the ballast tanks out, but forced the sub upwards. The change was only two degrees. Those two degrees changed the precarious balance that had been achieved between the upper curve of the *Key West* and the knife edge keel of the *Nord Hakata*. The seventeen-thousand-ton ship shifted suddenly, knocking aside the puny orange ladder and men holding on to it.

Jordan tumbled backwards, barely managing to catch his foot in two of the rungs. His grinder fell two stories down and bounced off of the towed array cowling with a clang. He found himself hanging upside down and swinging into the side of the sail.

Lewis flailed arms and legs to keep his balance, dropping his grinder as well. The swinging of the jury-rigged sling swung his left leg between the jagged rent in the *Nord Hakata*'s side and the sail. There was the sickening sound of a cleaver shearing meat. Lewis screamed in pain and shock as his leg was severed just above the knee. Blood sprayed arterial red through the spot light beams. The impact threw the skinny petty officer off the sling. Before anyone could move, he slammed into the deck. His unconscious body bounced once and slithered into the water directly between the joining of the hulls. The freighter rolled more and the water stained red and gray.

"Shit!" screamed Jordan as he swung a second time against the sail, his arms wrapped around his head to minimize the damage to his face.

Dorsett, the COB, and Daly all raced towards the swinging man, heedless of the danger. The impact with the sail slowed the swinging and Nicholas came to a stop at the midpoint. He still was above the reach of any of the men on deck.

"Try not to move," Chief Dorsett called up to the upside-down man.

"I bry not ta'" mumbled Jordan through a crushed nose.

Three more sailors hurried up from the hatch and ran towards the sail.

Daly grabbed two of them and pointed.

"Get a hold of those ropes. We're going to need you to lower him down. Beckett, you and I will catch him if he falls before he gets in reach."

Gunny Doc ran a hand through his thinning hair.

"We lost ET1 Lewis during the shift. MM2 Jordan has a busted nose, hairline fracture in his right arm I think, and probably a concussion. COB and Chief Dorsett are trying to set up the rig a little better. But if the freighter moves much more, we are going to lose more sailors."

Land frowned.

"Doc, no matter what we do, we are going to lose a lot more sailors. All of us if we can't get free. I want to save as many as we can. How are the other casualties?"

"Other than the two deaths, the worst is Valencia. I set the leg the best I can but I haven't got the X-ray machine working yet. Electrical division is working on it but Chief Gallindo thinks it's a solid-state item that is the problem. We don't run that thing very often.

"Five twisted or sprained ankles and a possible fractured skull. Everybody else has stitchable lacerations and a metric butt ton of bruises."

Dorsett took the headset from Galecio.

"Captain, we have a new problem."

Sound-powered phones do not convey emotion well. However, if the emotions are strong enough they convey them well enough.

Land was leaning against the secondary plot as he listened and wincing at the tone of the chief's voice.

"How bad?"

"That shift opened up the fracture line on the freighter. It now is extending below the waterline. The freighter is now taking on water. And the rain has started up again."

"How fast is the water getting in?"

"Can't tell for certain. I'd say ten to twelve gallons per minute. It isn't really bad yet. Unfortunately..."

"Understood. It is going to get worse. And faster. Time to cut the fairwater free."

Land could almost see the chief shaking his head.

"Not enough. I've got the guys trying out an idea. An interesting idea. I'll fill you in once I see if it is doable."

Land shuddered but kept his voice even. "Keep me informed."

"Roger, topside out." Dorsett brushed rain-soaked hair from his eyes and passed the headset back to Galecio.

"Stupid and crazy. Even if this interesting idea works, it is stupid and crazy."

The sandy-haired petty officer nodded in agreement as he strapped the chest section of the headset on. Galecio shrugged,

"Not like we have many other options. Most of us probably can't tread water long enough for the sharks to get us."

Dorsett snorted and walked over to the gaggle of sailors working on a pile of silver chains and multicolored metal containers.

Half an hour later an interconnected series of four one-ton chainfalls was hooked to the cut section of the freighter's hull about two stories above the deck of the sub. The other ends of the chainfalls were attached to the deck cleat aft of the sail.

"Crazy and stupid. Best explanation I have for that."

The new CO had come topside to see the damage and work for himself. By now, the air from outside had fully circulated through the submarine so there was no more danger from the virus topside than below. Unlike below though, everyone was soaked with rainwater and sea spray.

"If it works..." began Chief Dorsett.

"It's still crazy and stupid. Good to see that you have everyone except the two guys pulling the rig all the way back. If this lets go under strain, that chain is going to cut someone in half."

"That's why I have Daly and Jones in combat helmets and body armor under the life jackets. If it smacks them, the armor should mean they only get broken ribs."

"Only?"

"Beats getting cut in half. Best we can do. Desperate times and all that. Besides, their vests will keep them afloat. Needs of the Navy."

Commander Land nodded. "Not quite wooden ships though I get your meaning." He turned and headed back into the ship. "You get that fairwater out of there. I'll make sure the ship is ready as soon as you are."

"I'll be fine. I've got to get back up there. Nose has even stopped bleeding." Jordan pushed Gunny Doc away from himself, wincing as his injured arm took the pressure. He held out the blood-soaked rag as if to prove his point.

"Concussions do not simply go away."

"Concussion'll be the least of my worries if I don't get back up there. We are going to sink if I can't get us out of this."

Gunny Doc shook his head. "Other guys are working it. Whole thing is not on your shoulders."

"Yeah it is. And on the shoulders of everyone else here.

Something I realized while I was hanging there. This is all our responsibility. Every one of us took that oath. Protect and defend, true faith and allegiance. My responsibility..."

"Is to get better." Gunny Doc pushed the rising sailor back into the wardroom seat. "You can only do so much, take so much on. There are over a hundred other guys out there working this. They can handle it. They took the oath too. As you said, everyone's responsibility."

"They're the only family I've got left now!" blurted Jordan suddenly. "Everyone else, they're dead."

The corpsman nodded his head. "Yes. We are all a family. Always have been. Trust everyone here with my life. Hell, my wife said that she might not like some of them, but she'd trust our kids' lives with them. A family works together, though. Each person does what they can when they can and pulls the extra when someone is sick or hurt, like you. So let your family do this for you. Your job, as I said, is to get better."

Daly gathered the slack out of the draw chain and verified that everybody but Jones was well back.

"On my call...heave!"

The two sailors strained and drew the chain towards them. The ratchet rotated and drew all slack out of the combined chainfalls. There was a moan from the torn metal above the fairwater.

"Again. Heave!"

The chains quivered, drops of rain sparkling like diamonds as they shook from the tightened metal. The freighter's hull plating moved a few inches more, then stopped.

"Again!"

The metal chains quivered in time to Daly and Jones's muscles. This time the metal did not move at all. Daly shouted over his shoulder.

"We need to cut more of the hull back. That's all we seem to be getting."

Chief Dorsett took a hard look at the situation.

"Keep the tension on them. That way as they are cut, you can pull them back more."

Daly countered while keeping the chain taut.

"That's going to put someone in the line of fire. Not sure we should do that. Safety you know."

"At this point, if we don't take risks, we are all going down with the ship. We'll stay as safe as we can."

Dorsett gestured to two of the sailors behind him.

"Rig up. We have got to get more of the metal cut back. At least another foot I'd say."

The sailors didn't argue. They grabbed the safety harnesses and stepped into them. Within minutes the two were on the repaired makeshift sling and attacking the torn hull with cutting wheels.

Land had returned below and was now massaging his forehead with one hand, trying in vain to drive off the headache that continued unabated.

"Sir, even with the continuous low-pressure blow, we've dipped another degree and a half. Much more and the midpoint of the screw is going to clear the water. Once that happens..." the diving officer's voice trailed off.

"We won't have enough of the screw in the water to pull us out. With the blow in place, how fast are we sinking forward?" asked Land.

"I'd guess about a degree every fifteen minutes. I'd say about another forty-five minutes, maybe an hour before things get really bad."

Land sighed heavily. "Shit."

He turned to the control room phone talker.

"Inform topside that they have to hurry. We have to get free in less than an hour."

The phone talker gulped and passed the message to the topside party.

"Trim party, sir."

"What?" Land look around. "Who said what?"

One of the A gangers who were attempting to fix the hydraulic leak on the destroyed number two scope raised an oil-covered hand.

"I said trim party, sir. Send people opposite of where chief of the watch is trying to trim the boat."

Exasperated, Land said "I know what a trim party is."

"Get everyone who isn't working on directly saving the ship aft. Take as much heavy stuff as we can. Sure, it's not a huge amount, but it will..."

"It will throw the balance point aft," interrupted the chief of the watch.

He gestured around. "Sir, he's absolutely right."

"Hell, just ten or twelve guys can cause a pretty good change when we're trying to level the boat. Getting three quarters of the crew and as much stuff as they can carry should give us three, maybe even four extra degrees aft."

"Not sure it will give us quite that much. That freighter masses a lot more than the water we take in for ballast."

Land continued as he pulled the 1MC mic down.

"However, everything helps."

He keyed the mic and ordered everyone not engaged in life saving damage control to head to the engine room and take everything they could with them.

Ten minutes later the diving officer reported, "Seems to be working, sir. She's actually gained a degree and doesn't seem to be sliding down quite as fast. It's something."

Land look around at the now nearly deserted control room and nodded.

"It's something," he agreed.

"Bring them down handsomely. I don't need another sailor in the drink or dead."

Chief Dorsett turned to Galecio.

"As soon as they are down and back here, tell control to rotate the planes. I think if they give them a ten or fifteen down angle that we will definitely be able to pop the plane free from the freighter."

"Aye, Chief," replied the tired Galecio.

Galecio had been the first guy up topside and had been stuck on the phones for the last several hours. The collision had occurred shortly after he had finished the evening shift. Poor sleep from the previous weeks and the long hours were beginning to catch up with him. He watched for the chief's signal, then contacted control.

"They acknowledge. They are going to start by trying just to level the planes out. Then they will go for the down angle."

To minimize the chance of breaking anything, the chainfalls had been unhooked from both the torn hull plating and the submarine, then stowed aft of the escape trunk.

"Level the fairwaters," ordered the diving officer.

The helmsman pushed forward on the control column. Above

the watchstanders' head a low groaning noise began. The control column began to vibrate as the fairwater planes pushed against the shattered metal of the freighter.

Topside the sailors put fingers in their ears as the metal on metal screech reached a crescendo. Suddenly the fairwater plane's steady movement halted.

"She's fighting me hard, Dive. Can't seem to get it to move anymore."

The helmsman was nearly standing and shoving the column with all his might. The diving officer leaned in and added his weight.

"It's caught!" shouted one of the sailors and pointed. "That beam is ripping into it."

Dorsett blanched and turned to Galecio.

"Tell them to stop!"

Exhaustion had caught up with the phone talker, and he did not hear Dorsett's order. He did not pass the information. Not until the second time the chief yelled at him.

Unlike earlier submarines, the 688-class fairwater planes were not hardened for under ice operations, and the hydraulic system was overall lighter. The force of the freighter's structural beam pushing downward combined with the hydraulic pressure attempting to raise the plane added up to a failure point. With an almost silent hiss, the metal packing ring of the fairwater plane's primary hydraulic cylinder failed and sprayed inside the sail. The yellow-orange fluid was the lifeblood of the system, and without its pressure the helmsman slammed the controls forward.

"Chief, I've lost the planes. No response to the controls," he continued as he moved the aircraftlike control yoke back and forth freely.

The diving officer turned toward the phone talker just as the word came in.

"Sir, topside reports that a structural beam has jammed against the fairwater and recommend securing operations."

"Bit late for that," interjected the diving officer. He turned to the CO.

"Sir, we have lost fairwater control. Probably a hydraulics failure."

"If it isn't one thing," Commander Land said, his shoulders drooping slightly. He straightened and turned to the A Gang chief.

"Get a team up there. See what happened and if it can be repaired quickly."

The A Gang chief grunted slightly.

"If it can't be fixed fast, it ain't probably gonna matter."

Then he briskly walked out of control and headed aft to grab his team.


"Two more frigging feet. Two more at most," Daly commented as he and Chief Dorsett examined what they could see of the situation.

The structural steel had probably torn free from the wall of the hold when the *Key West* had impacted with the freighter. During the operation to level the planes, the starboard fairwater plane's trailing edge had caught it. Now the steel had ripped into the thin metal over the fairwater plane and jammed.

"We are most definitely not going to be moving that with the chainfalls. Not enough leverage since we would need to pull from about ten feet out in the water to get the right angle."

Dorsett rubbed his chin.

"Interesting."

Daly shook his head.

"Do not say that. We have got to do something. Prybars?"

"Won't have enough oomph," said the COB as he walked over to the two M Division sailors.

"Need something that will really kick that thing in its ass."

"That plane's sitting a lot closer to level than when we started," mused Dorsett.

"More oomph. What if we put a guy in a harness up on the starboard plane and beat it with Thor Senior? Get the chainfalls hooked back up to pull downward on the hull as someone beats that support out of the way?"

"Gee, and I thought that Thor Senior was not supposed to exist."

The COB scowled up at the taller chief.

Dorsett shrugged.

"I wasn't the one who brought it on-board. Was here before most of the guys were as far as I know. The thing is not exactly part of the ship's manifest, so we don't advertise it."

"In other words you hide it so only you guys can find it."

The COB grunted again.

"At this point we might as well try everything. The A gangers are trying to remove a maintenance plate in the sail so they can access the plane's hydraulic equipment. The plates are buckled pretty badly though. You send one of yours up to beat on that with Thor Senior. Work the problem from as many angles as we can."

"I think I'd rather use one of the torpedo guys instead."

Minutes later, Machinist Mate Second Class Halstead, known affectionately among the rest of the Weapons Department as "Wall," was hoisted to the edge of the starboard fairwater plane. Though he was on the tall side for a submariner, it was the fact that his shoulders were nearly three and a half feet and his bicep measured twenty inches that encouraged the nickname. He tossed one end of a safety rope around the forward edge of the plane. Another sailor connected the ends together.

"Hooked up," the sailor on deck called.

Wall smiled and snapped his harness to the safety line with a click. He double checked the connection before leaning over and reaching out with his gloved hands.

"Pass it up."

The hammer was a thing of rumors and legends. The name itself, Thor Senior, was a play on the name associated with the short six-pound sledgehammers found in the damage control kits. Those hammers somewhat resembled the popular comic look of Mjölnir. Thor Senior, on the other hand looked nothing like the comic. Three feet of handle and a twenty-pound head, the hammer was huge and unwieldy. Like mermaids and the lost city of Atlantis, it was often spoken of but rarely seen.

With a grunt Wall pulled the hammer up. He rested the head on the plane and tied the hammer's safety line around his waist. Normally tool safety lines were attached to the wrist. There was no way that Halstead was going to risk dislocating his shoulder or elbow if he slipped doing this. Finally he pulled his set of safety glasses down over his face and squared off.

"Ready up here," he shouted down.

Dorsett popped a thumbs up sign to Wall, then turned to Jones and Daly.

"Give me tension on the chains. Just tension. Don't start pulling until Wall starts smacking that thing."

The two mechanics chorused an "Aye, Chief" and bent to the task.

"Halstead; whenever you are ready!"

Everyone cringed as Halstead began swinging the hammer, reciting at the same time the ballad of John Henry.

Much of the impact of the hammer transmitted through the beam as it struck. Metal carries vibrations a long way and the beam was still attached to the rest of the freighter's structure. Each hit jarred the torn metal and the multitude of microfractures in the hull a bit more, the kinetic energy opening them up slightly each blow.

Wall's rather enthusiastic assault on the beam and the pull of the chains on the torn hull combined to force the beam free before the ballad was complete. As soon as the beam tore free, the planes pivoted down. The sudden elastic release of the structural member transmitted a massive tremor through the cargo hold. Four cracks along the ballast chamber wall failed. Water began to pour into the hold from the vented-to-sea ballasting system.

Halstead fell forward, losing his grip on the hammer as the fairwaters pivoted. The safety line on his harness tightened up and left him standing parallel to the deck of the *Key West*. Thor Senior fell for a foot, then stopped as its safety line tightened. Wall grunted with effort as the line and gravity pulled on his body. A sailor raced to the hanging hammer and grabbed it.

"We got it Wall. Release the line."

A set of hands pushed the hammer back upwards to slack the safety line.

Halstead fumbled a second with the connection point, then released it with a grunt.

"Whew. Okay, now can we get me down?"

The rumble of the inrushing water caught everyone's attention topside. Water frothed through the rents in the outer hull and sloshed over the deck of the *Key West*, bright white in the glare of the spotlights. The sailors helping get Wall down scrambled back.

"Get him down now!" screamed the COB. He glanced back to Galecio and noted the now awake petty officer was already relaying the new issue to control.

Two sailors scrambled back to Wall and unhooked the safety rope around the planes. Wall's legs slid forward as the hoist crew pulled the line tight. They dropped him unceremoniously back to the deck as soon as his legs were pointed down. He collapsed into the rushing water as the tension of the line slacked unexpectedly.

COB waved his right arm at the group around the sail area. "Get out of there. Come on. Everyone back."

Dorsett tapped the guys on the back as they passed.

"That's everyone," he yelled.

Without any weight on them, the fairwater planes pivoted back to their neutral horizontal position as they were designed to do. The design maintained the planes level with the hull in the case of a control failure to prevent the drag of two huge metal walls against the water. Shuddering, the entire sub tipped downward as the weight of water in the freighter began dragging it towards the depths.

Daly ran past Dorsett.

"What are you doing," Dorsett screamed.

"Fairwaters are clear. We've got to slack the chains and unhook at least one or we're going to be fighting that thing as it sinks," he said and pointed at the freighter.

The petty officer reached the chainfall attached to the deck and kicked the release free. The chain sang as it released tension. Daly then ran to the farthest chainfall he could reach and attempted to unhook it.

Dorsett knew that there was no way one man would be able to unhook the chainfall alone in this situation, not with the freighter moving so much.

"Fairwaters are reported clear. We are at eight degrees and falling. Sir, she's taking us down!"

The diving officer stared intently at the dive angle indicator bubble as it slowly drifted farther down.

Land leaned forward and clapped him on the shoulder. "All back emergency. Open her up. We'll make it."

Water sprayed and churned as the prop, almost half out of the water, fought to drag the *Key West* backwards from the death trap she was caught under.

The COB cupped his hands and shouted over the roar of the seething water.

"Dorsett, come on. Get your two butts below. All of this is going to get wet really fast."

Dorsett grabbed the chainfall Daly was working on and lifted. He ignored the COB's plea.

"Get it unhooked or you and I are swimming home."

Grunting, Daly acknowledged the situation.

"Almost got it. Lift a little higher."

Suddenly the pivot lock sprang open. The yellow chainfall it had been attached to tore out of Chief Dorsett's hands and slammed into the side of the *Nord Hakata*. A hollow *bong* sounded at the mass of metal hit. Daly grabbed up one of the chainfalls and Dorsett grabbed the other. They both began running. Water lapped over their feet as they raced uphill towards the escape trunk hatch.

"Ten degrees. Ten and a quarter. That bitch is going to push us under."

The diving officer kept a running status of the ship's angle.

"Crew's Mess. Get that hatch shut now!" Land empathetically told the control room phone talker.

Warm seawater sprayed through the open upper hatch, blinding Chief Dorsett as he scrambled to shut it against the incoming flood. Daly reached a second hand up and pulled as well. With a clang the metal skirt slammed into place, cutting the water off. The chief rotated the hand wheel and braced himself as the submarine suddenly angled down hard.

"Eighteen degrees. Props clear of the water."

"Flood the ballast tanks. Maybe we can get below her and then pull out."

The forward quarter of the *Nord Hakata* slammed into the Indian Ocean as the support of the *Key West* disappeared. The already gravely wounded freighter broke, the front third snapping off cleanly. Water rushed into the new openings. The connecting passages between the cargo compartments had been left open during the frenzied panic of the abandon ship. None of the surviving crew had been concerned that the freighter might flood and that the open doors would allow water to travel easily between the huge spaces. Survival, no matter how small a chance, had come first.

"Conn, sonar. Indications of the freighter breaking up. Sounds of high speed flooding."

Land glanced over at the curtain separating the sonar shack from the rest of control.

"Go active."

The force of the rushing water spun the forward portion of the freighter away from the stern, opening a small passage between the two sections. The massive bow of the *Nord Hakata* tore free of the rest of the ship and rolled off of the *Key West*. The submarine's bow bobbed upward and her screw slammed into the ocean. The screw bit hard into the water and dragged the ship sternward. Personnel bounced as the ship's angle suddenly leveled out.

"Freighter has broken. The forward section is swinging away from us," the sonar supervisor reported excitedly.

"Roger sonar. Dive, back full. I want to make sure we clear the area of immediate danger."

The off-watch crew packed every available space in the galley and mess deck of the ship, waiting to hear the news. Jordan, a green sling holding his right arm to his chest, Daly, and Chief Dorsett sat near the front.

"Captain on deck."

The crew braced to attention as best they could in the crowded spaces.

"At ease," Commander Land said as he slid through the sailors to stand at the front of the group.

"We have been able to regain contact with Fleet and inform them of our situation. Reception is poor and spotty. We were only able to get contact using the AM antenna that radio and the ETs managed to cobble together."

Land inclined his head to the haggard group of sailors that had restored the ability to communicate with the world.

"No guarantees that we will be able to continue getting in contact with them. Overall, consider that we are on our own.

"Additionally, we will not be able to maintain the *Key West* at sea in her current condition. Too much damage to her. The sail is trashed. There is no way to open the clamshell doors to get up inside and use it to look around. When this happened to the USS *Hartford*, it took cutting equipment from another ship to get it open. We don't have another ship."

Sailors nodded but remained silent.

"Both scopes and the ECM mast are damaged and unworkable. The sail sonar was destroyed in the collision so we can't dive and still see what's above us very well. Sonar sphere was undamaged but that's less effective for looking at the near surface. The weapon shipping hatch cowling was crushed so that access is unusable."

He paused and looked around at his men.

"Overall we are now a really poor surface ship with bad handling characteristics. The bright side is that the GPS system is still working and we do have AIS on some vessels. As all of you have seen with the new watchbill, we have people topside with binoculars watch for ships so we don't have another run in with a target."

Several of the crew laughed at the weak joke.

"Fleet reiterated that the infecteds are still, and will continue to be, a major danger on land. To survive we are going to need to find a place to anchor the ship that is unlikely to have infecteds. And it has to be fairly close since we are in bad condition. We lost contact with Fleet just after they restated the warning and have not been able to pick them up again. It is up to us to determine an island that meets our requirements.

"No matter what our situation is, all of you swore an oath. We are still sailors sworn to protect our nation. Right now that means finding a way back home, and we can't do that safely on the *Key West.*

"I intend to steam in a small circle here until after the sun rises this morning. At that time we will have determined where we are going. I want each and every one of you working on this. This takes priority. We have to find a new home today, or there will be few tomorrows."

The sun peeked over the horizon and bathed the USS *Key West* in reddish light. Broken fairwaters gently rocked on the bent and battered sail as she steamed uncertainly toward a distant island over a wine-dark sea.

# The Killer Awoke

## JOHN BIRMINGHAM

The killer awoke, surrounded by strangers. An IV line dripped clear fluid through a long, thick needle punched into the back of her right hand. The strangers—all women, she thought dully—leaned in, their faces anxious. She ignored them. Stared instead at her hands as they lay in her lap on a thin hospital blanket. The left hand was bandaged. The other, the one with the IV line, looked strong, even masculine. The nails were cut short. Calluses disfigured her knuckles and the heels of both palms. Like the women gathered around her bed, those hands were completely alien to her. She had no idea who she was.

"Cathy? Are you all right?"

"Doctor," somebody called out.

The strangers, three of them, seemed to launch themselves at her, and she tensed up, but they simply wanted to comfort her.

"Doctor. Come quickly. She's awake. And she looks much better."

She felt soft hands patting her down, stroking her like you might comfort a child who's suffered a bad fright. *Cathy*—was that her?—Cathy tried not to panic or to show how much she didn't want any of these women touching her. Her wounded left hand throbbed painfully. She pulled it away from them, clutching it to her chest.

These women looked like freaks, not the sort of people she'd want as friends. And then, she remembered. They weren't her friends.

They were her mission. And her name wasn't Cathy. It was Caitlin.

Falling back into the pillows, recovering from a moment of vertigo, Caitlin Monroe composed herself. She was in a hospital bed, in a private room, expensively fitted out. The women did not look like they belonged there. The youngest wore a brown suede jacket, frayed at the cuffs and elbows and festooned with colorful protest buttons. A stylized white bird. A rainbow. A collection of slogans: "If you can't be a unicorn, just punch a Nazi." "Who would Jesus Bomb?" "Resistance is fertile."

Caitlin reached a squeeze bottle by the bed.

Her heart lurched when she remembered why that hand was bandaged.

She'd been bitten.

Panic sweat suddenly covered her, warm and greasy. Panic, or infection?

"I'm sorry," she croaked, trying to slow the trip hammer of her heart. "What happened to me?"

She received a pat on the leg from an older, red-haired woman wearing a white T-shirt over some sort of lumpy, rustic jumper that looked like it'd been hand-woven from alfalfa sprouts and wizard beard.

*Celia.* Her name was Celia and she'd chosen the strange outfit to show off the writing on her T-shirt, which read, "If you are not outraged you are not paying attention."

"Doctor!" cried the woman in the doorway.

*Maggie.* An American, like Caitlin. And there the similarity ended. Maggie the American was short and barrel-chested and pushing fifty where Caitlin was tall, athletic and young.

Using the bandaged hand, she felt around under her blanket and came up with a plastic control stick for the bed. She held it up awkwardly.

"Try this," she said to the young girl she knew as Monique. A pretty, raven-haired Frenchwoman. "The red call button." Then, gently touching the bandages that swaddled her wounded hand, she asked, "Where am I?"

"You're in a private room, at the Pitie-Salpetriere hospital in Paris," explained Monique. "Paris, France," she added self-consciously.

Caitlin smiled weakly. "S'okay. I remember Paris is in France." She paused. "And now I am too, I guess. How did I get here?"

The large American woman standing over by the door to her room—*Maggie, try to remember her fucking name!*—turned away from her post.

"Fascist asswipes, that's how. Attacked us outside of Calais."

She seemed to choke on her outrage, suddenly coughing and spluttering until Celia smacked her a couple of times on the back.

"Alt Right Nazis," explained Monique. "And you were *magnifique!*"

"I was?"

"Oh yes," the French girl enthused. She looked no more than seventeen years old, but Caitlin knew her to be twenty-two. She knew a lot about Monique. The others chorused their agreement. "You stood up to them, Cathy. You fought them very bravely. Even though you were sick with the flu. They were not so brave. One bit you."

Caitlin tried to reach for any memories of the incident but it was like grabbing at blocks of smoke.

She remembered very little of the last week.

She did recall a military flight from Egypt to London. The infiltration brief.

This girl Monique. She was not the target, but she knew the target. A suspected bioterrorist.

"I see," she said, but really she didn't. "So I beat on these losers?"

Monique smiled brightly for the first time.

"You are one of our tough guys, no? It was your surfing. You told us you always had to fight for your place on the waves. *Really* fight. You once punched a man off his board for...what was it...dropping in?"

Caitlin felt as though a great iron flywheel in her mind had suddenly clunked into place. Her cover story. To these women she was Cathy Mercure. Semi-pro wave rider. Ranked forty-sixth in the world. Part time organizer for the Sea Shepherd Conservation Society, a deep green militant environmental group famous for direct and occasionally violent confrontation with any number of easily demonized eco-villains. Ocean dumpers, long line tuna boats, Japanese whale killers. They were all good for a TV friendly touch up by the Sea Shepherds. But that was her cover. Her jacket. Quickly stitched together and liable to fall apart if anybody pulled on the wrong thread.

She took a sip of cool water and closed her eyes for a moment.

That's how she knew this was bad.

Echelon never put anyone in the field without due preparation. But she'd been yanked out of her deep cover run against al Banna's network and thrown at these wingnuts on half-a-moment's notice, with a ten-minute briefing and a surprisingly painful shot in the ass of some unnamed antiviral magic potion that gave her the worst dose of flu she'd ever had.

Caitlin cursed softly under her breath. She had no idea what day it was. No idea how long she'd been out, or what had gone down in that time.

"Are you all right?"

It was the French girl, again, Monique. The reason she was here, with these idiots.

"I'm cool," said Caitlin. "Do you mind?" she asked, pointing at the television that hung from the ceiling. "I feel like I'm lost or something. How'd the protest march go?"

"Brilliant!" said the red-headed woman. Aunty Celia. "We really took it up to the Nazis."

"Really?" said Caitlin, feigning enthusiasm. "That's great. Was there anything on the news about it?" she continued, pointedly looking at the television.

A flick of the remote and the TV screen lit up.

"Can we watch the Beeb then?" asked Celia. "My French you know, it's not too good."

Caitlin's hand was throbbing and her head was starting to spin. She desperately needed a moment to herself, to get her shit together. She forced herself to breathe slowly. Stilling her racing thoughts. Her flu had mostly cleared. She hadn't turned rabid. She needed to reestablish real-time contact with Echelon. Overwatch must have arranged for her to jump the line if she was in a private hospital room. She did remember that hospitals were already turning people away when she was London.

"Eh up? What's this then?" blurted Celia.

Everyone fixed on the screen, where an impeccably groomed Eurasian woman with a perfectly modulated BBC voice was struggling to maintain her composure. "...the quarantine, which was not agreed to by Washington, will be enforced by NATO using all means necessary according a spokesperson from the prime minister's office. Outbound commercial flights are either returning to their points of origin or diverting to Halifax and Quebec in Canada, or to airports throughout the West Indies, where the plague is reportedly nearly as advanced as on the continental U.S."

The women all began to chatter at once, to Caitlin's annoyance. On screen the BBC's flustered anchorwoman said that the U.S. President and Vice President had been evacuated "under fire" from the capitol. A hammer started pounding inside Caitlin's head as she watched the reporter stumble through the rest of her read.

"...U.S. forces are heavily engaged at Guantanamo Bay, using heavy weapons on hundreds of naked victims."

Interesting word, thought Caitlin. Victims.

She couldn't help staring at her bandaged hand.

"It's a goddamn coup is what," coughed Maggie, her angry compatriot. She was one of those squat women who always looked like a bunched fist. She coughed a couple more times, before sniffing and going on. "This plague is a cover, a false flag operation. We all saw you get chewed on by that crazy guy, Cathy, and you just stomped him outta the game. He was just some poor mental patient they used. You didn't get no super rabies. It's a fascist coup for sure. A cover story to justify the Right seizing power."

Caitlin felt sick, but not with the flu, or the "rabies" that was nothing of the sort. She was nauseated and light-headed with the realization of just how close she'd come to turning into one of those "victims."

The man who'd bitten her was naked and insane. A snarling berserker with knives in his eyes and a face full of blood from the man he'd just bitten.

No, she shuddered.

He hadn't just bitten that dude.

He'd locked jaws on his throat and torn away a huge gobbet of flesh.

She realized that the background buzz of the hospital had died away. She heard a metallic clatter as a tray fell to the floor somewhere nearby. Caitlin had a passing acquaintance with the Pitie-Salpetriere. There had to be nearly three thousand people in this hospital and at that moment they were all silent, the only human sounds came from the television sets which hung in every room and ward, a discordant clashing of French and English voices, all of them speaking in the same clipped, urgent tone.

"The prime minister has addressed Parliament calling for calm and promising to devote the full resources of the British Government to resolving the crisis. A Ministry of Defence spokesman confirmed that British forces have gone onto full alert and a curfew is now in place. Troops have orders to shoot anybody breaking the curfew."

"Aye it's a coup all fuckin' right," Aunty Celia said quietly to herself.

The reporter was about to speak again when she stopped, placing a hand to one ear, obviously taking instructions from her producer.

"We have just received these pictures from a drone operator in New York a short time ago."

The screen filled up with surprisingly clear, full color imagery of New York. The video was much sharper than the mil-grade stuff Caitlin had seen over the years.

"This picture shows the centre of New York, as of twenty-three minutes ago," said the reporter. "Centralized authority appears to have collapsed on Manhattan."

Caitlin recognized Times Square from above. She quickly estimated the height of the drone as being less than five hundred feet. The drone pilot was threading his craft through the upper floors of the city's high rise towers. Her brief curse was lost in the gasps and swearing of the other women. Fires burned throughout the Square where hundreds of cars had smashed into each other. Smoke and flames also poured from the surrounding buildings. Buses and yellow cabs had run up onto the footpath and in some cases right into shop fronts and building facades. But most upsetting were the people. The streets seethed with humanity, as always, but humanity lost in the howling wastelands of madness. You could tell immediately who was who. The infected were naked. Their prey was clothed. The greatest city in the history of the world had fallen to an unholy bloodswarm of madness and savagery.

Caitlin Monroe, a ten-year veteran of Echelon's blackest and most secret operations had seen nothing to match this horror.

A harried-looking man wearing a white coat over a dark suit appeared at the door and pushed past Maggie. Pole axed by the TV news, she barely noticed him. The physician seemed to do his level best to ignore all of them, including Caitlin, even as he questioned her. A name tag on his white jacket read "Colbert."

"Any pain? Discomfort? Anything?" he asked in French, addressing the query to his Apple Watch, which he was examining as though it was the most fascinating trinket in the world.

"No, Doctor," she said in French. "My hand hurts, but not too much. My neck is sore but..."

She stopped short. Monique was staring at her and Caitlin cursed. Cathy Mercure could not speak French. That was part of her cover.

*Shit.*

"And you have had no more symptoms of the flu? No skin irritation. No psychotic ideation."

"My neck...is just stiff and sore," she said, slowly in English. "I have a headache but I think an aspirin would fix that."

Monique stared at her as if she had grown a new head. The others were still fixated on the BBC. Vision from all over the U.S. More scenes from an American apocalypse.

"But you told us you could not speak French," Monique said.

"Fookin' 'ell, look at that."

"Ms. Mercure, I'm afraid I have some bad news for you..." Dr. Colbert, still mechanically checking his watch, had lapsed back into his native tongue.

*No shit, Sherlock,* thought Caitlin.

Monique, like the doctor, was also phase locked in her own little world.

"But you *told* us. You insisted you could not speak French."

Caitlin stared at her, as the world broke up into jagged mirror shards of meaning and insanity. She improvised as best she could.

"I don't speak it very well. It's embarrassing to even try. You guys are like so hard core about it, with all the eye rolling and the shrugging. I mean, you know, *lighten up.*"

The doctor saved her by cutting her off at that point, speaking in English again.

"Excuse me. But we will need this bed. The hospital is turning people away. Sick people. Now is not twenty questions time. Now is—"

*"Fook me!"*

Aunty Celia's extra loud cry finally brought everyone's attention back to the TV, where a top-down image of Manhattan was displayed. Caitlin momentarily thought it might have been archival footage of the 9-11 attacks. Great plumes of black smoke curled away from collapsed high-rise buildings that burned at their cores like active volcanoes. But quickly she saw there were too many of them, too widely spread over the island, at least eight or nine that she could count immediately.

"...if repeated across the country, the death toll might run into the millions," read the anchorwoman.

"Everyone's gone," said Maggie in a croaky voice. "This is fucked. What's *happening*?"

*I seem to recall you thought it was a fascist coup, you granola-eating fucknugget,* Caitlin thought.

"...At any one time many thousands of aircraft are aloft over the U.S., many of them above densely populated cities."

The coverage switched to grainy video taken from a weather cam, somewhere high above Manhattan. As Caitlin watched, numb and disbelieving, a Singapore Airlines jumbo jet ploughed into the side of the Chrysler Building, one wing spinning off-screen. The screen switched to a video of a supertanker slamming into a wharf in a city she didn't recognize. The front half of the tanker crumpled back in on itself while the water around the vessel churned white and dockside cranes began to topple. And then... the moment of detonation amidships, a blossom of white light spilling from the ruptured hull, like the birth of a dwarf star.

Maggie started swearing at the TV again, a stream of disconnected curses. "Aunty" Celia softly repeated the same thing over and over again.

"Fookin' 'ell...fookin' 'ell..."

Every time she said it, she folded and unfolded her arms. Monique, on the other hand, refused to even look at the screen anymore.

"You said you could not speak French at all," she said. Her voice had turned hard but brittle.

Caitlin Monroe had been an Echelon field agent for nearly five years. She had been intensively trained for three years before that. Her entire adult life she had lived in a crazy maze where every step she took, every corner she turned, she faced the possibility of betrayal and death. She had adapted to a contingent existence where nothing was taken for granted. She had faced her own potential annihilation so many times that the idea of dying was completely passé. At least on a normal day.

But this was a thousand fucking miles away from being a normal day and for once Caitlin found the idea of her life ending to be a completely novel and unsettling experience. It stuck in her mind, a barbed, immovable object that tugged painfully whenever she tried to pull at it.

The television went blank. The screen a dead black void.

Two words of white, plain type appeared.

TRANSMISSION INTERRUPTED.

"Holy shit, it's happening here now!" said Maggie.

"No!" said Caitlin, cutting off an outbreak of panic. "Just wait."

STAND BY FOR AN ANNOUNCEMENT
BY HM GOVERNMENT.

"Check the French news channels," she said.

Monique stopped glaring at her long enough to flip channels with the remote. As Caitlin had expected, the continental stations were still broadcasting.

"It's nothing," Caitlin assured them, rubbing at her throbbing temples with her good hand. "The British government has taken control of the news broadcasters. It's standard procedure in a national emergency. Just watch."

A single, high-pitched tone filled the room for one second before the TV screen came back to life. A vaguely familiar man was sitting at a desk in book-lined room with a British flag prominently draped from a pole behind him. His eyes were haunted and even beneath a very professional makeup job his skin looked blotchy and sallow.

"G-good evening," he stammered. "I am afraid I must inform you that the prime minister is dead."

Colbert wasn't kidding about needing the bed. An hour later, still swaddled in bandages, trailing one rogue sensor lead that had become entangled with her unwashed hair, Caitlin Monroe was still in character as Cathy Mercure, attempting to sign herself out of the Pitie-Salpetriere. A hospital was the last place you wanted to be during any sort of plague outbreak but her motley collection of social justice ninjas had closed around her like a fist slowing her exit through hospital corridors now crowded with terrified locals.

Caitlin wasn't surprised at the fearful undertow already running so strongly in the Pitie-Salpetriere. The infected were here. On the way down to checkout she witnessed half a dozen pedal-to-the-metal, full-bore freak-outs. One was just a panicky idiot, some bug-eyed Parisian screaming about the end of days before disappearing down the hallway with her enormous, deeply dimpled butt swinging free in the rear of a badly strung hospital gown.

But at least she was wearing the gown.

Twice, in the distance Caitlin caught sight of medical staff trying to subdue naked lunatics, thrashing and screeching with rabid rage.

"I'll be a lot better off out of here," Caitlin assured her companions.

Apart from Monique, who remained suspicious after discovering Caitlin's hidden gift for her native tongue, the others weren't doing much better than the unhinged locals. Maggie blabbered endlessly about needing to phone her sister in Connecticut, stopping only to sneeze a couple of times. And Celia had started praying. Praying and swearing.

"Our fookin' father, who art in fookin' 'eaven..."

Caitlin was considering whether it might be time for a little freaking out on her part too. She didn't know what to make of the news out of the States. Things had been rough back home, last she remembered. But it had turned psychotic there now. She had to run to ground as soon as possible, reestablish contact with her controller.

A single television, suspended from the ceiling in the main waiting room, had drawn a huge crowd, all muttering and gasping at every new revelation from the France24 news service. Caitlin ignored it. Monique tugged at her elbow, saying in French, "I want to speak to you."

"Bugs," said Maggie.

They both turned to her.

The dumpy American was scratching at her arms hard enough to draw blood.

"Get them off me," she cried. "Cockroaches! Spiders!"

She made a sort of strangled scream and began tearing her clothes off.

"Maggie, what is it?" Monique asked as Caitlin started to back away, looking for a weapon.

She might have no memories of the last few days, but she remembered this from the London briefing. Carriers with late stage infection manifested symptoms of...what did the Echelon briefer call it? Fornication? No, dumbass. For-MIC-ation. Paresthesia. A feeling of ants under the skin.

Maggie was wailing, tearing at her stupid protest T-shirt.

She'd ripped it halfway off when her eyes rolled up in their sockets, her lips skinned back from her teeth and she snarled like a rabid dog.

Then her head suddenly burst open.

Caitlin ducked at the sound of a gunshot.

Ropey strands of Maggie's blood, bone chips and gobbets of brain tissue splattered everybody within two yards. As Maggie's oversized, half naked and utterly lifeless frame began to drop to the floor, Caitlin was already in midair, having launched herself without thought towards the nearest cover. She sailed over the counter, crashing bodily into the nurse on station there. A cheap pink radio exploded on top of a filing cabinet. The screams began as the hundred or more people crammed into the foyer finally realized that somebody was shooting into their midst, but Caitlin was already on the move, belly crawling towards an open door which she hoped would give on to another exit point.

She felt a hand on her ankle and lashed back with a heel strike. It was Monique. Her face was an offal pizza, covered in glistening chunks of Maggie. The blow caught the French girl heavily on one cheek and she cried out in pain. Caitlin swore and reached back behind her, grabbing Monique by her collar and roughly dragging her up into a crouching run. She slipped once on the gore that now coated her hospital slippers.

"*Move*," she yelled. "If you want to live, move your ass!"

Behind them, a riot. She heard two muffled shots and the crash of breaking glass, barely masked by the uproar of the terrorized crowd. A frightened nurse stood in their way, her eyes wide and staring. Caitlin elbowed her aside and made for a doorway behind her.

Crashing out into a corridor, they ran headlong into a couple of security guards, one fat and wheezing and the other some wrinkled old scrote who looked like he might have started his career as a public security professional back in the days of the Maginot Line.

"That way," yelled Caitlin, throwing a glance back over her shoulder, where she caught the briefest glimpse of pandemonium in the hospital foyer. Snaking around the guards, she sped up again, turning left and right, slamming through a series of swinging rubber doors without regard for who or what she might find on the other side. She'd let go of Monique and didn't much care whether she was keeping up or not, as she blew through yet another set of swinging doors, crashing into an orderly pushing a trolley. It tipped over and fell to the tiles with a great metallic clattering of medical instruments and stainless steel bowls. Never stopping, Caitlin swooped down on a foil package, slipping it into her sleeve as she hurried on.

"Wait, Cathy, wait,"

Monique was still with her.

Monique sounded as though she was about to start demanding answers and looked like she might just put down roots on the spot where she'd slid to a halt. A formidable gray-haired woman in a matron's uniform started moving towards them with her head down and eyes glaring murderously. She put Caitlin in mind of a big blue bulldozer.

"What the hell are you doing?" asked Monique. "What is going on?"

The matron was getting naked, that's what. She was squirming and scratching and snarling just as Maggie had done.

Before Caitlin could answer, or even just spin around and keep running, the same heavy rubber doors swung inwards and two men, both of them armed, muscled through. They were dressed in suits, one of them heavily bloodstained, and their eyes swept the room, quickly settling on their quarry. Caitlin knew there was no chance of running.

Two bullets took the formidable-looking matron in the chest, rendering her a whole lot less formidable as her body crashed into a wheelchair and dropped to the floor, twitching and pulsing extravagant amounts of blood onto the yellowing tiles. Monique screamed and ducked, covering her ears with both hands. Her cries were lost in the bedlam as more patients and medical staff flew into a panic. Having no cover and no safe exit, Caitlin took the only option left. She attacked.

"Monroe!" the nearest man, barked. "Stand down! Safe word: *Screenplay*. Stand down."

There was nothing conscious about her response. Years of training had programmed Caitlin to react to the order without thought or delay.

"I'm Bateman. Station Two," the man said, as her arms fell to her side. "This is Le Clerc. DGSE. We have to get you and Ms. Duroc to a holdfast at Noisy-Le-Sec."

She almost spun up into action at that. Echelon did not work with the *Direction générale de la sécurité extérieure*. They were the enemy. Everyone but Echelon was the enemy.

And Noisy-Le-Sec?

The only time Caitlin had ever been inside the grim, stone fort, she'd been a prisoner.

"Cathy? Who are these men?" Monique demanded to know. "Did they kill Maggie? Why do they want me?"

"Don't move," said the French man. Le Clerc. He was painted in blood and gore, just like Monique. His weapon was pointed at the French girl, however, not at his American opponent.

Caitlin could not let go of that.

Echelon was not a normal agency. The operational arm of the Five Eyes—an alliance of the major English-speaking democracies against, well, everyone else—Echelon was a half mythical sword, locked in a black box at the dark heart of Anglo-Saxon power realism. At least that's how the French thought of them. Caitlin had heard the recordings from the heart of the Élysée Palace. Echelon and DGSE did not cooperate. Ever.

And yet, here they were.

"I have Larrison on a secure sat channel for you," said Bateman. "But we have to get moving. This facility is compromised."

He took a phone from the pocket of his jacket, paying her the compliment of doing so very carefully and slowly. He was a station pogue. She was not just a field operator. She was a Tier One asset.

The satellite phone was heavy. The orange screen already lit.

She hit a button and half a second later the phone connected her to Wales Larrison. Her supervisor.

"Caitlin? You still with us?"

"Wales?"

She was surprised how much her voice shook, betraying the stress and trauma of the last few days, Hell, of the last hour.

"Wales," she said. "What the fuck is going on?"

"We've gone to Case Plan Jericho," he said, as she started walking in a tight group with the other agents and Monique. The French girl was muttering fiercely in her own language at Le Clerc. The DGSE man shrugged expressively a couple of times but did not say much more. He offered her a bloody handkerchief to wipe the gore from her face.

Jericho, she thought. A plan for the Fall. Caitlin shook her head. Not in denial. She had seen the evidence of the accelerating collapse with her own eyes.

It was just hard to imagine it was happening, was all.

"Confirm code?" she asked, almost robotically.

"Graveyard. Island. Sorrow. Salt," Larrison replied. For a moment the words meant nothing to her. It had been so long since she had committed that sequence to memory, so unlikely that she would ever have to recall it, and her thoughts were so unsettled by the events of the day that Caitlin almost froze.

Then the response came to her, as though unbidden.

"Darkling hope," she said.

It *was* Larrison, and Case Plan Jericho was live.

"Go with Bateman and Le Clerc," he said. "And make sure Monique Duroc does not get away from you."

They hurried down a service corridor. The only soul they encountered was a janitor who stuck his head out of a closet for a moment, saw them, freaked the hell out, and slammed the door closed. Caitlin ignored him, her eyes locking on Monique.

"Is she a primary?" she asked quietly.

"No," Larrison said. "But her brother is a person of interest and she had a cell call to him this morning. He is a person of great interest. We need her at Le Sec. If Paris falls, we can hold out there."

*Holy shit.*

Caitlin thought it, but said nothing for a moment.

"Confirmed," she said at last. "Escort to Le Sec."

She was about to cut the call when Wales spoke again.

"Caitlin, your immunization. It worked? You were exposed

to the blood borne pathogen when you were bitten. You're still good to go?"

"Still got my pants on and I haven't bitten anybody," she said. "Not even peckish."

"Good. Be aware that Bateman and Le Clerc have not been immunized."

She regarded the thick smears of drying blood on Le Clerc's face. "Thanks."

Caitlin cut the call as they emerged from the corridor through another set of swinging plastic doors into what looked like the ER. It was a medieval vision of Hell on Earth. A writhing mound of human bodies had piled up at the exit where a hundred or more people had been trapped while trying to escape. They could not all fit through the sliding doors at the same time, and nobody was inclined to wait patiently while a dozen naked, blood drenched fiends raked and tore at the edge of the crush. Caitlin, who had seen some shit in her time, froze for a second, paralyzed by horror as a ravening cannibal pulled a small limb, a child's arm she thought numbly, from the living heap as though tearing off a chicken wing.

Monique screamed, and for half a heartbeat Caitlin thought she had cried out in distress at the sight of the dismembered child, but the tenor of her cry—a shriek of pain and outrage and deeply personal horror—drew the assassin's attention away from the atrocity at the exit.

Le Clerc had turned.

He was already half naked, his suit jacket and shirt torn asunder. He must have given up on his pants because he'd gone full zombie, sinking his teeth deeply into the forearm of the French girl. Bateman was frozen in shock, his gun hanging uselessly by his side as he watched on inertly.

Caitlin grabbed the only ranged weapon to hand, a stainless steel bowl, and launched it with great force like a bright metal Frisbee directly at the Frenchman's head. It bounced off with a dull metallic clang but did little to distract him. Monique thrashed about his jaws like a fish caught on a hook. Caitlin stripped the silver wrapping away from the disposable scalpel she'd picked up a minute earlier and focusing her *kiai*, her war shout, into the very center of her target, she closed the short distance between them as quickly as she could.

To those few normal, mortal beings around her who saw what happened, she moved as fluid blur of violent action, suddenly airborne, one long leg pistoning out and into the sternum of the berserker. Le Clerc flew backwards, ripping a long, ragged strip of meat from Monique's arm as he went. His head struck a metal oxygen tap on the wall with a wet crunch and he began a slow drop to the ground, trailing a greasy organic smear down the wall. Without pause Caitlin's whole body swept around in a small, self-contained tornado, one foot lashing out to strike squarely at a zombie which had been drawn by the prospect of a new feeding station at this all-you-can-eat buffet. Its arms reaching for her, broken fingers hooked into bloodied claws, this "victim" opened wide its jaws as though to close them entirely around Caitlin's head.

Turning tightly with the direction of the kick, Caitlin shot out her free hand, grabbing the nearest wrist, extending it up and slamming her other arm in under the elbow to snap the vulnerable joint with a terrible wet cracking sound. It made no difference, other than taking one potential grappling tool out of the fight. In the final extremes of infection and violent dementia, the zombies apparently cared not one single fuck for pain compliance. In a flash, her weapon hand whipped backwards and she opened up his throat with the razor sharp scalpel. A geyser of hot, contaminated blood spilled out in a rush as Caitlin continued to spin, dragging the bulk of the infected around off its feet, improvising a quick and dirty body drop to the filthy tiled floor of the ER. The thing was still thrashing away, trying to get a grip on her even as its lifeblood gushed out in a river. Caitlin raised one booted foot and stomped down twice, hard on its skull. It crunched under her heels and the zombie stopped moving.

Funny, how quickly she'd come to think of them as zombies, not victims.

"Nooo," cried Monique. The French girl's shriek was a raw, animal sound. Within it roiled pain, violation, horror and outrage. Her face, a mask of dark, primal emotions distorted as though mashed by a rough, invisible hand.

"Get them off me, get them off me."

"She's turning," Caitlin shouted at Bateman. "Put her down."

"But the mission."

"Is blown. Shoot her."

But Bateman, doubtless operating under strict instructions to get the French girl back to Noisy Le Sec even at the cost of his own life, was phase locked. He half raised his gun, then lowered. Raised it again, hesitated, looked at Caitlin with his eyes wide and imploring.

Monique, or what had been Monique, was on him, biting and snarling, before he could react. They went down in a tangle as Caitlin wrenched Le Clerc's gun from his hand. His trigger finger was broken. The protruding bone had caught the guard before the weapon could fall away. Caitlin's hand closed around the grip and she pulled the gun free.

Two loud, flat cracks rang out and Monique slumped over Bateman. He was crying and howling. It was a human cry. He hadn't turned.

Caitlin climbed slowly back to her feet, scanning the room, which was still in deranged chaos. But nobody was close enough to threaten her directly. With a slight shift in stance, she swung around, and double-tapped the man at her feet, even though his life was already bleeding out of him. Almost no thought went into the action. The assassin had long ago stopped counting the number of men and women whose last seconds she'd seen through crosshairs or iron gunsights.

A hot flush washed over her, dizzying, unexpected.

She let her gun hand fall to her side, tired of it all.

She could end all of this now, she thought. Just put the muzzle of Le Clerc's gun under her chin and...

An enormous cracking sound.

Then, the shattering of glass.

The window wall at the front of the ER had given way under the press of so many bodies. Survivors and killers, infected and soon-to-be all spilled out of the madhouse into the night air.

Instantly Caitlin could hear the sounds of the dying city. Sirens, explosions. Screaming. Gunfire. The screech of tires and crunching industrial uproar of cars plowing into each other, into buildings and obstacles. Into people.

The terrified, hysterical crowd surged through the newly opened portal to what must have seemed like safety. Some of them died on jagged fangs of broken glass. Some fell under the trampling feet of those behind them. Others were ravaged by the infected.

For a moment she stood alone. A still presence in the widening gyre of violent madness.

A man in a white coat, a doctor most likely, emerged from the swinging doors behind Caitlin, and took a few hesitant steps in her direction, but a shake of her head and a casual wave of the pistol in his direction arrested any further advance. His face, already gray, turned ashen at the scene into which he'd stumbled.

He disappeared back into the depths of the hospital.

Her moment of weakness passed. Caitlin quickly searched Bateman, finding his weapon and a few spare mags. She stripped a leather jacket from a dead woman, plucked the last of the sensor leads from her own filthy hair. The reloads went into a zippered pocket.

She scanned the room, raising Le Clerc's pistol to shoot down a zombie that had turned away from the pile of screaming bodies still trapped in the remains of the crush. One round to the head.

She checked the load on both guns.

Counted the number of "victims" between her and escape.

Outside, early evening had come with a hard chill and she shivered inside the jacket, thankful for its warmth.

Caitlin Monroe, a professional killer, raised both pistols.

She chose her first target, and went to work.

# About the Authors

**John Ringo** brings fighting to life. He is the creator of the Posleen Wars series, which has become a *New York Times* best-selling series with over one million copies in print. The series contains *A Hymn Before Battle, Gust Front, When the Devil Dances, Hell's Faire,* and *Eye of the Storm.* In addition, Ringo has penned the Council War series. Adding another dimension to his skills, Ringo created nationally best-selling techno-thriller novels about Mike Harmon (*Ghost, Kildar, Choosers of the Slain, Unto the Breach, A Deeper Blue,* and, with Ryan Sear, *Tiger by the Tail*).

His techno-thriller *The Last Centurion* was also a national bestseller. A more playful twist on the future is found in novels of the Looking-Glass series: *Into the Looking Glass, Vorpal Blade, Manxome Foe,* and *Claws That Catch,* the last three in collaboration with Travis S. Taylor. His audience was further enhanced with four collaborations with fellow *New York Times* best-selling author David Weber: *March Upcountry, March to the Sea, March to the Stars* and *We Few.*

There are an additional seven collaborations from the Posleen series: *The Hero,* written with Michael Z. Williamson, *Watch on the Rhine, Yellow Eyes* and *The Tuloriad,* all written with Tom Kratman, and the *New York Times* bestseller *Cally's War* and its sequels *Sister Time* and *Honor of the Clan,* all with Julie Cochrane. His science-based zombie apocalypse Black Tide Rising series includes *Under a Graveyard Sky, To Sail a Darkling Sea, Islands of Rage and Hope* and *Strands of Sorrow*. A veteran of the 82nd Airborne, Ringo brings first-hand knowledge of military operations to his fiction.

**Mike Massa** has lived a diverse and adventurous life, including stints as a Navy SEAL officer, an international investment banker and an Internet technologist. His greatest adventures, though, have been in marriage and parenthood. Mike is a university cyber security researcher, consulted by governments, Fortune 500 companies and high net worth families on issues of privacy, resilience and disaster recovery. He lived outside the U.S. for several years (plus military deployments!) and has traveled to over eighty  countries. Mike is pleased to call Virginia home, where he passionately follows the ongoing commercial space race, looks forward to family holidays and enjoys reading the latest new books by his favorite SF&F authors.

**Sarah A. Hoyt** is a novelist, a blogger and a columnist for PJ Media. She also works as instapundit.com's "night DJ." She's published thirty some novels in Science Fiction, Fantasy, Mystery and Historical fiction. Her novel *Darkship Thieves* won the Prometheus Award in 2011. She's also published over one hundred short stories, in anthologies and markets like *Asimov's, Analog* and *Weird Tales*. When not writing, she haunts diners and museums in Denver, Colorado.

**Robert E. Hampson**, Ph.D., is THE (brain) scientist behind the science fiction for more than a dozen writers. He has assisted in the (fictional) creation of future medicine, brain computer interfaces, unusual diseases, alien intelligence, novel brain diseases (and the medical nanites to cure them), exotic toxins, and brain effects of a zombie virus. His science writing (as both Rob Hampson and under the pseudonym, Tedd Roberts) ranges from the mysteries of the brain to surviving the Apocalypse, from prosthetics to TV and movie diseases, and from fictional depiction of real science to living in space. His recent forays into short fiction (as Tedd

Roberts) are included in *Science Fiction by Scientists* (Springer), *Riding the Red Horse* (Castalia) and *Black Tide Rising* (Baen).

Dr. Hampson is a Professor of Physiology and Pharmacology with over thirty-five years' experience in animal and human neuroscience. His professional work includes more than one hundred peer-reviewed research articles ranging from the pharmacology of memory to the effects of radiation on the brain. He is also leading a clinical team which is developing a "neural prosthetic" to restore human memory following damage due to aging, injury or disease.

**Travis S. Taylor** ("Doc" Taylor to his friends) has earned his soubriquet the hard way: He has a doctorate in Optical Science and Engineering, a doctorate in Aerospace Systems Engineering, a master's degree in Physics, and a master's degree in Aerospace Engineering, all from the University of Alabama in Huntsville. Added to this is a master's degree in Astronomy from the University of Western Sydney (Australia) and a bachelor's degree in Electrical Engineering from Auburn University (Alabama). Dr. Taylor has worked on various programs for the Department of Defense and NASA for the past two decades.

He is currently working on several advanced propulsion concepts, very large space telescopes, space-based beamed energy systems, next generation space launch concepts, directed energy weapons, nanosatellites, and low cost launch vehicle concepts for the U.S. Army Space and Missile Defense Command. Dr. Taylor was one of the principal investigators of the Ares I Flight Test Planning effort for NASA Marshall Space Flight Center and was the Principal Investigator for the NASA Marshall Space Flight Center and Teledyne Brown Engineering effort to study and develop a Pluto-Kuiper Belt orbiting probe using nuclear electric rocket engines.

In his copious spare time, Doc Travis is also a black belt martial artist, a private pilot, a SCUBA diver, and races mountain bikes. He has also competed in triathlons, is a marathon runner, a CrossFitter, and has been the lead singer and rhythm guitarist of several hard rock bands. He has written or cowritten over twenty science fiction novels, various short stories, two textbooks, and over a dozen technical papers. Dr. Taylor has appeared and starred in several television programs including the History Channel's *The Universe and Life After People*, National

Geographic Channel's hit shows *Rocket City Rednecks* and *When Aliens Attack*, and The Weather Channel's *3 Scientists Walk into a Bar*. He currently lives with his wife and two children in north Alabama just outside of Huntsville in view of the Saturn V rocket that is erected at the U.S. Space and Rocket Center.

**Michael Z. Williamson** is a best-selling and award-winning SF and fantasy author, best known for the Freehold universe. He has consulted on disaster preparedness for various theatrical productions, private clients and the DoD. The latter are woefully unaware of the impending zombie threat. A veteran of the U.S. Army and USAF, his hobbies include fine Scotch, antique swords and firearms. Having successfully outgunned the nations of Iceland and Barbados, he is currently in an arms race with Bermuda. He lives in central Indiana, where the postglacial terrain offers a good, clear field of fire. He can be found online at MichaelZWilliamson.com.

**Jody Lynn Nye** is a writer of fantasy and science fiction books and short stories. Since 1987 she has published over forty-five books and more than 140 short stories, including epic fantasies, contemporary humorous fantasy, humorous military science fiction, and edited three anthologies. She collaborated with Anne McCaffrey on a number of books, including the *New York Times* bestseller, *Crisis on Doona*. She also wrote eight books with Robert Asprin, and continues both of Asprin's Myth-Adventures series and Dragons series. Her newest books are the third Lord Thomas Kinago adventure, *Rhythm of the Imperium* (Baen Books), a humorous military SF novel, and *Wishing on a Star* (Arc Manor Press), a contemporary fantasy. Jody runs the two-day intensive writers' workshop at DragonCon. She and her husband are the book reviewers for *Galaxy's Edge* magazine.

**Brendan DuBois** of New Hampshire is the award-winning author of twenty-one novels and more than 160 short stories. His second science fiction novel, *Red Vengeance*, was published in June 2017 by Baen Books, and its sequel, *Black Triumph* was released in 2018. He is currently working on a series of works with *New York Times* best-selling author James Patterson.

His short fiction has appeared in *Playboy, Analog, Asimov's Science Fiction Magazine, Ellery Queen's Mystery Magazine, Alfred Hitchcock's Mystery Magazine, The Magazine of Fantasy & Science Fiction,* and numerous anthologies including *The Best American Mystery Stories of the Century,* published in 2000, as well as *The Best American Noir of the Century,* published in 2010.

Two of his short stories have appeared in Gardner Dozois's *The Year's Best Science Fiction* anthologies. His novel, *Resurrection Day,* won the Sidewise Award for Best Alternate History Novel of the Year.

His stories have twice won him the Shamus Award from the Private Eye Writers of America, and have also earned him three Edgar Allan Poe Award nominations from the Mystery Writers of America. He is also a *Jeopardy!* gameshow champion.

Visit his website at www.BrendanDuBois.com.

☙ ⊖ ❧

National best-selling author **Robert Buettner** was a Quill Award nominee for Best New Writer of 2005, and his debut novel, *Orphanage,* Quill-nominated as best SF/Fantasy/Horror novel of 2004, has been called a classic of modern military science fiction. His ninth novel, *The Golden Gate,* is set in the near-present, but has a giant space ship in it just like his first eight. Various critics have compared his writing favorably to the work of Robert Heinlein, which proves you can fool some of the people some of the time.

He was a National Science Foundation Fellow in paleontology; served as a U.S. Army intelligence officer, prospected for minerals in Alaska and the Sonoran desert, and has been General Counsel of a unit of one of the United States' largest private multinational companies.

He lives in Georgia with his family and more bicycles than a grownup needs. Visit him at www.RobertBuettner.com.

☙ ⊖ ❧

**Dave Freer** lives a largely self-sufficient life on a farm on Flinders Island—a remote island off the south coast of Australia, where he spends too much time shooting, fishing or diving for spiny lobster and abalone and not enough time writing.

Once upon a time—when dinosaurs roamed the earth—he spent a couple of years in the army in South Africa. Both he and army survived, but neither were quite the same afterwards. When he got out he trained as a fisheries scientist, and spent a lot of time messing about in boats and being in and under water. Somehow he blundered from this into writing SF and fantasy, and has authored or coauthored about twenty books.

His latest novel from Baen Books is *Changeling's Island*—which, besides being a YA fantasy set on Flinders Island, also made the Fantasy and YA shortlist for the Dragon Awards.

He is something of an expert on zombies because—as one of the local volunteer Ambulance Officers—when he gets called out at three a.m., he is one. Your sympathy should be reserved for the patients and his fellow Ambulance officers.

A veteran police officer, **Griffin Barber** is also a lifelong Speculative Fiction fan and gamer.

He's had several short stories published in the *Grantville Gazette* and penned a well-received novella for RSI's website called *A Separate Law*.

The novel *1636: Mission to the Mughals*, coauthored with Eric Flint, is available from Baen Books.

**Michael Gants** is a quality inspector of nuclear systems. He is a proud retired USN submariner, trained in the maintenance and upkeep of nuclear power plants. During his time in the military he visited twenty-five countries on five of the seven continents. He has been around the world and through every ocean. He has also been an insurance salesman, computer programmer, journalist, air conditioner mechanic, small business owner, small craft boarding specialist, an aquarium maintenance personnel for Ripley's Aquarium, and Navy antiterrorism trainer. He and his amazing family now reside in Southeast Tennessee with several fur babies.

**John Birmingham** has published lots of books. So many that he sort of loses track of them. He wrote features for magazines in a decade before publishing *He Died with a Falafel in His Hand*, working for *Rolling Stone*, *Playboy* and the *Long Bay Prison News* amongst others. He won the National Award for Nonfiction with *Leviathan: The Unauthorised Biography of Sydney*. He started writing genre novels because they were way more fun. His first alternate history was the Axis of Time series, in which he sends a carrier battle group from the future back to World War II to kick Hitler's butt. Then he made America disappear in *Without Warning*, and imagined the worst superhero ever in his *Dave vs. the Monsters* series. His most recent series of books that improve with altitude are the *Girl in Time* novels. He blogs at the cheeseburgergothic.com and can be found on Twitter as @JohnBirmingham.

Editor **Gary Poole** has worked in the entertainment and publishing industry for his entire adult life. He's worked directly with John Ringo and several other authors on over a dozen novels and anthologies. He is also a film and television screenwriter, the managing editor of a successful alternative newsweekly in Tennessee, cohosts a popular radio morning show, and has voiced well over three thousand radio and television commercials.

21982318892449